Playful Activities for
READING
INESS

Laying a Foundation for Literacy

Gryphon House
www.gryphonhouse.com

BULK PURCHASE

Gryphon House books are available for special premiums and sales promotions as well as for fund-raising use. Special editions or book excerpts also can be created to specifications. For details, call 800.638.0928.

DISCLAIMER

Gryphon House, Inc., cannot be held responsible for damage, mishap, or injury incurred during the use of or because of activities in this book. Appropriate and reasonable caution and adult supervision of children involved in activities and corresponding to the age and capability of each child involved are recommended at all times. Do not leave children unattended at any time. Observe safety and caution at all times.

Table of Contents

Acknowledgments

Years ago, I read this quote from Irene Gaskins, founder of the Benchmark School: "Expert teachers become experts because they are always honing their skills. They regularly read and discuss with colleagues professional books and journals and seek answers to questions about how to better meet the needs of their students. The inevitable outgrowth of these professional learning activities that are based on research about what works in classrooms is better instruction for all children." I took this to heart and have been on my professional journey ever since. I'd like to acknowledge my colleagues who have joined me along the way.

Coming from middle grades, it was Erica Fulmer and Laura Lindemann who showed me the way to early childhood. Erica let me in on the playfulness of lessons with young children while at the same time implementing expert, intentional literacy instruction. Laura opened my eyes to systematically teaching young children to do a whole host of things through modeling and guided practice.

My early search for professional learning led me to Marcia Invernizzi at the University of Virginia, who opened my eyes to young children's reading development. Many thanks to Virginia Coffey and Liza Taylor, a dynamic mother-daughter duo, and Alisha Demchak—all three are extraordinary early childhood educators. While my list of collaborators is long, I am especially indebted to Gail Lovette and Steph Tatel for challenging me and helping me grow as an educator. I have come to rely on our discussions and our collective search for insights on teaching young children to read and write.

Lastly, I am deeply grateful for the many young children in my life—past, present, and future—and perhaps most especially for Preston and Bella. Having first-row seats to their journeys in learning to read was one of the true pleasures of my life.

CHAPTER ONE
Setting the Stage

A child's early years build the foundation for their success in school and life. Since Head Start was established in 1965, more and more children have had the opportunity to participate in early childhood education, and these prekindergarten experiences can have long-lasting positive effects (Magnuson and Duncan, 2016). Since the National Institute for Early Education Research's (NIEER) first report on prekindergarten in 2002, access to state-funded prekindergarten has dramatically increased. This increase in access has occurred alongside important research findings and subsequent educational policies and standards. Today, all but six states contribute to prekindergarten programs, equaling approximately 1.64 million children (NIEER, 2021). Moreover, NIEER reports total state funding surpassed $9 billion for the first time in the 2019–2020 school year.

Snapshot on Research and Policy

Research over the last three decades has provided guidance on literacy instruction and assessment in early childhood classrooms across prekindergarten and kindergarten. Some key reports, both meta-analyses and syntheses of this body of research, have provided us with valuable resources to guide our work with young children. For example, the National Education Goals Panel published a research-based report, *Reconsidering Children's Early Development and Learning: Toward Common Views and Vocabulary* outlining learning indicators and expectations for young children across five developmental domains (Kagan, Moore, and Bredekamp, 1995), including phonological awareness and print awareness. In 2000, the National Reading Panel report mapped out the research to date across the component reading skills of phonemic awareness, phonics, vocabulary, fluency, and comprehension. In 2008, the National Early Literacy Panel report reviewed research specific to the foundational skills prekindergarten children need to develop for later success in elementary school. Paulson and Moats (2018) note that "the job of all early childhood educators is to deepen their understanding of the processes involved in children's learning so they can do the best job possible." In addition to providing you with activities to develop young children's literacy skills, this book also seeks to help deepen your understanding of literacy learning.

Snapshot on Literacy Standards in Early Childhood

Acknowledgement of these foundational literacy competencies has notable implications for early childhood educational standards and, as a result, educational practices. In 2002, Good Start, Grow Smart, a federal initiative to improve early childhood education, called upon states to develop standards such as those in K–12 education. The release of the report of the National Early Literacy Panel in 2008 resulted in many states developing or revising their early childhood guidelines to reflect research evidence. Head Start established the *Head Start Early Learning Outcomes Framework: Ages Birth to Five* in 2015 (U.S. Department of Health and Human Services, Administration for Children and Families, Office of Head Start, 2015), and the National Governors Association and the Council of Chief State School Officers developed the Common Core State Standards in 2010 (NGA and CCSSO, 2010). Throughout this book, I'll refer to these two sets of standards to ground each chapter in what children are expected to learn in our early childhood classrooms.

Snapshot on Foundational Literacy

Children are inundated with print every day. Print is everywhere, and children start developing ideas about print before they enter our early childhood classrooms. For example, young children make scribbles and even letter-like shapes in attempts to mimic the readers and writers in their lives. Children then begin to notice marks on the page and start to learn how to make some letters, especially those in their names. At this point, you'll notice a variety of symbols making their way into their writing. For example, take a look at kindergartner Janya's story about recess with her friends on the playground.

You'll notice children engage in pretend reading as they practice concepts about print. They'll turn pages in a book, label pictures, and perhaps even retell a favorite story they've heard many times. As they learn more about our written language, they'll start to notice the letters on the page and even words. They'll learn to write special words, such as their names, by heart.

Take a look at the story here written by a prekindergartner about visiting her cousins over the summer. She used mock linear writing infused with words special to her: *mom*, *dad*, and *love*.

It is our responsibility as early childhood educators to nurture this literacy growth and harness young children's natural curiosity. The process of learning to read and write a language is not like learning to listen to and speak a language. Think about it this way. Human speech dates back to 100,000 years or so, but an alphabetic writing system wasn't invented until around 3,800 years ago. Even then, the alphabetic writing system wasn't widely used until about 500 years ago. While oral language is learned naturally through immersion during the early years of life, reading and writing must be directly taught over several years.

The Simple View of Reading as a Framework for Developmental Trends

We'll explore a model known as the Simple View of Reading to help us understand the factors involved in learning to read and write (Gough and Tumner, 1986). To understand written text, a reader relies on components: word decoding and language comprehension. Seems simple, but it is anything but. In fact, each of these components of the simple view is complex and multifaceted.

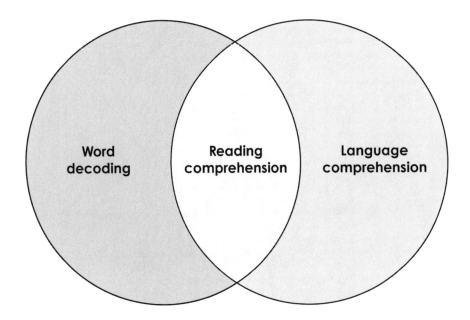

WORD DECODING

In the left circle of the Venn diagram is *word decoding*. This component involves the ability to decode printed letters and words into pronounceable words. To do this, readers must rely on their understanding of the sound structure of our language, *phonological awareness*, and the letter-to-sound correspondences. This process of connecting sounds to letters to make words leads to a critical awareness called the *alphabetic principle*—the awareness that letters are connected to sounds that we use to read (decode) *and* write (spell) words. To grasp the alphabetic principle, young children must have phonological awareness, and, more specifically, they must be able to recognize individual sounds in spoken words. They must also have a growing knowledge of letter-sound correspondences (what we often refer to as *phonics knowledge*). With these two parts working together harmoniously and with increasing automaticity, children begin to build a small corpus of words that they can recognize at first sight, meaning they don't need to decode them—they recognize them right away. Word-recognition abilities are especially important as children begin learning to read and write.

Let's unpack word decoding with a child decoding a word such as *run*. The child says the sounds the letters represent, holds those sounds in their memory, and blends to make the whole word *run*. As the child makes this pronounceable word, they also connect to the meaning of the word and think of children running. Eventually, that same child will not need to decode *run* upon encountering it. The word will become part of that growing corpus of words they know at first sight.

LANGUAGE COMPREHENSION

Now let's look at the right circle of the Venn diagram, the language-comprehension component. Children build their language comprehension alongside word decoding. Language comprehension is the ability to understand the meanings of spoken words, phrases, sentences, and longer connected texts, meaning the things we *hear* rather than what we *read*. As children listen to a story, for example, they need to orchestrate many language skills. They need to call upon vocabulary knowledge as well as their understanding of language structures, for example, how *but* connects ideas or how an introductory clause such as "once upon a time" functions in a sentence. They must understand verbal reasoning, such as inferring a word's meaning or a character's motives, and have some background knowledge.

Let's think back to our example of *run*. Now let's say a child heard someone say, "I need to run to the store." The child knows the word *run* means "to move fast," and they know that in the context of that sentence that someone needed something fast. At the same time, they know that their parent, for example, doesn't literally run to the store. The parent might drive in their car to the grocery store or walk to the corner bodega, but in most cases they wouldn't literally run. So, the child makes an inference using their verbal reasoning. They infer that the person needs something from the store, and they want to get it quickly.

READING COMPREHENSION

Now let's go back to our Venn diagram. Notice reading comprehension is represented by the overlapping circles in the middle. Reading comprehension depends on *both* word decoding and language comprehension. It is possible to have strong language comprehension but still experience obstacles to understanding what you read if you struggle recognizing words. On the flip side, it is possible to have strong recognition of the words in a written text but still experience obstacles if you don't have the language comprehension to support understanding. Successful reading comprehension requires both components.

Let's say a child is reading about bodies of water and reads the sentence, "The water runs in the river." If the child cannot read the words, reading comprehension cannot occur. If the child can read the words but has difficulty making the leap from *run* as "moving fast" to water rushing in a river, then the meaning of the sentence might be lost.

Importantly, this does not mean we focus solely on word decoding in the early years and language comprehension in the later years. Across all grade levels, and even during the prekindergarten and kindergarten years, we must provide literacy instruction that ensures children become decoders, build oral-language skills, and develop background knowledge to support their ability to understand written language in the books of our early childhood classrooms.

What Does This Mean for the Children in Your Classroom?

What does this mean for the children in your classroom? In the prekindergarten classroom, you can expect the children to start recognizing letters, especially those in their names. They will begin to grasp concepts about print such as identifying the front and back of a book, distinguishing the print from the illustrations, and understanding that text moves from left to right. Your prekindergartners will also begin to develop a level of phonological awareness, such as identifying rhyming pairs—*cat* and *bat*—or categorizing words that begin with the same sound—*fish-face-fan*. They will enjoy listening to stories, engage with story lines, and learn new concepts.

By the end of kindergarten, children typically recognize all or most letters, including upper- and lowercase. They will also know the sounds of single letters, especially consonants, and will know some short vowel sounds. Many kindergarten curricula teach children to decode simple consonant-vowel-consonant words, such as *cap, bet, mop, hug, lid*. Their oral-language comprehension exceeds their reading comprehension, meaning they can understand texts while listening that they would not be able to understand if reading, due to their limited word-recognition skills.

How Does Assessment Fit In?

Informed and integrated assessments can help you gather the necessary information to plan effective, engaging, and developmentally appropriate literacy instruction for the children you teach. Through assessment, you will identify what they already know and what they need to learn. You can use screening measures to efficiently assess children's levels of performance on indicators that predict future achievement. For example, in prekindergarten, three key early literacy indicators are alphabet knowledge, phonological awareness, and rapid naming: rapid picture, color, letter, and digit naming. You can also use tools developed to monitor progress and help you identify children who are *or* who aren't learning at an appropriate rate. Your assessments should help you target your instruction and best meet the needs of all children in your classroom.

How Does This Inform My Instructional Practice?

As noted in the International Literacy Association's position statement *What Effective PreK Literacy Instruction Looks Like*:

> *"Children will need to learn the technical skills of reading and writing. Letter knowledge, phonological awareness, and an understanding of speech–sound correspondences are essential for children to learn how to become readers and writers. However, it is critical for children to also learn how to use these tools to better their thinking and reasoning. Developing oral language comprehension and engaging children in meaningful oral discourse is crucial because it gives meaning to what they are learning"* (Neuman, 2018).

Developmentally appropriate practice is a core concept guiding early educators as we create learning environments where children can explore. In 1987, the National Association for the Education of Young Children (NAEYC) put out a position statement on developmentally appropriate practice, stating such practice would include rich learning environments that encourage learning and exploring. In 2009, *Developmentally Appropriate Practice in Early Childhood Programs Serving Children from Birth through Age 8* pointed to the importance of a rich learning environment plus intentional instruction of skills (Copple and Bredekamp).

Broadly, the early childhood classroom should be:

- developmentally appropriate;
- explicit, with concepts explained directly and clearly with concise language;
- intentional, with thoughtfully chosen activities based on research, assessment, and a preplanned sequence of study; and
- part of a playful learning environment.

Developmentally appropriate practice necessarily includes intentional assessment as well as instructional practices that support children's learning of key foundational competencies. This book homes in on key foundational *literacy* competencies.

Current practice in early literacy instruction is increasingly informed by several key studies and policy documents, such as the report of the National Early Literacy Panel. Armed with an understanding of the processes involved in early literacy and language development, early childhood educators can intentionally plan activities, create literacy-rich learning environments, and provide purposeful (and fun) opportunities to support children's growing literacy knowledge. Children need to engage in instructional experiences, including opportunities to practice, that integrate their interests with early literacy activities across these six foundational literacy competencies:

- **Oral language** to foster both expressive and receptive language as well as verbal reasoning
- **Phonological awareness** to develop their understanding of the sound structure of language
- **Alphabetic code** to build children's letter-sound connections and ultimately achieve the alphabetic principle
- **Foundational fluency and word recognition** to provide opportunities for letter-to-sound connections while blending words and print conventions as they engage with books
- **Reading aloud** to foster their appreciation and comprehension of text while simultaneously developing vocabulary and world knowledge
- **Early writing** to apply sound-to-letter connections when writing and to explore writing as a means of communication

ORAL LANGUAGE

As mapped out in the Simple View of Reading, oral-language abilities contribute to learning to read. Moreover, they predict future academic achievement and life outcomes. Young children are building their oral vocabulary as well as relationships across words. In fact, a child's oral vocabulary grows at warp speed between the ages of two and five, resulting in an *expressive vocabulary* (words they can say) of a few thousand words by age five and a *receptive vocabulary* (words they understand) of thousands more. Oral-language development also includes implicit understandings of grammatical rules, such as pronouns and verb tense, as well as syntactical rules used to put words in the sequential order of a sentence. Each of these oral-language components are interrelated and develop simultaneously as children gradually learn to talk and communicate on increasingly complex levels. The oral-language activities in chapter 2 provide children with opportunities for targeted practice and orchestrate these components through conversations and by following directions—calling upon Dana Suskind's "three Ts" (2015):

- Tuning in to children's interests

- Talking with children (both child-directed and adult-directed)

- Taking turns in conversation

PHONOLOGICAL AWARENESS

Children start to develop phonological sensitivity in infancy as they learn the speech sounds of their home language. During the prekindergarten years, they play with speech sounds through language play, especially with rhyming and alliterative books. With this, they begin to develop phonological awareness. This awareness follows a developmental sequence along a linguistic hierarchy, starting with awareness of rhyme, word, and syllable, then moving to onset-rime and phoneme.

Across the sequence, children become more refined in their understanding of the sound structure of language. Children often become aware of sounds through rhyme play. They begin to notice it's not just about a *mouse* in a *house*, but that *mouse* and *house* sound the same at the end—they rhyme. Early in the sequence children begin to determine word boundaries as they orally segment the words in spoken sentences such as, "I went to a party," with five words. They begin to hear syllables within words as they clap the two syllables in the word *party*: /par/

/tē/. Later in the sequence, they start looking within the syllable as they segment beginning sounds. For example, they segment a word such as *mop* into its *onset* (beginning sound) /m/ and *rime* (the vowel and what follows) /ŏp/. Finally, they focus within the rime and segment all sounds, or *phonemes*: /m/ /ŏ/ /p/. When you help children develop phonological awareness, you are influencing their later reading and writing development. The activities in chapter 3 foster phonological awareness across this linguistic hierarchy.

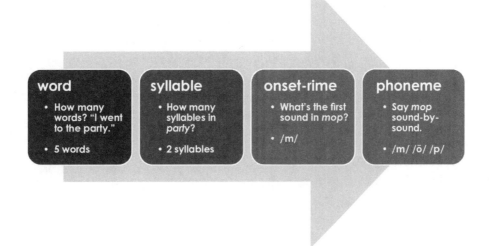

ALPHABETIC CODE

Building a child's understanding of the alphabetic code involves recognizing and naming both upper- and lowercase letters as well as recognizing the paired association between a letter's name and its sound. Ultimately, letter name and sound fluency give a child a real advantage when learning to read and write. In other words, children need to be accurate *as well as* automatic, or quick, identifying letter names and providing letter sounds. More than quick and accurate letter knowledge, children must learn to connect letters with their sounds when they decode and spell words. This is known as the *alphabetic principle*, the understanding that letters are connected to the sounds that make up our words. With this in mind, the activities in chapter 4 work to build quick, accurate letter naming and letter-sound production.

FOUNDATIONAL FLUENCY AND WORD RECOGNITION

Young children just starting out on their journey as readers and writers are working to build their concepts of print. Understanding how to navigate written texts is a foundational skill. For example, young readers begin to understand that we read books moving from the front to the back and from the left page to the right. We start in the upper-left corner of a page and read text from left to right. When they write, they'll begin moving left to right (even if with scribbles!) and will use a return sweep when they get to the end of a line.

As they learn more about letter sounds and build an awareness of phonemes, they will begin to build a bank of known words through activities that provide many opportunities to read highly frequent words, such as *she*, *was*, and *in*, as well as decodable words, such as *cat*, *bat*, and *that*.

They will start to read decodable books and poems as they practice reading and decoding words. In chapter 5, you'll see activities that build these early concepts about print as well as activities that foster the alphabetic principle and later word recognition.

EARLY WRITING

As children are building the foundational skills of writing, they explore through both less structured writing activities and very structured activities that help them learn more about the form and function of print. For example, less structured activities, such as drawing about a shared experience like a class trip to the park and then using scribbles or letter-like forms, can help children explore the differences between illustrations and print. They can also explore the global form of print, such as left-to-right writing and the return sweep (moving from one line of text to the next). More structured activities help children learn the formation of uppercase and lowercase letters as well as the application of letter-sound connections when writing words. Taken together, children's early writing ultimately leads to the acquisition of the alphabetic principle. The activities in chapter 6 encourage children to form letters, begin to apply their letter-sound knowledge to spelling words, and explore writing for authentic purposes such as class books or lists.

COMPREHENSION, VOCABULARY, AND WORLD KNOWLEDGE

Learning to read requires the orchestration of many skills. Word decoding from the Simple View of Reading pulls in skills such as phonological awareness and alphabet knowledge. In early grades, we tend to focus on the skills of word decoding to help children learn to read the words on a page. This makes sense because reading comprehension is primarily constrained by decoding.

Skills in language comprehension are also necessary for learning to read. Comprehension requires children to understand the meanings of words and sentences while also integrating their knowledge of the world. The influence of language comprehension on reading comprehension—our ultimate goal—increases over time (Catts, Hogan, and Adlof, 2005). In early childhood classrooms, read-alouds are a mainstay in fostering language comprehension. Children's books with sophisticated vocabulary, concepts that extend world knowledge, and sentence complexity provide rich learning opportunities. The activities in chapter 7 work toward these goals: building vocabulary and world knowledge alongside early comprehension skills.

Ultimately, through application of decoding *and* spelling to a word and its meaning, children develop the alphabetic principle. One way to think about this is the interplay of sound, spelling, and meaning. Take the word *chop.* The sounds, or phonological information, for *chop* include the three different phonemes that, when combined, produce the oral form of the word *chop*: /ch/ /ŏ/ /p/. The spelling information for this word consists of the visual representation of the sequence of letters *(C-H-O-P)* that, when combined, form the spelling of the word *chop.* Finally, the meaning, or *semantic information*, includes the definition of the word *chop* (to cut something into pieces) and understanding how *chopping* carrots into pieces with a knife is different from *cutting* paper into pieces with scissors. These connections are at the heart of the alphabetic principle, a key foundational skill for early literacy.

Core Practice in Early Childhood Classrooms

All of the upcoming chapters are focused on activities that acknowledge developmental trends and current research on early literacy. In addition, I've vetted hundreds of activities to ensure that the ones included in this book also reflect developmentally appropriate practices of early childhood classrooms. In particular, the activities include hands-on engagement, purposeful play, and read-alouds. They are all activities you can read today and use tomorrow.

HANDS-ON, USE-TOMORROW ACTIVITIES

Hands-on activities are alive and well in early childhood classrooms. We believe in their power to keep our young learners engaged and active. We know children are more focused and motivated to learn when they are engaged with both their minds *and* their hands. Hands-on activities make learning less abstract for our young learners and can also provide an opportunity to improve fine motor skills. The activities in this book encourage active engagement and many are hands on.

Each set of activities begins with a brief introduction to connect to the purpose, so you can see how the activity fits within your early reading and writing instruction. Each activity includes tips to prepare before the activity, explicit steps and language to use during the activities, considerations to modify activities for children who may have difficulty grasping concepts, and ideas for wrapping up the activity and extending. Throughout these activities, you will see things to look for—or how to observe children's learning and gauge their understanding.

PURPOSEFUL PLAY

The activities come from a stance of purposeful play. As Mraz, Porcelli, and Tyler (2016) said, "Play isn't a luxury. It's a necessity." Not only does play offer multiple opportunities for children to reach various standards—be they the Common Core State Standards or the Head Start Early Learning Outcome Framework—but play also provides children with opportunities to engage in discussions and build oral language, turn-taking skills, and literacy skills in authentic (and fun) ways in an environment where they feel safe taking risks.

READING ALOUD

In their landmark review *Becoming a Nation of Readers* (1985), the Commission on Reading call reading aloud to children "the single most important activity for building the knowledge required for success in reading." In this book, every chapter includes ideas for literature connections. For example, the sentence "It kinks, coils, and curls every which way," from *Hair Love* by Matthew A. Cherry, can be used to develop concepts about print as children practice tracking left to right. *Mary Wears What She Wants* by Keith Negley provides a context for learning the word *courage* and the related word *courageous*. *Strictly No Elephants* by Lisa Mantchev introduces acceptance and tolerance while also acting as a backdrop for a syllable sort with animal names to build phonological awareness.

Nonfiction, too, is highlighted. Books such as *Give Bees a Chance* by Bethany Barton support learning how bees help plants grow while also using *bees* as a springboard for the letter-sound connection of *B* to /b/. *Living Things and Nonliving Things* by Keven Kurtz supports development of the science concept of living versus not living and builds world knowledge as well as serving as a jumping-off point for matching rhyming pairs like *rock/sock* and *plant/ant*.

Summary

Young children's overall development is complex and multifaceted. In early childhood classrooms, we observe them grow and learn across physical, cognitive, emotional, and social development. During these early years, they learn to communicate, form relationships, and explore the world around them. Each child comes to your classroom with different experiences, especially when it comes to literacy. The opportunities you provide the children in your classroom are critical in building the foundation they need for their future reading and writing success. To this end, chapters 2 through 7 provide you with more than one hundred activities informed by research in early literacy and specially selected based on developmentally appropriate early childhood practices. Lastly, chapter 8 details how early childhood teachers bring all of these critical literacy practices to their classrooms to provide valuable learning opportunities for the children in their care.

Let's get started!

2

CHAPTER TWO
Developing Oral Language

This chapter zeroes in on building children's oral language. Not only is oral language critical for comprehension, vocabulary, and concept development, it also contributes to literacy skills such as phonemic awareness, which in turn contributes to phonics. To begin, let's take a look at the early literacy standards from the Head Start Early Learning Outcome Framework and the Common Core State Standards that address oral language. As you can see, these standards span oral language elements such as conversing and asking questions to increasing the breadth and depth of word meanings and how words fit together in messages.

HEAD START EARLY LEARNING OUTCOME FRAMEWORK 36-60 MONTHS	COMMON CORE STATE STANDARDS KINDERGARTEN
■ Demonstrates interest and understanding when participating in language activities and games (36 months) ■ Initiates and responds in conversations with others (36 months) ■ Participates in simple conversations with others that are maintained by back-and-forth exchanges of ideas or information ■ Engages in simple conversations by expressing own feelings, thoughts, and ideas to others (36 months) ■ Asks and answers simple questions in conversations with others (36 months) ■ Shows ongoing connection to a conversation, group discussion, or presentation (60 months) ■ Demonstrates understanding of a variety of question types, such as "Yes/No" or "Who/What/When/Where" or "How/Why" (60 months)	■ Participates in collaborative conversations with diverse partners about kindergarten topics and texts with peers and adults in small and larger groups: • Follows agreed-upon rules for discussions • Continues conversation through multiple exchanges ■ Confirms understanding of a text read aloud or information presented orally or through other media by asking and answering questions about key details and requesting clarification if something is not understood ■ Asks and answers questions to seek help, get information, or clarify something that is not understood

HEAD START EARLY LEARNING OUTCOME FRAMEWORK 36-60 MONTHS	COMMON CORE STATE STANDARDS KINDERGARTEN
■ Maintains multiturn conversations with adults, other children, and within larger groups by responding in increasingly sophisticated ways, such as asking related questions or expressing agreement (60 months) ■ Categorizes words or objects, such as sorting a hard hat, machines, and tools into the construction group (60 months) ■ Discusses new words in relation to known words and word categories, such as "The bear and fox are both wild animals" (60 months) ■ Identifies shared characteristics among people, places, things, or actions (60 months) ■ Identifies key common antonyms and identifies 1 or 2 synonyms for very familiar words (60 months) ■ Shows an ability to distinguish similar words, such as "It's more than tall, it's gigantic" (60 months)	■ Determines or clarifies the meaning of unknown and multiple-meaning words and phrases based on kindergarten reading and content: • Identifies new meanings of familiar words and applies them accurately (for example, knowing *duck* is a bird and learning the verb "to duck") • Uses the most frequently occurring inflections and affixes (for example, *-ed, -s, un-, pre-, -ful, -less*) as a clue to the meaning of an unknown word ■ With guidance and support from adults, explores word relationships and nuances in word meanings: • Sorts common objects into categories to gain a sense of the concepts the categories represent • Demonstrates understanding of frequently occurring verbs and adjectives by relating them to their opposites (antonyms) • Distinguishes shades of meaning among verbs describing the same general actions (for example, *walk, march, strut, prance*) by acting out meanings • Uses words and phrases acquired through conversations, reading and being read to, and responding to texts

As discussed in chapter 1, the Simple View of Reading demonstrates the importance of oral language to later reading achievement (Gough and Tunmer, 1986). "Language has the power to shape our consciousness and it does so for each human child, by providing the theory that [they use] to interpret and manipulate their environment" (Halliday, 1993). In the first years of life, children develop foundational understandings of the sound system of language (*phonology*), the meanings of words across contexts (*semantics*), the way we put words together to communicate (*syntax*), the meaning units of words (*morphology*), and the rules that guide the way we communicate with each other (*pragmatics*).

Young children are experiencing intense growth in language development. To put this into perspective, children in prekindergarten know between one thousand and ten thousand words (Shipley and McAfee, 2015). By the time they enter first grade, many of them have learned an average of 14,000 words (Carey, 1978). Putting it another way, the children in our prekindergarten classrooms, on average, are acquiring somewhere between one thousand and three thousand words per year. This means they are acquiring as many as eight new words a day!

This rate of intense growth, unfortunately, is not universally so. In a classic study, Hart and Risley (1995) estimate that some children heard three million more words than other children by the age of three, and by the time they reached kindergarten, some heard 30 million more words than other children. The sheer difference in number is astounding, but that only paints part of the picture. There was also a notable difference in the contexts in which these words were used and in the interactions with caregivers. Moreover, adult clarification of words within the course of conversation is associated with increased vocabulary (Weizman and Snow, 2001). Our early childhood classrooms are filled with children across a range of language skill, and this chapter focuses on ways to support children's language growth. Some of these activities will be a part of the fabric of your everyday routines, and others will be part of more explicit, intentional instruction.

Everyday Routines

One goal of the early childhood classroom is to turn ordinary exchanges into rich language experiences. Oral language is developed even when teachers don't intentionally focus on building vocabulary or conversation skills. Consider the following five practices to build your everyday routines: recasts, expansions, and questions; sophisticated words; and narrations.

RECASTS, EXPANSIONS, AND QUESTIONS

We have an important role to play in children's language development. When we respond to what children say, we let them know that we care about their thoughts, their stories, and their contributions. The linguistic quality of our responses is equally important. McGinty and Justice (2010) suggest recasts and expansions as ways to support language growth and provide timely feedback. Recasts allow you to correct children's ungrammatical language use while also acknowledging what they've said. Expansions involve this same acknowledgment while also adding detail to their message.

Questions serve many purposes, such as information gathering. When it comes to language development, our purpose in questioning is about encouraging children's participation in sustained, meaningful conversations. McGinty and Justice (2010) suggest using topic-continuing questions and *wh-*questions, with preference given to *wh-* questions. *Wh-* questions have been shown to be very helpful in supporting oral language, especially in prekindergarten and kindergarten. Moreover, we can consider the type of *wh-* questions. Closed *wh-* questions—*who, what, when, where*—usually require only a one-word response, but they still play an important role in early childhood classrooms because they keep children engaged and help you check for understanding. Open-ended *wh-* questions—*why*—require more detailed responses and help foster language growth.

As you think about incorporating these language-support practices, here are three important considerations. First, be selective with your recasts and expansions within an oral exchange. This keeps the exchange more natural, and when it comes to recasting, less is more. Second, keep the child's level of understanding in mind. You don't want to jump too many levels of language complexity. Third, give *wh-* questions priority with a slant toward open-ended ones.

SOPHISTICATED WORDS

Young children love a big word! Using big, or sophisticated, words encourages interest in words and a motivation to learn new words. Sophisticated words are words that aren't likely to be encountered in typical, everyday conversation. Using sophisticated words for familiar words you use every day can expand children's breadth and depth of vocabulary. This practice can increase the number of words they know and link new words to familiar ones. This type of word learning may seem incidental, but the teaching is not. Rather, teaching sophisticated words includes deliberate, thoughtful decisions.

You can intentionally include sophisticated words by pinpointing specific familiar words you can gradually replace with more sophisticated synonyms. Include appropriate explanations when needed, and make sure your language is child friendly and comprehensible. In addition, you'll want to consistently use words throughout the day and provide opportunities for children to use these words, too. To get started, think about the everyday routines in your classroom that would lend themselves to more sophisticated synonyms. Here are some ideas.

- Actions in your classroom:
    - Words to consider using when possible: *arrange, collect, distribute, gather, pause*
    - Instead of telling children to *walk* to get in line, say *hustle.*
    - Instead of asking children to *pass out* papers, say *distribute.*
    - Instead of suggesting children *make* a tower of blocks, say *construct.*
- Group time:
    - Words to consider using when possible: *contribute, cooperate, determine, express, participate*
    - Instead of asking children to *think about* a response, say *consider.*
    - Instead of asking children to *make* a circle, say *create.*
    - Instead of asking children to *get together* on the group rug, say *collect* or *gather.*
- Children's behaviors:
    - Words to consider using when possible: *courteous, impolite, resolve, respectful, thoughtful*
    - Instead of saying someone is *tired*, say *exhausted.*
    - Instead of saying someone is *thankful*, say they are *grateful.*
    - Instead of describing someone as *happy* or *nice*, say they are *delighted* or *pleasant.*

Lane and Allen (2010) provide specific examples of this deliberate introduction to sophisticated words in a kindergarten classroom. During morning meeting, the class charts the weather each day. The teacher appoints a "weather watcher," and the children discuss the weather as *cloudy* or *cool.* As the year moves on, the teacher deliberately makes a switch from "weather watcher" to *meteorologist,* and children report on the *forecast* as *overcast* or *brisk.* She incrementally brings in sophisticated words, provides clear explanations, has children repeat the words frequently, and encourages them to use the sophisticated words.

NARRATIONS

Self-talk and parallel talk are common narrations in early childhood classrooms and may very well be part of your everyday routine already. These strategies provide a descriptive narrative with expansions to build children's understanding of language. Basically, these are descriptions of what you are doing or what the children are doing. With self-talk, you will describe what you are doing. For example, you might say, "I am collecting our papers. Now I'm hanging them up so we can see all of our drawings. I know I'll enjoy seeing them displayed." Parallel talk involves you narrating what a child is doing. When the children line up for recess, for example, you might say, "You are lining up. I see you standing still and patiently waiting for everyone to collect. Plus, you all have your coats for recess because it is brisk this morning."

Oral language is developed even when we do not intentionally focus on building vocabulary or conversation skills. Each of these practices—recast, expansion, question, sophisticated words, and narration—can be a powerful language builder as part of your everyday routine. Placing intentional focus on building oral language can greatly influence not only the quantity (size) of a child's vocabulary but also the quality (depth of understanding). The activities outlined throughout the remainder of this chapter home in on understanding language and following directions, getting children to engage in conversation, teaching vocabulary, and building relationships across words.

Understanding Language and Following Directions

When children enter prekindergarten around the age of three, they know more than a thousand words. They are still learning to listen and pay attention to what they hear. Listening is a core factor in a child's ability to follow directions, and following directions is a part of everyday life in the classroom and beyond. To follow directions, you have to hear and attend to what is being said, understand the pronunciation and meaning of the words, interpret the sequence of steps that must be followed, and seek clarification when needed. The following activities provide practice in following directions through popular games. These are just a few suggestions; there are many other games that encourage listening and following directions, such as Red Rover and Red Light, Green Light.

ACTIVITY Simon Says

▢ Get Things Ready

This is a great game. You don't need to do anything to play, just a game plan for the directions you'll pose. You can play inside or outside. Just make sure there is room to move around.

▢ Make an Introduction

"We're going to play Simon Says. You have to listen very carefully! If you hear 'Simon says,' you have to do what Simon says. But if you *don't* hear 'Simon says,' then don't do anything. So, we'll listen for the words 'Simon says' and then what Simon says to do!"

▢ Now for the Model

"Watch me. Let me show you what to do. Simon says touch your shoulders. I'm going to touch my shoulders because I heard the words 'Simon says.' (Touch your shoulders.)

Simon says turn around. I'm going to turn around because I heard the words 'Simon says.' (Turn around in a circle.)

Jump on one foot. I'm not going to do anything because I didn't hear 'Simon says.'

Ready? I'll be Simon. You should only do what I say when I say . . . (Wait for response.) That's right! Simon says!"

▢ Let's Get Some Practice

Continue playing as you give them one-step directions, occasionally including "Simon says." Provide guidance and reminders. To start, you might find you need to direct them on the next step to establish understanding and/or narrate what they are doing to reinforce the directions of the game. I usually invite children to be Simon after we all get the hang of it. Some versions of Simon Says have children sitting down or leaving the group if they make a mistake; I don't play that way. Children continue to play to practice their listening and language comprehension skills.

▢ Wrap It Up

"What great listeners! You listened closely to Simon's directions to decide whether you should follow his directions."

> **Flex the Activity!**
> Turn Simon Says into multistep directions. You can start with two-step directions. I like to work up to three-step directions. Use sequence words by saying, "Simon says, first touch your toes, then touch your head." Or you might say, "Simon says, first touch your toes, then touch your head, and last turn around." You can also incorporate letter formation by asking them to make an *S* or *M* with their bodies.

ACTIVITY Polar Bear

▢ Get Things Ready

This is a popular poem widely used with various animals or toys. I switch it up based on a theme, child interest, or a recent read-aloud. All you need is the poem. I always have it written on chart paper. I sometimes take pictures of the children making the movements and post the photos by the lines.

> *Polar Bear, Polar Bear*
> *Polar bear, polar bear, reach up high.*
> *Polar bear, polar bear, touch the sky.*
> *Polar bear, polar bear, bend down low.*
> *Polar bear, polar bear, touch your toe.*
> *Polar bear, polar bear, turn around.*
> *Polar bear, polar bear, touch the ground.*

▢ Make an Introduction

"We're going to learn a new rhyme today! It's called 'Polar Bear, Polar Bear.' This rhyme tells us things to do, so we have to listen carefully to know what the rhyme tells us."

▢ Now for the Model

"Watch and listen. I'm going to say the rhyme and follow the directions." Recite the poem and make the movements.

▢ Let's Get Some Practice

Recite the poem a few times. For the first couple of recitations, invite the children to join you only in following the directions. Then begin inviting them to recite chorally with you.

On subsequent days, you might tell them to listen carefully because you will mix up the directions. To do this, you'll mix up the rhyming couplets. For example, switch the third and fourth lines:

> *Polar bear, polar bear, touch your toe.*
> *Polar bear, polar bear, bend down low.*

You can also google "Teddy Bear, Teddy Bear." You'll find YouTube videos of versions as songs for you and the children to watch and sing.

▢ Wrap It Up

"We listened closely today! We said our polar bear rhyme and listened so we could follow the directions. Let's reach up high and touch the sky to celebrate!"

Connect to a Book!

I chose to use *polar bear* here because I have recently read *The Lonely Polar Bear* by Khoa Le. I could choose other animals for other occasions, such as *arctic hare* while exploring poems in *Ice: Poems About Arctic Life* by Douglas Florian, *humpback whale* while exploring ocean animals in *The Big Book of Blue* by Yuval Sommer, or *snowy owl* after reading *Over and Under the Snow* by Kate Messner.

ACTIVITY Mother, May I?

Get Things Ready

While you don't need to prepare to play this classic game, I usually have some supports prepared, especially for children who are first learning to play. I teach the children that they must ask to make a movement and must give a number of times they'll make the movement. I also post pictures of movements they can make, such as hop, twirl, or crab walk. After they grasp this, I'll add animals. For example, they'll first have to ask to hop two times. Then I'll add animals, so they hop like a bunny two times.

Make an Introduction

"We're going to play a game called Mother May I. You have to listen closely during this game! You'll listen to what the 'mother' tells you to do. One of us will play the mother. Then you have to ask, 'Mother, may I?' This is important. You can't move until you ask, 'Mother, may I?' You are trying to move closer and closer to mother. The first one to make it to mother wins. To move, you have to ask to move and say how many times. Look at my poster of ways you can move. You can take steps or hop." Point to pictures as you say each movement. You can add new movements as they learn the game, but I usually keep it to two or three movements when we are learning.

Now for the Model

"To play the game, everyone stands in a row at this end of the room." Collect a small group of children in a row at one end of the room. Starting out with a few to demonstrate will make the first few times you play go more smoothly. "And one friend will be mother. Mother stands at the other side of the room. I'll play mother first. Look at me. I'm going to move to the other side and put my back toward you so I can't see you. You will take turns asking mother if you can move. Remember, you have to say, 'Mother, may I?' Mother can say yes or no! But if the answer is no, mother will give you another movement to make. When you ask 'Mother, may I,' you have to say a movement and how many times you'll do it. So you might say, 'Mother, may I take two steps?' Keyshawn, you will start us off. Say, 'Mother, may I take two steps?'" Keyshawn asks. "Yes, you may. Now, Keyshawn, since I said yes, you can take two steps toward me."

Let's Get Some Practice

Continue giving each child in the row turns as they work their way toward you. Support as needed and encourage them to ask, "Mother, may I?" and say how many movements. I usually play at least twice and invite a new group up for a second round. Eventually, children will play the role of mother.

Wrap It Up

"Nice work asking to move and listening for mother's directions! Amelia asked to move, and when mother said no, she listened for

Look For

With any of these activities, you will be watching for the children to follow directions without prompting. You can also start listening for how easily they express themselves. For example, in Mother May I, you can look for their ease at articulating the movement they want to make. As you add animals, you can see if they are able to add an additional piece of information to their request.

mother's directions. Let's remember who made it to mother today: Javier and Amelia! You can play this game at recess. Let me know if you need help."

ACTIVITY Charades

Get Things Ready

Make a set of action cards and a set of location cards using pictures. Action pictures could be writing, reading, jumping, chewing, cutting, spinning, clapping, snapping, nodding, or shaking. Location pictures would highlight places in your classroom such as tables, the group rug, library, science center, or sign-in desk. Put each set in a separate basket.

Make an Introduction

"We're going to play a game today called Charades. In this game, you act things out, and your friends guess what you are doing. They will have to name the actions you are doing. An action is something you do with your body. See this basket? It has pictures with actions in them. Let's take a look." Show each picture and name the action. Invite the children to repeat the action. Have them show you how to make each action. "Now let's look at this basket. This is the location basket." Show each picture and name the location. Invite them to repeat the location. "Ready to play Charades?"

Now for the Model

"Watch me. I'll go first. You're going to guess my action! I'll pick an action card and a location card. Then I'll make the action at the location. If you guess, keep it in your head. Let me show you how Charades works first." Perform your action at your location. "Now you might know what I'm doing. This is what you'd say. Here's my sentence: I am jumping at the library. Say it with me. 'Ms. Hayes is jumping at the library.'"

Let's Get Some Practice

Invite one child at a time to come up and choose an action and a location. Name any picture they can't remember. Then encourage the children to guess the action and location by using the sentence frame: ___ is ___ at/in the ___.

If children can easily play this level of Charades, you can have them pick two cards from each set. Then the group will have to guess the two actions and locations using sequence words and the appropriate pronoun in the second sentence. For example, you might say, "First, Ms. Hayes jumps at the library. Then, she writes at the at the group rug." Or you could add a third set of pictures with position words, such as *under, over,* and *beside.* So, you might write under the table.

Wrap It Up

"Charades is so fun! You named your friends' actions and the locations, like Amelia nodding at the sign-in desk."

Getting Children to Engage in Conversation

Typically, children love to talk! They just don't always know how to discuss what they are learning with you or with each other. As early childhood teachers, we are helping children learn about letters and sounds, forming letters, and counting objects. But we are also actively teaching them how to talk with, and listen to, each other. Before we head into our activities, let's look at about three common ways to get children talking and sharing: equity sticks, talking partners, and gallery walks.

EQUITY STICKS

Equity sticks are an easy, cheap way to encourage participation with an eye toward equitable participation. All you need is craft sticks (or anything easy to manage), a permanent marker to write one child's name per stick, and two jars or cups. When you facilitate a discussion, randomly pull out an equity stick and invite that child to participate. Then put that child's stick in the other jar. This will help you keep track of who you've called on and who has gotten a chance to share.

Over the course of a week, I like to chart children's participation. I do this with an equity chart. I make a chart with their names on the left and then a column for each day of the week. I keep it with me all day and make a tally mark each time I call on someone or someone volunteers. Then at the end of the week, I ask myself about who is participating the most and the least, and I try to see any pattern as to why. I use this to set goals for myself for the next week about who I need to invite to share more and how I can best support them.

TALKING PARTNERS

Turn and talk and think-pair-share are two strategies commonly used across elementary grades and beyond. They work well in early childhood classrooms, too. They are quick, easy ways to get children talking with each other to build understanding. These brief interactions also provide children with stopping points to process and consolidate their learning. Moreover, children can clarify their own thoughts as they listen to their partner's thinking. Through these talking partnerships, children play an active role in their learning. The main difference between the two strategies is that think-pair-share includes an initial step of thinking to yourself before turning and talking with your partner.

As with anything, you will teach procedures, model expectations, and provide plenty of practice with an anchor chart as a reminder of the procedures. Here are some additional tips to get you started:

- I like to start with simple questions first, for which children will easily have an answer and can turn for a brief talk before coming back to share. For example, you might ask about their favorite food.

- Children might benefit from sentence stems. So, if you are having them talk about their favorite food, your stem could be, "My favorite food is . . ."

- You can pose two related questions to encourage children to add on to the conversation. For example, you might ask, "What is your favorite color? What is something that is that color?"

- Once children get the hang of it, ask open-ended questions. I've always found this transition to be easier when connected to a read-aloud and a familiar topic.

- Then encourage them to elaborate and have some back-and-forth. You might teach them how to agree and disagree and how to be active listeners.

- You will want to be sure to monitor their conversations and give them feedback on how to talk with each other, take turns, actively listen, and keep the conversation going.

- Lastly, you'll want to allow time for some sharing afterward.

GALLERY WALKS

A gallery walk involves children exploring a text, problems, or images that are displayed on posters or chart paper around the classroom. Typically, children write comments, ideas, or answers on the posters, and then groups move around the room exploring other groups' work. While I've not tried gallery walks in prekindergarten, I have used them in kindergarten. They can provide a meaningful purpose for collaborative thinking and shared learning, but things need to be kept manageable for our young learners. One adaptation that has been helpful is to have them work on something as a group and then explain their work one group at a time rather than walking around the room to see how other groups approached a problem.

Here's how it might work. Let's say you've given groups of children pictures to sort into those that begin with various consonant sounds. Each group is responsible for a different sound. As they make their decisions, they glue their pictures on their posters and maybe even attempt to label their pictures. Upon finishing, each group explains their final poster by talking through their pictures with the same initial sound to the class. You'll see instances throughout the following activities (and the activities throughout this book) where equity sticks, talking partners, or gallery walks are suggested.

ACTIVITY I Spy

Get Things Ready

Collect several objects or pictures that relate to a theme. Just make sure your theme is familiar to the children. Or you can always play I Spy on the fly with everyday objects in your classroom.

Make an Introduction

"We're going to play I Spy today! You have to listen closely to the clues about what is described so you can make a guess."

Now for the Model

"Look at my animals." Display the animal objects you've collected. "It's a collection of our favorite zoo animals! I am going to choose one of the animals with my eyes. This way you won't know which one I chose. Then I'm going to give you clues about the animal I spy. Here's my first one. I spy an animal that has brown spots. It looks like a horse with a very long neck and short horns." Add additional clues if children need more information.

Let's Get Some Practice

Continue playing I Spy by giving children turns to spy an animal. You can use equity sticks to choose children. You might need a sentence stem to get them started: "I spy an animal that . . ." Remind them that they are choosing with their eyes.

Wrap It Up

"You all know a lot about zoo animals! You gave great clues to us as we played I Spy. I have one more clue for I Spy. I spy an animal that is nocturnal. Remember, *nocturnal* means they are active at night and rest during the day. That's right. A leopard!"

ACTIVITY Mystery Bag

Get Things Ready

You'll need either a collection of objects and/or pictures related to the same theme. Plus, you'll need your trusty mystery bag! In this game, I use the five senses to help. So, you might have a chart of the five senses for a quick reference.

Make an Introduction

"We are going to play Mystery Bag. This time we'll use our five senses. Remember, our five senses are touch, taste, see, smell, and hear. Our senses are going to help us describe the things I've collected in our mystery bag! Our bag has different kinds of foods."

Now for the Model

"I'll go first. I'm going to choose an object from the mystery bag. This is a banana." Hold the banana up for the group to see. "I'm going to use my five senses to describe it. I see that its long and shaped sort of like a C. It is yellow. It feels smooth. I can't taste or smell this one, but I can think about how a real banana smells or tastes. A banana tastes sweet. Can we hear bananas? Haha! No."

Let's Get Some Practice

Continue to play the game by inviting children to take turns choosing from the bag. Support their descriptions by asking questions about the five senses or prompting them to describe and then referencing your five-senses chart. You might provide sentence stems such as "It looks like . . ." You can also play this game by having one child choose an object and not show it to the group. Then they provide clues using their five senses for the group to guess.

Wrap It Up

"What a great job describing our foods today! You thought about your five senses so you could describe each food with lots of details."

> **Flex the Activity!**
>
> If my objects and theme lend themselves to sorting the objects after, I will encourage the children to sort the objects into groups of things that are alike or different. Then you can compare and contrast, count, and graph the groups. Or you might have a Question of the Day to vote on a favorite animal from an animal theme or a favorite food from the mystery bag example here.

ACTIVITY A Picture Is Worth a Thousand Words

Get Things Ready

Collect a variety of photographs that have a lot of detail. I usually collect them based on the themes of our classroom study. I like to laminate them so I can use them each year, or you can have a collection that you present using your classroom projector.

Make an Introduction

"We're going to look at some pictures and talk about the things we see happening in them. We can also think about our own experiences doing some of these things or seeing these things, to make personal connections. Remember, making personal connections help us learn about new things."

Now for the Model

Hold up a photo. "This is a photograph of a forest. Let me tell you about the things I see. I see tall trees with green leaves. The leaves will change colors in the fall when the season changes. Do you see any animals? I see a bird. I see three birds in this photograph. I have a birdfeeder at my house and see lots of birds. I've seen a red bird like this one at my house." Point to the bird in the picture. "It's called a cardinal." Continue to talk about what you see and make connections, occasionally inviting the children to engage with the photograph.

Let's Get Some Practice

You can continue with this photograph or show them a different one. Ask questions to help them elaborate as they talk. Here are some general questions or prompts:

- What do you see?
- What is this/that called?
- Have you been to a ___?
- Tell me about a time you ___.
- What do you know about ___?
- What do people do at a ___?

Wrap It Up

"We talked a lot about what we saw in our photographs today. You gave so many details! You might want to use one of these photographs to write about in your journal. We already know we have a lot to say about them!"

> **Connect to a Book!**
> After exploring a wordless picture book and telling a companion story, you can choose an especially detailed page to unpack. For example, in *Window*, illustrated by Marion Arbona, there is a picture of a busy city street filled with activity and plenty of details to get a conversation going. Or look at one of the silly pages of *Mayhem at the Museum*, illustrated by Luciano Lozano, where the art of the New York Metropolitan Museum of Art comes alive.

ACTIVITY Name, Tell, Do

Get Things Ready

Collect five or six objects or pictures. Again, I like to do this based on a theme. I usually use my mystery bag for this, but you can also collect items in a basket.

Make an Introduction

"Today we'll play a game called Name, Tell, Do. We're going to talk about the pictures I have in my basket. The first thing you'll do is pick a picture and say the name of what's in the picture. Next, you will tell us something about it. Last, you'll show us what people do with it. Before we start, let's take a look at our pictures. These are all pieces of clothing you'd wear in the winter when it's cold and snowy." Take out all pictures, name them, and have the children repeat. Always encourage them to use complete sentences, so you might need sentence stems ready, such as "This is a . . .," or "These are . . ."

Now for the Model

"I'll go first. I'll pick a picture from the basket. First, I name what's in the picture. These are snow pants." Show the picture. "Next, I'll tell you something about snow pants. You wear snow pants when you are playing in the snow to help you stay warm and dry. Last, I'll do something I'd do when I wear snow pants. I'm going to pretend I'm sledding when I wear my snow pants. Let's all pretend we are sledding in our snow pants!" Pretend with the children. "Now, it's your turn to name, tell, and do." I usually narrate what they are doing when they pretend.

Let's Get Some Practice

Invite children to take a turn using your equity sticks. Remind them of the steps after they pull out a picture. You might say, "First, name what you see. Next, tell us something about it. Last, pretend to do something," as they share. I usually like to have everyone pretend the "do" step before moving to the next child and picture. If a child has difficulty, you can name what's in the picture. Say, "These are mittens. What are they called?" Or if they have difficulty telling you something you use the item for, you might say, "You wear mittens to keep your hands warm when it's cold outside. How are mittens used?" Or you might show them something to do with mittens and narrate what you are doing by saying, "I'm going to put my mittens on to keep my hands warm while I make snowballs. I'm going to scoop up some snow and make a ball by patting it." Encourage the child to pretend to put on their mittens and make snowballs.

Wrap It Up

"Everyone, nice work naming the clothes, telling us something about them, and pretending to do something with them. You might want to use one of these pictures to write about in your journal. You already have a lot to say about them!"

> **Look For**
>
> As with all of these activities, you will be looking for instances of children keeping a conversation going as they use their words to describe and communicate. Pay close attention to and make note of children who need more support and prompts from you or their friends. In these cases, you might want to intentionally buddy up with them during moments of free play or exploration to recast, expand, and question. Or you might want to provide more narration during the times you are with that child or a group that child is in.

ACTIVITY Tell Me More!

Get Things Ready

Collect pictures of things based on a theme or topic of great interest to children. Or you might take pictures during a shared experience such as a nature walk or share pictures of everyday things children will be familiar with such as a busy grocery store.

Make an Introduction

"It's fun to listen and talk to each other. It's fun to have a conversation. A *conversation* is when we listen to what someone tells us and then we say something to add to their idea. Conversations help us learn new things, and they help us make friends! Let's have some conversations!"

Now for the Model

"Here's a picture of you all at recess on the playground. I see some of you on the swings and some of you running around. I see the slide and the sandbox. I'm going to tell you what I like to do when I'm at a playground. I like to play in the sandbox when I go to a playground. I like having dump trucks that I can fill with sand and then dump the sand out. What do you like to do on the playground at recess?" You'll want to keep the conversation going by providing a narration of the conversational "moves" you are making. It might sound like this:

Keyshawn: I like to go down the slide.

You: I'm going to say something that adds to Keyshawn's idea. I can tell him that I like to slide, too. Then I'm going to ask him a question. [to Keyshawn] I like to slide, too. I really like slides that are tall so I can slide fast. Do you like tall slides that make you go fast?

Keyshawn: Yes!

You: Now I think I'll ask him to tell me more. [to Keyshawn] What other kinds of slides do you like?

Keyshawn: There's this one at the playground near my house that curves around like this. I like that one, too.

You: I liked how Keyshawn and I learned that we both like tall slides that make us go fast. I also liked how Keyshawn told me about the curved slide at the playground near his house. We had a conversation! We gave each other a lot of details about our ideas so we could learn more about each other.

Let's Get Some Practice

You can either continue with the same picture or use a new picture. Support the conversation using the same process as described in the model. To help support children in keeping a conversation going, you could distribute Unifix cubes. Give each child two or three cubes of one color, meaning, for example, give two red to one child and two blue to another. You can challenge the group to build a tall tower of cubes as they add a cube with each contribution they make to the conversation.

Wrap It Up

"We had conversations today! Remember, a *conversation* is when we listen to what someone tells us and then we say something to add to their idea. We learned a lot about each other today. Amelia and Javier love to swing high. Keyshawn and I love tall slides to go fast. We also built a tall tower to show how many turns we took in our conversation. Let's try to add one more cube next time!"

ACTIVITY Say It with a Puppet

Get Things Ready

For this activity, each child will need a puppet, so gather up all of the puppets you have. If you only have a couple, no problem. You can easily make stick puppets or sock puppets.

Make an Introduction

"Today we're going to play with our puppets! Our puppets are going to have conversations. Remember, a *conversation* is when we listen to what someone tells us and then we say something to add to their idea. Our puppets want to get to know each other!"

Now for the Model

"Let me show you how we can help our puppets have a conversation. I have two stick puppets. I'm going to move them up and down to pretend they are talking. They are going to have a conversation. This puppet is Ralph, and he'll talk in a high voice. This one is Stuart, and he'll talk in a low voice. But you can do whatever you want with your puppet. You can give them names and have them talk in a baby voice or a robot voice or even your own voice. I'm going to start by having them greet each other.

Ralph: Hi! I'm Ralph. What's your name?

Stuart: I'm Stuart. I'm five years old. How old are you?

Ralph: I'm five, too! I'm going to play in the sandbox. Do you want to come?

Stuart: Sure!

Ralph: I like to put sand in my dump truck and dump it out. What do you like to do at the playground?

Stuart: I like the sandbox. I don't have a dump truck.

Ralph: Tell me what you like to do in the sandbox."

Let's Get Some Practice

Distribute puppets and pair the children. I tell them where they can pretend their puppets are. They might be on the playground or in their classroom. It just needs to be a universally familiar place. Then I tell them they need to do two things: have their puppets greet each other and then find out something new about each other. Go around the partnerships and support their conversations as needed.

Wrap It Up

"You did such a great job helping your puppets have a conversation. I noticed your puppets greeting each other. I also noticed many of your puppets sharing things about themselves, like Aaliya's puppet was named Sunshine, and Sunshine's favorite snack is a fruit roll."

ACTIVITY Pretend Interview

Get Things Ready

Decide on a person you will pretend to be for children to interview. You could choose to highlight a job or a character from a book. For example, if you are in the middle of a weather unit, you could pretend to be a meteorologist. Or if you've just read a book with a character children can easily relate to, you can pretend to be that character. For example, in *A New Home* by Tania de Regil, two children move to a new city. If you choose someone based on their job, then you will need to build the children's background knowledge about the job. If you choose a character, then read the book and engage the children in a conversation about the character. You might want to dress up or have props to really play the part and add to the fun.

☐ Make an Introduction

"We're going to do a pretend interview. An *interview* is when you ask someone questions to learn about them. I'm going to pretend to be the little girl in our story who moves to New York City."

☐ Now for the Model

"Remember how we talked about the things she might miss or why she was nervous and sad? So, you might ask questions about what she will miss or how she feels about going to a new school. You might ask, 'What do you miss about Mexico City?' I can answer, 'One thing I'll miss is grilled corn. We eat it on a stick!'"

☐ Let's Get Some Practice

Encourage the children to ask you questions. You can support them in asking you questions about more things you miss, new favorite things in New York City, how you like your new school, whether you have made new friends, and so on.

☐ Wrap It Up

"Nice job interviewing our character from *A New Home* today! We learned some new things about her. You can pretend to be a favorite character and ask a friend to interview you."

> ### Connect to a Book!
> A number of books highlight different professions, such as *Clothesline Clues to Jobs People Do* by Kathryn Heling and *Lisette the Vet* by Ruth Mac Pete. Any book from The Questioners series by Andrea Beaty provides some insight into a profession. These books are fun introductions to different professions that could complement others such as *I Want to be a Veterinarian* by Laurie Driscoll, which provides more information about what veterinarians do through the lens of a boy taking his dog to the vet. Either way, these books can provide fun backdrops to your explanation of different professions.

ACTIVITY What Do You Think?

☐ Get Things Ready

After you've read a book or a few books, you can have them on hand and invite children to share their opinion about the books.

☐ Make an Introduction

"Today we'll look at a book we've already read and share our opinions about it. We all have things we like and things we don't like as much. These are called our *opinions*. We'll share our opinions today."

Now for the Model

"Here's our book *Cake* by Sue Hendra. I am going to share my opinions. Remember, *opinions* are the things we liked or didn't like as much. When we share our opinions, we also want to explain why. So, here's my first opinion. There were so many things I liked about this book. I liked it when Cake was shopping for a special hat to wear to the party because I liked seeing Cake in all of those funny hats. I also liked not knowing for a couple of pages about the hat he ended up with because I got to guess a little bit about what it might look like. One thing I didn't like was when the friends at the party wanted to eat Cake. I know I love to eat cake at a party, but in this story, I thought Cake was invited because he was a friend. I just shared my opinions. I talked about the things I liked and the things I didn't like as much in our book *Cake*. Now, you will share your opinion."

Let's Get Some Practice

"We are going to think-pair-share. The first thing you'll do is think. You are going to think about your opinions about the book. So, you will think about things you liked and things you didn't like as much. You may only have things you liked. That's okay. We don't always have to have things we like *and* things we don't like. When your partner shares their opinion, you can agree with them or disagree with them. Remember how we agree. We stay, 'I agree because . . .' And, when we disagree, we say, 'I disagree because . . .' Okay everyone. Let's think." After you give the children a minute to think, have them pair up with their talking partners and share. Move around and support the partners' conversations as needed.

Wrap It Up

"Nice job today sharing your opinions! It sounded like most of us had opinions about the things we liked in this book. And, a lot of us like the part when Cake shopped for hats! I agree with you all because it was pretty funny! Some of you disagreed with me and liked the part in the end when Cake had to run for it. That's okay. We won't always agree with each other."

Teaching Vocabulary

Early vocabulary is a powerful predictor not only of children's later language development but also their reading skills, school readiness, and overall academic success. Considering its importance and the varied vocabulary knowledge the children bring with them to school, you will want to intentionally make vocabulary learning a part of your school day. Creating a language-learning classroom is a good first step. But what are best practices for facilitating vocabulary learning? Keep these principles in mind:

- Be systematic as you choose words intentionally and build upon them over time.

- Be explicit with your explanations of new words.

- Provide plenty of opportunities for vocabulary use during classroom activities.

- Offer frequent active *and* guided practice with the words.

- Include periodic reviews.

- Observe children's use of the words.

Chapter 6 will go into more detail about teaching specific words. In the following activities, we will focus on teaching words for grammatical purposes, such as verb tense and pronouns. These same guidelines apply as we'll be intentional about our choices, explicit in our explanations, and thoughtful about the opportunities we provide for practice and review. First up are pronouns.

ACTIVITY What's the Pronoun?

Get Things Ready

Gather together eight to ten objects, and write a short, simple sentence about each one using names of the children in your classroom as the subject of each sentence. Write each sentence on a sentence strip, and make sure to have some sentences with more than one child as the subject. If children need support recognizing written names of their friends, you can include pictures by their names. I usually have a few premade sticky notes with pronouns already written on them, such as *he, she, we*, and *they*. Once the children use these pronouns easily, you can incorporate others such as *his, her, your*, and *their*.

Make an Introduction

"We're going to play a game with something called pronouns. A *pronoun* is a word you can use instead of someone's name. (Note: At this point, I'm keeping this to personal pronouns.) We use pronouns because it can be quicker, and then we aren't saying someone's name over and over. We know Amelia likes to swing. Amelia likes to go down the slide, and Amelia likes to run around with her friends at recess. Instead of saying Amelia over and over, I can say, 'Amelia likes to swing, and she likes to go down the slide.' *She* is a pronoun." Show the sticky notes with *he, she, we*, and *they*. "The pronoun we usually use for a boy is *he*." Point to *he* and say *he* again. "The pronoun we usually use for a girl is *she*." Point to *she* and say *she* again. "When we are talking about a group, we use *we* or *they*." Point to each pronoun as you say it.

Now for the Model

"Watch me. I'll show you what we are going to do. I'm going to show you an object and a sentence I wrote about the object. You'll notice my sentences are about all of us! Here's my first sentence and the object. My object is a toy slide. My sentence says, 'Amelia and Keyshawn like to slide.'" Point and read the sentence. "Read it with me. 'Amelia and Keyshawn like to slide.'" Point and read again. "This sentence is about more than just one of you. It's about two of you: Amelia and Keyshawn. So, I need to use *we* or *they*. I'm going to choose *they* because it is about Amelia and Keyshawn. You use *we* if you are also included. So, I'm going to get my *they* sticky note and put it here. *They*. What's my pronoun? *They*." Encourage a choral response. "Now I'll read my sentence again, but this time I'll use my pronoun. '*They* like to slide.'" Point and read the sentence.

☐ Let's Get Some Practice

Continue with your objects and sentences. Hold up your object and name it. Then point and read your sentence. Invite children to point and read with you a second time. Then show your sticky notes. Point and read *he*, *she*, *we*, and *they*. To help them distinguish between *we* and *they*, you could pose questions such as, "What if Keyshawn read this sentence? 'Amelia and Keyshawn like to slide.' He'd use the pronoun *we* because it includes him." If children have difficulty, reduce the number of choices.

☐ Wrap It Up

"We'll continue to practice our pronouns. Using the right pronouns when you talk and write will help others understand what you are talking about or writing about. Let's pay attention to the pronouns we use today. Oh! I just used one. I said, 'Let's pay attention to the pronouns *we* use today.'"

> ### Connect to a Book!
>
> There are some books that are fun reads that emphasize pronouns, such as Brian Cleary's *I and You and Don't Forget Who*. I've found that book fun with some pages to emphasize for my young learners, but generally I've found that one hard for them to follow. Another option for our younger learners is *If You Were a Pronoun* by Nancy Loewen.

ACTIVITY More Than One

☐ Get Things Ready

Collect objects from around the room, such as plastic letters, blocks, stuffed animals, and pencils. You just need a few of each so you can discuss the concept of more than one.

☐ Make an Introduction

"Today we are going to think about when a word is plural. *Plural* means more than one. So, we will be talking about people, places, or things when we have only one and when we have more than one—when those things are *plural*, more than one."

☐ Now for the Model

Place a pencil in front of you on the floor. Then say, "I have a pencil. I have only one pencil. Now look." Lay down another pencil. "Now I have two pencils. When I have more than one pencil, I have to add /s/ to the end of the word. This lets you know I'm talking about more than one. I make it plural. One pencil. Two pencils." Make sure to emphasize the /s/ at the end of *pencils*. "Say it with me: one p. . ." Pause and encourage them to finish the singular *pencil*. "Two p . . ." Again, encourage them to finish the word but this time the plural *pencils*.

> ### Connect to a Book!
>
> I've found that just about any book can connect to plurals by just hunting for them as you reread a story. Counting books are especially good for this, such as Christopher Danielson's *How Many?* But just about any book will work. For example, *My Dog Bigsy* by Alison Lester and *Don't Think About Purple Elephants* by Susanne Merritt are fun books with loads of regular plurals. (Bigsy chases animals on the farm, and a little girl can't stop thinking about purple elephants.)

Let's Get Some Practice

Continue by talking about one thing and then more than one by adding the /s/ to make a plural. This is an oral task, so we aren't writing anything. You may have objects such as pencils and letters, but you can also put yourself in the middle of the group (*teacher*) or put three children in the middle (*students*). You can consider one chair versus many chairs or one table versus many tables. If children have difficulty, provide the word and have them repeat.

Wrap It Up

"Nice job thinking about plurals. Remember, plurals let us know we are talking about more than one of something. I am one teacher, but you are many students." Emphasize the /s/ in *students*.

ACTIVITY When Did It Happen?

Get Things Ready

All you need to get going with this activity is chart paper and markers. Make a T chart.

Make an Introduction

"Today we're going to think about things you did when you were little, before you started school. We'll also think about things you'll do when you are older, when you are a grown-up."

Now for the Model

"Look at my chart. On this side of the chart, I'm going to write things I did when I was little." Write *things I did when I was little*. "On the other side, I'm going to write things I will do when I'm older." Write *things I will do when I'm older*. "Okay. First, I'm going to think about things I did when I was little. When I was little, I learned how to tie my shoes. So, I'm going to write *learned* on this side: things I did when I was little." Write *learned*. " I also played." Write *played*. "When I'm talking about things I did when I was little, I have to change the word. I changed *learn* to *learned*. I changed *play* to *played*. Now I'll think about things I'll do when I'm older. When I'm older, I will drive a car. So, I'm going to write *will drive* here: things I will do when I'm older." Write *will drive*. "When I'm talking about things I'll do when I am older, I have to use the word *will* before I tell you what I do."

Let's Get Some Practice

Ask children about things they will do when they are older. On the chart, write *will* ___. Then have the group say what they'll do in a complete sentence: I will ___when I am older. Some ideas of things they'll do are cook dinner, buy groceries, or go to the movies. Then ask them about things they did when they were little. On the chart, record what they say with the –*ed* ending for the regular past tense verb. Then have them say what they did in a complete sentence: I ___*ed* when I was little. Don't worry about irregular verbs. You have established that the word will change. This still holds true with irregular verbs, such as *eat/ate*. Some ideas of things they did when they were little might be played with particular toys, loved a certain movie, or learned to write their name.

▢ Wrap It Up

"We thought about things we did when we were little. Remember, we had to change the word a bit when we talked about things that happened when we were little. When you said you *played* with trucks when you were little, you changed *play* to *played*." Point to *played*. "On this other side, we thought about things we will do when we are older. We use the word *will* when we are talking about things you *will* do when you are older, like when you said you *will* cook dinner when you are older." Point to *will cook*.

ACTIVITY Tell Me a Story

▢ Get Things Ready

Write sequence words on a chart or on the board: *first, next, then,* and *last.*

▢ Make an Introduction

"Today you'll tell stories with a friend. When you tell your story, you'll use words that will help your friend understand your story better. You'll use the words *first, next, then,* and *last.*" Point to each word as you say it. "This will help your friend know what happened first, what came after, and what happened last."

▢ Now for the Model

"When you turn and talk today, you'll take turns sharing your stories. We'll tell a story about something we did over the weekend. Watch me. I'm going to tell my story to a partner." Choose an equity stick to pick a partner. "Today, Javier will listen to me tell my story. While I share my story, listen carefully for the words *first, next, then,* and *last.* I made a cake this weekend! First, I read the recipe. Next, I got all of my ingredients together. Then, I made my batter and cooked my cake. Last, I ate a slice!" As you are telling your story, point to the words on the board as you use them. Note: you might decide to have your partner also tell a story while you support them using the sequence words.

▢ Let's Get Some Practice

Have children turn to their talking partners to share their stories. Use whatever method you like for who goes first, such as peanut butter-jelly partners. Remind them to use their words *first, next, then,* and *last.* Move around the group and support their stories as necessary. Sometimes children have difficulty coming up with stories. If this happens, you can show them a simple sequence of four events to prompt their story. Here's an example.

☐ Wrap It Up

"You are great story tellers. I heard you using *first*, *next*, *then*, and *last* while you told your stories. This helped your friend know what happened first, what came after, and what happened last."

Connect to a Book!

Wordless picture books provide a sequence of events for practice using sequence words. You could use the book *Hike* by Pete Oswald or *One Little Bag* by Henry Cole. *Hike* follows a little girl throughout a day when she goes on an epic hike, and *One Little Bag* follows one little bag that is used and reused multiple times.

ACTIVITY Can You Find It?

☐ Get Things Ready

Create shapes with different colored paper. You'll want a second set of shapes for you. Tape the shapes around the area where you will meet with children. I've found it helpful to have a list of positional words at the ready that I can refer to and use.

☐ Make an Introduction

"We're going to play Can You Find It? You'll find shapes I've hidden around the room. To help you find them, I'll use positional words. Positional words are words that describe where something is. These are words such as *under*, *behind*, or *in front*."

☐ Now for the Model

"Look at my shapes." Display your set of shapes and say each one as well as its color, such as *yellow circle*. "If you already see some of these shapes, don't say anything! Let me show you how to play the game. I'm going to look around the room to find one of the shapes. I'm not going to say anything when I see one." Move slowly around the room as you look. Then come back to the group. "Now, I'll give you clues and use positional words. The shape is *near* our art easel. I'm going to choose a friend to find my shape." Pull an equity stick. "Finnigan, the shape is *near* our art easel." Wait until Finnigan moves near the art easel. "Look *under* our art easel." Encourage Finnigan to look under the art easel. "What shape did you find? Everyone, did you notice my positional words? I said *near* and *under* the art easel to help Finnigan find the shape."

Look For

With all of these activities, you'll listen for children's easy use of these words. When you notice a child having difficulty using the correct plural form of a noun or tense of a verb, recast their comment to demonstrate the correct grammatical usage. If you notice a child is confused following directions with positional words, intentionally use expansions that include positional words, such as "Get a pencil from the cup that is *on top of* the table," or "Get a dry-erase board stacked on the shelf *under* the coloring paper."

Let's Get Some Practice

Give children time to walk quietly around the room and find a shape. Remind them to use only their eyes and not to say anything. Have them come quietly back to their spots once they find a shape. Choose two children using your equity sticks. Have one of them give directions to help the other one find a shape. Encourage the child giving directions to use positional words. Continue until all of the shapes are found.

Wrap It Up

"You did a great job using positional words to find our shapes! We found our yellow circle under the art easel and our green square on top of our mailboxes. Let's pay attention for positional words today."

Building Relationships Across Words

Learning new words involves both conceptual knowledge and vocabulary knowledge. Children learn how vocabulary is categorized and labeled. In other words, they learn a new word, such as *jaguar*, and then its category: animals or, more specifically, jungle animals. As they learn more jungle animals, their categories become more defined. They may learn about tigers, boa constrictors, panthers, monkeys, gorillas, and lizards. They might have a new category of big cats, such as jaguars, panthers, and tigers. Then they learn about other big cats, such as cougars, cheetahs, and lions. They learn how big cats are different from house cats. Thinking about how words are related helps to accelerate and deepen word learning. The following activities will help children build these relationships and, at the same time, get them talking!

ACTIVITY Categories

Get Things Ready

Print out pictures of things that would be in a category. For example, you might think about places and have pictures of a beach, a school, a zoo, a celebration party, and a farm scene. Put the pictures in a basket. The goal is having something children will be able to provide details about and can keep a conversation going as they add on information. I usually have five or six pictures on hand, one for modeling and the rest for practice.

Make an Introduction

"We're going to talk about categories today. A *category* is a group of things that are alike in some way. I might put *people* into categories by how old they are. You would be in the *children* category, and I would be in the *adult* category. We're going to talk about the pictures in my basket to think about other categories."

Now for the Model

"Watch me. I'll go first. My picture is of a playground. My category is 'things I see at the playground.' I can use the picture to help me think about things I see at the playground. I would see swings at the playground. I would also see benches for people to sit on at the playground. What else might I see?" Encourage responses. "Those are all things I would see at the playground. They would all go in my *playground* category. What's something that would not go in my category? I'm thinking a giraffe. I might see people walking dogs or see squirrels in the trees, but I would not see a giraffe!"

Let's Get Some Practice

Continue with new pictures, such as pictures of a beach, a farm, a school, a zoo, and a celebration party. Choose a new picture and have the children name the place. Then pose the question, "What are some things you would see at a ___?" I often like to build a Unifix tower. (See the "Tell Me More!" activity on page 27). If you need a new, fresh way to encourage children to add on, you could collect pennies in a cup or tally each response. Use questions to encourage additional responses. You might simply ask, "What else would you see?" But you can also provide some choices, if needed, by asking, for example, "Would you see a tractor or a slide at a farm?" You can also ask what they would *not* see. You may only have time for one or two pictures. Keep the others on hand for another day!

Wrap It Up

"Nice job thinking about things that belong together in a category. Remember, a *category* is a group of things that are alike in some way. We had a big category of *places* and then thought about the things that would fit in our categories, the playground and our school. What's something that might be in both a playground and a school? Children! That's right."

Flex the Activity!

You can also think about categories for things you are learning in class. This is a double-duty activity; it gets children talking and it helps them review key concepts from your thematic units. For example, after you describe your playground scene, you add follow-up questions about the living and nonliving things in the picture. As part of the study, you might have an anchor chart about what living things need. This would allow you to ask an additional question: What do the living things in our picture need?

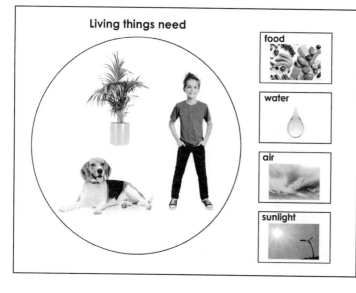

ACTIVITY Odd One Out

☐ Get Things Ready

Ready bags or envelopes with three or four objects or pictures. In each bag, place objects that are alike in some way with one that doesn't belong or is the "odd one out." For example, you might have a pencil, a crayon, and a marker in a bag with an apple. The apple is odd one out.

☐ Make an Introduction

"We're going to play Odd One Out. Today we'll figure out which picture doesn't belong and which pictures are alike in some way."

☐ Now for the Model

"I'll go first to show you how. First, I'll name each of the pictures in this envelope. I have a pencil, an apple, crayons, and a marker. Next, I need to figure out which pictures are alike. I know that we use pencils, crayons, and markers to write and draw. Then, I need to figure out the one that doesn't belong or the odd one out. The apple is the odd one out. It's a fruit and not something we use to write! That's silly. I'm going to put the apple over here. The pencil, crayon, and marker are all things we use to write and draw. That's the way they are all alike. My category is things we use to write and draw."

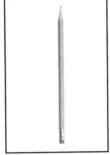  

☐ Let's Get Some Practice

Continue by showing the children another envelope with pictures. Make sure they name each picture first. Then, help them determine the items that are alike and the odd one out. Encourage them to use sentences to explain their decisions and name their categories. If children have difficulty, reduce the options to three. You can also put them in twos. For example, you might ask, "Are pencils and crayons alike, or are pencils and apples alike?"

☐ Wrap It Up

"Nice work playing Odd One Out today! You thought about things that are alike and thought about their categories. Then you found the odd one out! You can play this with your friends during centers."

ACTIVITY Concept Sort

Get Things Ready

Make picture cards based on your categories. These could be colors or shapes, or they can be related to a theme you're covering in your class. For example, if your goal is to highlight opposites, then you might have pictures of things or objects that have rough or smooth textures. Or, if your goal is to teach a concept and the related vocabulary, then choose the most important words such as *bike, bus, airplane, car, train,* and *boat* for types of transportation that can be sorted by mode of travel (land, water, air). For this example, I'm sorting shapes using pictures of shapes in our everyday environment by setting up a chart with my target shapes, gathering a set of pictures, and reading *City Shapes* by Diana Murray.

Make an Introduction

"We've been learning about shapes. Yesterday we read *City Shapes* by Diana Murray and talked about how we see shapes everywhere. Today we're going to sort pictures into groups by their shape. Let's review our shapes." Review circle, square, triangle, rectangle, and rhombus as you point them out on your chart.

▢ Now for the Model

"I'm going to go first to show you what to do. I'll pick a picture, name what I see, and look for our shapes. Here's my picture. It's a tall building called a skyscraper. This skyscraper is like a rectangle. It has four straight sides and four corners. It has two long sides and two short sides." Point out the straight sides, corners, and long and short sides. "So, I'm going to put the skyscraper in the rectangle group."

▢ Let's Get Some Practice

Continue by having children take turns picking a picture. As they select a picture, encourage them to name it and then identify the shape they see. If they can, encourage them to describe the shape, such as a square has four straight and equal sides and four corners. You can guide this with questions and expansions. If children have difficulty, reduce their choices by giving them two options, such as "Is it a circle or a square?"

▢ Wrap It Up

"Great job thinking about our shapes. They sure are everywhere! Let's review our groups." Take the time to talk about each group as you highlight the identifying characteristics of each shape.

Connect to a Book!

In my example, I've highlighted shapes. There are so many fun books about shapes, such as *Round Is a Tortilla* by Roseanne Thong, *A Trapezoid Is Not a Dinosaur* by Suzanne Morris, *Love, Triangle* by Marcie Colleen, *Circle Rolls* by Barbara Kanninen, and *Tangled: A Story About Shapes* by Anne Miranda. Or Mac Barnett's *Shape Trilogy* that highlights triangles, circles, and squares.

While this example sorts shapes, you can use concept sorts to explore any concept. You can reinforce living and nonliving things by reading books such as *Living Things and Nonliving Things* by Kevin Kurtz and the What Living Things Need series by Karen Aleo and then sorting pictures into living versus nonliving as you discuss why.

ACTIVITY Toss and Tell

▢ Get Things Ready

Make a picture cube. You can use a tissue box, a large foam die, and so on. Gather photographs or pictures related to your theme, and glue them on your picture cube. Or you can use a cube template (like the one on page 130) with your pictures on it, ready for printing and constructing. We're using this activity to encourage children to give details, so you'll want to choose pictures of familiar things that children will be able to use to extend their thoughts when talking about them.

▢ Make an Introduction

"Today we're going to play Toss and Tell! Here's our picture cube. To play, you toss the picture cube, name your picture, and then say as many things as you can about your picture." You will ask questions as children respond, having them name, describe, and explain something about the pictures, compare them to something else, or connect to them to their own experiences.

Now for the Model

"I'll go first to show you how to play. First, I'll toss the picture cube." Toss the cube. "Next, I'll name my picture. I landed on a caterpillar." Describe the picture. "This caterpillar is yellow with stripes. It is on a leaf, and I know caterpillars eat leaves." Add some things you know about the picture. "We've learned about caterpillars in class. They turn into butterflies." Compare to something else or connect to a personal experience. "I remember when I was younger. We had a kit where we fed caterpillars and they made chrysalises. When they turned to butterflies, we let them go outside."

Let's Get Some Practice

Invite children to take turns tossing the picture cube and telling. You will ask them questions as needed to help them add details.

- What is in the picture?

- What does ___ look like?

- What is ___ doing?

- Can you think of something that's like a ___?

- When have you seen a ___?

You could use Unifix cubes to encourage children to add details. You might challenge them to make a four-Unifix-cube tower. This would mean they name and describe and add at least two more details, such as explain, compare, or connect.

Wrap It Up

"Nice job describing our pictures during Toss and Tell! You all provided so many details and built our

Flex the Activity!

Toss and Tell is a great activity for reviewing things with defining characteristics, such as types of animals or types of books. For example, you might have a collection of recent read-alouds where you've been discussing what makes them fiction or nonfiction. The covers of those books can be the pictures on your picture cube. You can refer to a previously built anchor chart similar to this one to help guide their responses. Plus, you can add new book examples to your anchor chart straight from the picture cube!

Fiction
- not true
- made-up events
- made-up characters

Nonfiction
- true
- real events
- real people or animals

Possible fiction book covers for your picture cube:
- *The Very Cranky Bear* by Nick Bland
- *After the Fall* by Dan Santat
- *Lisette the Vet* by Ruth MacPete

Possible nonfiction book covers for your picture cube:
- *Living Things Need Shelter* by Karen Aleo
- *Living Things and Nonliving Things: A Compare and Contrast Book* by Kevin Kurtz
- *A Day in the Life of a Veterinarian* by Heather Adamson

four-cube towers! You can play Toss and Tell with a friend during centers. I'm going to put it in our science center."

ACTIVITY Opposites Class Book

Get Things Ready

Gather pictures of opposites. Here are the ones I usually use because they are easy to capture in pictures:

on/off	in/out	front/back	fast/slow
clean/dirty	open/closed	full/empty	soft/hard
wet/dry	thick/thin	above/below	night/day
hot/cold	long/short	top/bottom	inside/outside
big/little	happy/sad	tall/short	loud/quiet
asleep/awake	young/old	stop/go	smooth/rough

For this activity, you need one opposite card per child. I usually have each opposite pair printed on separate cards. Two children each get a card and find their pair. They then glue their opposite pairs on a page with the words written in a large font. You can also have sentence frames on each page for children to write their opposites: The opposite of ___ is ___. So, you might end up with a book with only the words or a book with sentence frames. You could also provide a mixture based on the support you want to give individual children.

Make an Introduction

"Today we are going to make a class book! We're going to make a book about opposites like the opposites in these books that we have read. To make our book, we first have to match up our opposites. I'll put out a few pictures at a time and choose friends to find the opposites. Then those will go on your opposite page!"

Now for the Model

"I'm going to lay out some pictures for us to find the opposites. I'll name them as I lay them down. Watch and listen: *off, hot, little, cold, on, big*. I'll go first. Here's what we'll say. 'The opposite of [pause] is [pause].' I'm going to pick *off*. The opposite of *off* is *on*. So, I'll put *off* with *on*. They are opposites." Put the pair together and off to the side a bit.

Let's Get Some Practice

As you take a pair away, bring a couple more pairs up. This will keep the number of pictures for the children to consider to a manageable number. However, feel free to lay out all pictures if you think that's okay for the children. Give each child a turn to come up and pick a picture. Support them by saying, "The opposite of ___ is ___ ," as they match the opposites. Once everyone has their matching pairs, have the children turn and talk to share their opposites with their talking partners. Encourage them to use their sentence frame. Now for the book! Pass out the pages for them to glue their matches and fill in the sentence frame, if you are using it. Encourage each child to share their page with the group by reading their page. Collect the pages and assemble the book, which can be as easy as stapling the pages together.

Wrap It Up

"We have a new class book—a book of opposites! I'm going to put our book in the library so you can read it."

Flex the Activity!

Opposites pair well with most classic games, such as Matching or Memory where you match opposite pairs, such as full/empty and smooth/rough. You can also play Bingo with opposites. Set up your Bingo board with a 3 x 3 array with pictures. Then pull from a deck of your opposite matches.

BINGO

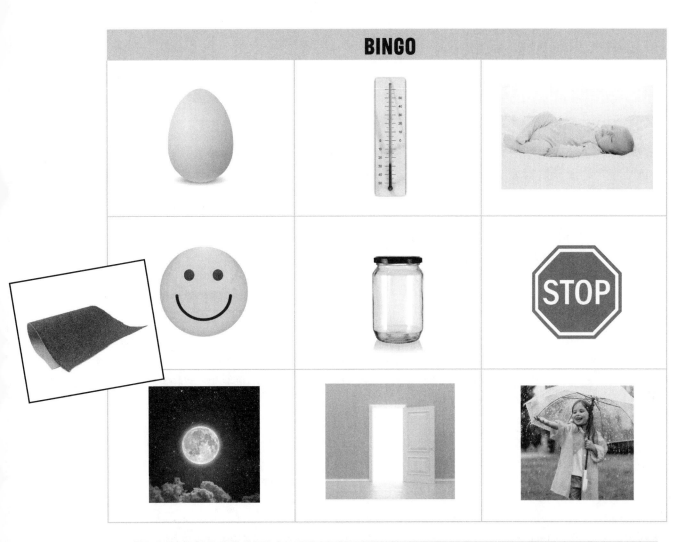

Connect to a Book!

Using opposites to connect to a book is an easy task. There are so many great books about opposites. Here are twelve of my favorites from more recent releases. They range from the silly *You Are Not Tall* to the graphically pleasing *Big Bear, Little Chair* to the informative *Opossum Opposites* to an opposite book that also introduces Spanish: *Marta! Big and Small.*

Big Bear Little Chair by Lizi Boyd

Big Bear, Small Mouse by Karma Wilson

Dot by Patricia Intriago

Double Take! A New Look at Opposite by Susan Hood

Drive: A Look at Roadside Opposites by Kellan Hatanaka

Good News, Bad News by Jeff Mack

Marta! Big and Small by Jen Arena

Opossum Opposites by Gina Gallois

Opposites: The Little Book of Big Friends by Agnes Green

Polar Opposites by Erik Brooks

The Hueys in What's the Opposite? by Oliver Jeffers

You Are Not Small by Anna Kang

ACTIVITY Word Association

Get Things Ready

Choose a vocabulary word you've previously introduced. Write it at the top of a piece of chart paper. I usually have a picture or group of pictures (or a recently read book) to represent the word on hand. A key to success with this activity is to have read and talked *a lot* about the topic related to your vocabulary word.

Make an Introduction

"We are going to talk about words we think about when we think about the ocean." Point to *ocean* on your chart paper. "This says *ocean*. I'll write the words we come up with here on this paper."

Now for the Model

"When I think about the ocean, a word I think about is *huge.* The ocean is a *huge* body of water. It's not just big. It's huge." Spread your arms wide. "I'm going to write *huge* under the word *ocean* on our paper."

Let's Get Some Practice

To help children start thinking, have them think-pair-share. Give everyone a minute to think about words that come to their minds and then pair up with their talking partner. They can then come back to the group to share. Encourage children to contribute. You could use your equity sticks or go around the circle. If children have difficulty, pull out your picture. Then you can ask them what they see. Encourage them to use complete sentences when they share. If needed, you can recast their response in a complete sentence. Write key words as they share. For *ocean*, you might expect words such as *dark, blue, wet, waves, whales*, and *fish.*

Wrap It Up

"We've collected a lot of words here for *ocean*. I'm going to put our pictures of oceans here, too. We will come back to these as we learn more about oceans!"

ACTIVITY Examples/Nonexamples

Get Things Ready

Choose a vocabulary word to explore, and then choose a variety of pictures to share, with some of the pictures acting as clear examples and others as nonexamples. This could be examples of specific shapes you are studying or examples of things found in nature. It's usually easy to come up with a good word based on things you are exploring as a class.

Make an Introduction

"We've been looking at *One Summer Up North* by John Owens and reading *The Hike* by Alison Farrell. In these books, the children explore nature. Nature is all of the things around us that are not made by people. It's things like plants, rocks, dirt, and animals. Today we are going to think more about this word—*nature*!"

Now for the Model

"I'm going to show you some pictures. We're going to put them into categories. Pictures that show something from nature will go in one category. They are examples of things from nature. Pictures that show something made by people will go in another category. They are nonexamples of things from nature. Watch me. Here's my first picture. It's a tree. Trees are not made by people. They are an example of something from nature. So, I'm going to give it a thumbs-up and put it in my examples of nature category. If I find a picture that is a nonexample, we'll give it a thumbs-down."

Let's Get Some Practice

Show each picture and say what's in the picture. Ask if it is an example of something from nature or a nonexample, and remind them to give a thumbs-up for examples and thumbs-down for nonexamples. Support as needed by asking if it is made by people. Ask for justifications of their answers by asking questions such as, "Why is this an example of something from nature?" or "Why is this a nonexample of something from nature?" Continue sorting into your categories of examples and nonexamples.

Wrap It Up

"Today we thought about examples of things from nature and nonexamples. Remember, nature is all of the things around us that are not made by people. Let's go over the examples of things from nature." Point and name each picture in your examples category. "Now let's review the things that were nonexamples." Point and name each nonexample picture.

ACTIVITY Guess What I'm Thinking!

Get Things Ready

Prior to doing this activity, it is helpful to have already completed one of the previous activities such as Examples/Nonexamples or Concept Sorts. I'm going to use Concept Sorts as my activity for this example. My concept sort will have the superordinate, or main, category of clothing and the subordinate categories of hot, cold, and rainy.

Make an Introduction

"Today we'll going to play Guess What I'm Thinking! We'll use our sort from the other day about the clothes we wear to keep us warm when it's cold, cool when it's hot, or dry when it's rainy."

Now for the Model

"I'll go first to show you how to play. I'm going to look at my chart first and choose a piece of clothing with my eyes. Remember, you are guessing, so I don't want to give it away! Then, I'll make sure I know if this is something I would wear when it's hot, cold, or rainy. Next, I'll say my clues. I am a piece of clothing. I have to say this because that's my main category. You wear me when it is cold. This is my second category. Now give at least one more clue to help your friends guess. You wear me on your head. Guess what I'm thinking!"

Let's Get Some Practice

Invite children to give their clues one-by-one using your equity sticks. Remind them to choose with their eyes. Then ask guiding questions. "What is your main category?" "What is your second category?" "What is your next clue?" Encourage them to give their clues in complete sentences. If a child needs support, say the sentence clue, such as "I am a piece of clothing," or "You wear me when it's rainy," and have them repeat for the group to hear. If children have a hard time guessing, have them look at the clothing pictures from your concept sort.

Wrap It Up

"Wow! You all did a great job guessing with our clues. Like Maria guessed *raincoat* when Josipa gave the clue, 'You wear me when it's rainy' This is a fun game. We'll play it again soon!"

To Sum It Up

Ever heard the saying, "Talk is cheap"? Perhaps in some circumstances it is, but not in an early childhood classroom. When it comes to laying a foundation for later literacy success, talk isn't cheap. It's priceless. In fact, oral language influences reading skills, school readiness, and overall academic success. Each of the activities in this chapter is offered to support children's oral-language development from understanding language and following directions to getting them to engage in conversation using new vocabulary to building relationships across words. These activities play a crucial role in fostering oral language and fit within a comprehensive framework that will help you lay the foundation for your developing talkers and thinkers *as well as* readers and writers.

3

CHAPTER THREE
Building Phonological Awareness

This chapter is devoted to the levels of phonological awareness across the prekindergarten and kindergarten years: rhyme, word, syllable, onset-rime, and phoneme. To begin, let's take a look at the early literacy standards from the Head Start Early Learning Outcome Framework and the Common Core State Standards that address phonological awareness. As you can see, these standards span the phonological continuum from rhyme to phoneme awareness.

HEAD START EARLY LEARNING OUTCOME FRAMEWORK—36–60 MONTHS	COMMON CORE STATE STANDARDS—KINDERGARTEN

■ Repeat simple familiar rhymes or sing favorite songs (36 months).
 	
■ Provide one or more words that rhyme with a single given target, such as "What rhymes with *log*?" (60 months).
 	
■ Produce the beginning sound in a spoken word, such as "*Dog* begins with /d/" (60 months).
 	
■ Provide a word that fits with a group of words sharing an initial sound, with adult support, such as "*Sock, Sara,* and *song* all start with the /s/ sound. What else starts with the /s/ sound?" (60 months).
	■ Demonstrate understanding of spoken words, syllables, and sounds (phonemes):
	
	  • Recognize and produce rhyming words.
	
	  • Count, pronounce, blend, and segment syllables in spoken words.
	
	  • Isolate and pronounce initial, medial vowel, and final sounds (phonemes) in three-phoneme (consonant-vowel-consonant, or CVC) words.
	
	  • Add or substitute individual sounds (phonemes) in simple, one-syllable words to make new words.

In chapter 1, you read about the development of phonological awareness skills from easier to more difficult—moving from the awareness of separate words in spoken phrases and sentences to syllables in words to initial sounds in single-syllable words to individual phonemes. The activities in this chapter address each of these levels and are presented in that order. Activities can be easier or harder based on the task itself, too. Take a look at this chart detailing common tasks we use for language play.

Common Tasks for Language Play

TASKS	EXAMPLES
Detection	Detecting or identifying a rhyming pair, such as *frog, log*
Generation	Generating a list of words that begin with the same sound /m/ such as *man, mop, mouse*
Blending	Blending the syllables *cup* and *cake* to make *cupcake*
Segmenting	Segmenting the initial sound /k/ in *cat*
Deleting	Deleting the /k/ from *cup* to get *up*

As you think about skill and task difficulty, be intentional about your instructional decisions. For example, let's say you are planning a series of activities to develop syllable awareness. You can begin with activities that have children blending syllables as you say them such as *cup* and *cake* blending into *cupcake*. As they become more successful with syllable blending, have them engage in activities where they segment syllables. For example, they can clap and say the two syllables in *table*—clap once with /tā/ and a second time with /bəl/. A deletion task might sound like this: "Say *snowman*. Now say snowman but don't say *snow*." (Answer: *snowman* without *snow* is *man*.) Increasing the difficulty in these activities allows the children the opportunities to develop a deep, firm understanding of these phonological skills.

We can also make activities easier or harder based on the words and materials we choose. Phonological activities are all oral, or sound-based. This can put a strain on a child's short-term memory. Consider this task: While playing an "odd one out" rhyming activity, a child has to remember the words *cat, log, hat* in order to determine *log* as the "odd one out" and the *cat-hat* rhyme. We can support children by using pictures and objects.

Our word choice is also important. Activities can be harder based on the type of word, the length of the word, and the novelty of the word. Let's take type first. It's easier for children to start thinking about syllables if we begin with compound words. Plus, I can make the abstract concept of syllables more concrete with pictures. Consider using pictures of *snow* and a *man* as you pull them together to blend for *snowman* or apart to segment into *snow* and *man*.

Now let's think about the length of a word. By length, I mean how many phonemes, or sounds, are in the word. The Common Core State Standards for Kindergarten have a benchmark of three-phoneme words, such as *cat*, *big*, and *hop*. It's easier for children to blend and segment two-phoneme words before moving to three-phoneme words. For example, it is easier for a child to blend /t/ and /ō/ to make *toe* than it is to blend /t/ /ō/ /d/ to make *toad* or segment *see* into /s/ /ē/ than it is to segment *seat* into /s/ /ē/ /t/. Remember, this practice is all oral. You can use pictures for this work, too, as you take a picture of a toe and cut it into two pieces that can be pulled together (blending for *toe*) or pulled apart (segmenting for /t/ /ō/).

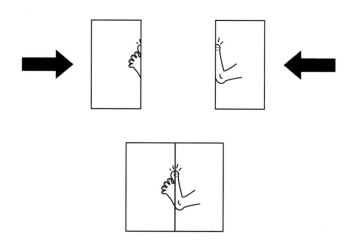

Another word choice consideration is the novelty of the word. While we want to build the children's vocabulary, we also want to think about our overall goals or purpose for the activities we use. Generally, children can handle phonological tasks more easily when they are familiar with the words (Metsala and Walley, 1998); in other words, they know the word's pronunciation and meaning. So, if our focus is on identifying rhyming pairs, then we would want to use words in the children's vocabularies to keep the eye on the prize. Use rhyming pairs such as *big-pig*, *nut-shut*, and *log-frog* rather than *big-fig*, *nut-rut*, and *log-bog* (with likely unfamiliar words such as *fig*, *rut*, *bog*). If you have children learning English as a new language, they may be less familiar with certain words. You can use pictures to support their learning.

Let's Start with Rhyme

Children begin to play around with the structures of words before they are even aware of it. In other words, they have an implicit sensitivity to phonology before they are able to intentionally consider the structures of our spoken words. They can detect differences in word structures and in syllables. Rhyme awareness is one of the first phonological skills children develop (MacLean, Bryant, and Bradley, 1987; Whitehurst and Lonigan, 2001). It makes sense, too. As children learn to speak, they learn the differences between words that sound alike such as *big* and *pig* or *dad* and *sad*. With the development of speech sounds, children begin to develop an awareness of rhyme. And, our everyday language play with young children helps to support this awareness.

Let's take a look at a timeline of rhyme development (Paulson and Moats, 2018). Two- and three-year old children begin to learn about rhyme as they listen to rhyming books, have fun with fingerplays, or sing songs and recite nursery rhymes. Three- and four-year old children begin to detect rhyme as they play "odd one out" games. This sensitivity to word structures—in this case, the way words end—is a first step toward developing metalinguistic awareness. *Metalinguistic awareness* is the conscious analysis of word structures. It isn't until this point that four- to five-year-olds can generate rhyme. The following rhyme activities move from awareness to detection to generation. These are ubiquitous activities many of us have seen in classrooms and used ourselves; their archival sources are sometimes not known. They are highlighted in this chapter because they each help provide targeted practice while engaging children in language play. The directions for each activity come from my own observations and practice about how to make them work best with young children.

Rhyme Awareness

Phonological awareness is an essential foundation for learning to read and write, and we'll start here with rhyme awareness. As noted previously, this level of rhyme understanding is often achieved in two- and three-year olds, but as you know, you'll have four- and five-year olds who haven't yet learned about rhyme. Rhyme awareness can be developed with the countless songs, fingerplays, and books that focus on rhyming.

Flex the Activity!

These rhyme-awareness activities are interchangeable—for example, the process for Read a Book with rhyming songs and whisper the rhyming words while you are singing.

ACTIVITY Say a Rhyme!

Get Things Ready

Choose short, easy-to-remember nursery rhymes. Some favorites are "Twinkle, Twinkle, Little Star," "Wee Willie Winkie," and "Little Bo Peep." You'll want to teach them to children before you do this activity so the focus can be on the rhyme and not learning the nursery rhyme.

Make an Introduction

"We're going to practice a nursery rhyme today. It's one we've already learned—'Twinkle, Twinkle, Little Star.' The fun thing about our nursery rhyme is that it has words that rhyme. When two words rhyme, they sound the same at the end. Listen to these words: snow and toe (say these words slowly and emphasize the ending sound /ō/). Since these words both say /ō/ at the end, they rhyme. They sound the same at the end. Say them with me—snow, toe. They rhyme!"

Now for the Model

"I'm going to say the nursery rhyme, and you are going to listen for the words that rhyme. When we hear rhyming words, we are going to stop and say them together. Listen to me first. I'm going to show you. 'Twinkle, twinkle, little star. How I wonder what you are.' Wait! I hear two words that rhyme: star and are. They sound the same at the end. They both end with /ar/. . . star, are (say them slowly and emphasize /ar/). Let's say the rhyming words together: star, are. Let's keep going. Listen. 'Up above the world so high, like a diamond in the sky.' I hear two more rhyming words: high, sky. They both end in /ī/ . . . high, sky. Let's say them together: high, sky."

Let's Get Some Practice

Continue with this practice with a new nursery rhyme you've already taught the children. Say the nursery rhyme and emphasize the rhyming words by saying them louder than the other words and elongating their rhyming ending. Identify the rhyming words and have children repeat them with you. Make sure to make note of the rhyming chunk (for example, /ī/ at the end of high, sky).

Wrap It Up

"We've thought about words that rhyme like *star, are*—they both end with /ar/—*star, are* (emphasize /ar/). Say them with me: *star, are*. We also talked about *high, sky*—they both end with /ī/—*high, sky* (emphasize /ī/). Say them with me: *high, sky*. We'll keep thinking about words that rhyme!"

> ### Look For
>
> As you engage children with rhyme awareness activities, pay attention who is participating and who is not. To make sure you understand a child's understanding of rhyme, call on individual children to provide the missing rhyming word (awareness) or make the rhyming match (detection). In fact, detection tasks, as opposed to awareness or generation tasks, seem to be more predictive of phonological skill.

ACTIVITY Sing a Song

Choose a short song to learn like "Itsy Bitsy Spider," "Rocco the Rhyming Rhino," and "Five Little Ducks." We also have many nursery rhymes set to music like "Twinkle, Twinkle, Little Star" and "Baa, Baa, Black Sheep." You'll want to sing these songs with children so they are familiar with them before doing the activity.

Make an Introduction

"We're going to sing 'Five Little Ducks!' We've already learned it, so let's sing it now. (Sing the song together with hand movement.) One reason I love this song is it has a lot of words that rhyme. When two words rhyme, they sound the same at the end. Listen to these words: *bee* and *me* (say these words slowly and emphasize the ending sound /ē/). Since these words both end with /ē/, they rhyme. Say them with me: *bee, me*. They rhyme!"

Now for the Model

"Now this time I'll sing it and sometimes I'm not going to sing one of the words. You'll sing the missing word! Let me show you what I mean. Listen. 'Five little ducks went out one day. Over the hills and far _____' (pause briefly and children will likely sing the word before you). The word here is *away*—over the hills and far away. Day and away rhyme. They sound the same at the end. Let's keep going!"

Let's Get Some Practice

Continue singing the song, pausing with the next rhyming word: "Mother duck said quack, quack, quack but only four little ducks came _____." Sing the song again and encourage children to fill in more rhyming words.

Wrap It Up

"That was fun singing! And, we got to think about rhyming words like *day, away*—they both end with /ā/—*day, away* (emphasize /ā/). Say them with me: *day, away*. We noticed two other words that rhymed. 'Quack and _____' (pause and encourage the children to give you the rhyming word—*back*). That's right. They both end with /ăk/—*quack, back* (emphasize /ăk/). Say them with me: *quack, back*."

ACTIVITY Read a Book

Get Things Ready

Choose a rhyming picture book like *Silly Tilly* by Eileen Spinelli. You will want to choose a book you've already read to the class multiple times. They need to be familiar with the text so that the focus can be on rhyming words rather than guessing what might fit.

Make an Introduction

"We're going to read one of our favorite books! This book is so funny, and it has a lot of rhyming words. Remember rhyming words sound the same at the end. Listen to these words: *day* and *May* (say these words slowly and emphasize the ending sound /ā/). Since these words both end with /ā/, they rhyme. Say them with me: *day, May*. They rhyme!"

Now for the Model

"*Silly Tilly*! (Make a big reveal!) When I read today, I am going to stop when we get to a rhyming word. Your job is to say the word. Let's whisper the rhyming word. Listen to me first so I can show you. 'Tilly was a silly goose, a daffy-down-and-dilly goose, who took her baths in apple ___' (pause briefly and then whisper *juice*). *Goose, juice*—they rhyme. They both end with /oos/— *goose, juice* (emphasize /oos/)."

Let's Get Some Practice

Continue reading and pause to let the children fill in the rhyming word. You can decide how they will say the word as you go. You might continue whispering, but you can also switch it up for fun. Sing like an opera star or talk like a robot. Be sure to highlight the rhyming words at the end of the page like *hat, cat, that* all end with /ăt/.

Wrap It Up

"We had fun reading *Silly Tilly* again! And, we got to think about rhyming words like *goose, juice*— they both end with /oos/. *Goose. Juice.* (Emphasize /oos/.) Say them with me: *goose, juice*. We noticed other rhyming words like *hogs* and _____ (pause and encourage the children to give you the rhyming word: *logs*. That's right. *Hogs, logs*—they both end with /ogs/. Say them with me: *hogs, logs*.

Rhyme Detection

As the children become more aware of rhyme, you can build in detection activities. This is a skill children generally grasp between the ages of three and five. So, the children across prekindergarten and kindergarten will benefit from detecting rhyme through fun rhyming games. Here are a few activities to get you started.

Connect to a Book!

Red Shoes by Karen English can help children think about growing up and passing things on to others. It can also be a springboard for some fun with rhyme detection. For example, children can match rhyming pairs (see Make a Match in this section) with color names like *blue-shoe*, *red-bed*, and *pink-sink*.

ACTIVITY What's My Group?

Get Things Ready

This activity is a sorting game where you sort pictures into rhyming categories, so you'll need a set of picture cards that will provide the children with at least two rhyming contrasts; do not use more than four contrasts. For example, you may choose to focus on words that rhyme with *mop* and words that rhyme with *bat*. You could choose the following pictures: *hop, stop, pop* and *hat, mat, cat*.

Make an Introduction

"Today we're going to play a game called What's My Group? In this game, we'll think about words that rhyme or sound alike at the end like *mop* and *shop*. They both end with /ŏp/. . . *mop, shop*."

Now for the Model

Set up the categories clearly delineating the groups. I often put a placemat on the floor for each one. For this sort, I'd put a picture of a mop on one placemat and a picture of a bat on the other. Model placing one or two rhyming pictures and emphasize the rhyming chunk. "I'm going to look for pictures that rhyme with *mop* or *bat*. Here's my first one. *Hat. Hat—mop. Hat—bat. Hat* and *bat* rhyme or sound the same at the end. They both end with /ăt/. *Hat—bat*. They rhyme! So, I'm going to put *hat* in my *bat* group."

Let's Get Some Practice

Have children say each picture as they place them into the correct rhyming category. If they don't know a picture or say the wrong picture name, tell them and have them repeat. For example, if they say *mouse* for *rat*, you would say, "This is a rat. What is it? A rat." Once they are finished sorting the pictures, have children "read" their pictures and talk about their rhyming words as you emphasize the rhyming "chunk" like the /ăt/ in *bat*.

Wrap It Up

To summarize your learning, you can have the children chorally name the pictures as you take them away, category-by-category, saying, "Today we thought about words that rhyme. Let's take away our words that rhyme with *mop*. Say it with me: *mop, hop, stop, pop*. They all rhyme—they all end with /ŏp/!"

ACTIVITY See You Later, Alligator!

Get Things Ready

Collect ten to twelve picture sets. For each set, you'll need three pictures (two rhyming pictures and one that doesn't rhyme with the other two). I usually keep my sets either clipped or organized in envelopes. You could also have them on slides you present with your projector. This is an oddity task, where children choose the odd one out.

Make an Introduction

"Today we're going to play a game called See You Later, Alligator! In this game, we'll think about words that rhyme or sound alike at the end like *bat* and *hat*. They both end with /ăt/—*bat, hat*."

Now for the Model

Lay out a three-picture set, and name each picture. "Here's my first group of pictures. I'm going to look for the two pictures that rhyme and say, 'See you later, alligator,' to the one that doesn't rhyme. Here are my pictures: *hat, mop, bat*. I know *hat* and *bat* rhyme because they both end with /ăt/. So, I'm going to say, 'See you later, alligator,' to *mop*!" Pick up *mop* and say, "See you later, alligator!" Place *hat* and *bat* side-by-side in a collection of your rhyming pairs.

Let's Get Some Practice

As you display each set, say the names of the pictures as you point to each one. Have children find the rhyming pairs and keep a collection of each rhyming pair. Then hold up the picture of the word that doesn't rhyme for a collective "See you later, alligator!"

Wrap It Up

As a quick review and reinforcement, you can have the children chorally name the pictures of the rhyming pairs, saying, "Today we thought about words that rhyme and said, 'See you later, alligator' to the words that didn't rhyme. Let's say our rhyming pairs." Point to each rhyming pair to guide the choral response, and from time to time reinforce the rhyming chunk (for example, "*Hop, stop*. Yes, they both end with /ŏp/!").

ACTIVITY Rhyme Detectives

Get Things Ready

For this activity, you'll need to collect either objects or pictures of rhyming pairs (for example, cat—bat). You can also do this activity orally without pictures or objects. Any way you choose, have prepared rhyming pairs.

Make an Introduction

"Today we're going to be rhyme detectives. We're going to play a game with rhyming words. Who's ready to be a detective? I am! Remember rhyming words are words that sound the same at the end like *cat* and *bat*. They both end with /ăt/—*cat, bat* (emphasize the /ăt/ by stretching the end of the words). I'm going to pick objects out of my basket, and you'll put your thumbs up if they rhyme and thumbs down if they don't rhyme. But first, let's name all of the objects so we all know what each one is called."

Now for the Model

"I'll go first. Watch me. I have *mop* and *stop*. I'm going to say the words again and ask myself if they rhyme (say mop and stop again but this time emphasize the /ŏp/ ending). *Mop, stop.* Thumbs-up (put a thumb up). They both say /ŏp/ at the end. They rhyme—*mop, stop.*"

Let's Get Some Practice

Pull out pairs of objects, making sure to mix it up with pairs that rhyme and pairs that don't. If children don't remember the name of an object or say the wrong name, tell them and have them repeat. Have children say each pair aloud and then put your thumbs up or thumbs down. For the first few times, name what they are doing to reinforce the game. For example, you might say, "You gave me a thumbs-down because *bee* and *log* don't rhyme." If they make a mistake, provide corrective feedback. You might say, "*Bee, tree.* They both say /ē/ at the end, so we would give them a thumbs-up. They rhyme. Let's do that one again. Say them with me: *bee, tree.* Yes, you give them a thumbs-up because they rhyme."

Wrap It Up

Reinforce rhyming pairs to wrap up the game. "Today we thought about words that rhyme. We used our ears to listen and find words that didn't rhyme like *plate, bee* (hold up the objects). And, we listened for words that did rhyme like *mop, stop* (hold up the objects). Say them with me: *mop, stop.* They rhyme. . . they end with /ŏp/. We are rhyme detectives!"

ACTIVITY Make a Match

Get Things Ready

Collect sets of four pictures. Within each set, one picture will be your target picture and the other three will include one that rhymes with your target and two that do not. Eight to ten sets are plenty for the game. You could mix and match the pictures, but having the sets prepped will help the activity move more smoothly. The goal with this activity is not to find the odd one out like in See You Later, Alligator! Instead, you are finding the one to keep in—to make a match.

Make an Introduction

"Today we're going to play a game called Make a Match. To make a match, you have to find two words that rhyme. Let's remind ourselves first about rhyming words. Rhyming words are words that sound the same at the end like *cat* and *bat*. They both end in /ăt/—*cat, bat* (emphasize the /ăt/ by stretching the end of the words). *Cat* and *bat* would make a match!"

Now for the Model

"Watch me. I'll go first (pull out your first set of four pictures). I have *cat, plate, eight, stop*. I'm going to make my match! *Plate, eight*. They both end with /āt/—*plate, eight*. They rhyme!"

Let's Get Some Practice

Show the four pictures in the set to the children, naming each one together. After they've all been named, say, "Make a match!" If a match is correctly made, then name what they did by saying, "Yes, *frog, log* is our match. They both end with /ŏg/. They rhyme." If, however, they have difficulty, you can support them by saying pairs together to see if they rhyme. For example, you might say, "*Frog, plate*. . . not a match. *Frog, cat*. . . not a match. *Frog, log*. That's a match. They both end in /ŏg/, so they rhyme. That's our match. Say them with me. . . *frog, log*." Or you can reduce your choices and have a set of three pictures.

Wrap It Up

After you've gone through all sets, chorally repeat the rhyming matches. "We made so many rhyming matches today! Great game. Let's say them together (say each match as you pull out the pictures)."

Rhyme Generation

Children who are more comfortable with rhyme detective should also work on rhyme generation. When a child can generate rhyming words, then that child has a solid grasp on rhyme. This is a skill children generally grasp at around five years old (Paulson, 2004). So, the children, especially our kindergartners, will benefit from activities that encourage rhyme generation. Here are a few to get you started.

Connect to a Book!

Rhyming Dust Bunnies by Jan Thomas is a book of rhyme generation. Children will enjoy generating rhyme as they join in a game of What rhymes with. . .? and finding out why Bob seems to be having trouble finding a rhyming word.

ACTIVITY Hot Potato

Get Things Ready

Generate a list of rhyming words so you'll be primed and ready to support the children. But truly, this is a low maintenance game, and one you could play in the spur of the moment. Gather children in a big circle and have something to pass around (for example, a small ball).

Make an Introduction

"We're going to play a rhyming game today called Hot Potato (show the ball). I'm going to say a word and pass the potato. We'll pass the potato around the circle. If you have a word that rhymes with mine, you can say your word when you get the potato. If you don't, just pass the potato along."

Now for the Model

"So, this is how you play. I'm going to start us off with this word—*cat*. Now I'll pass the potato to Javier, and he'll say a word that rhymes with *cat* like *hat* (pass the ball and direct Javier to repeat hat). Now Javier will pass the potato to Uniqua (have Javier pass the ball). She'll give us another word that rhymes with *cat* and *hat* or she'll pass the potato. That's how we'll play. We'll keep going until we get all the way around the circle."

Let's Get Some Practice

Start the game with *cat*. Pass the potato and encourage responses. Children can pass along, but you can also support those who can't think of a word by saying, "I'm thinking of a word that rhymes with *cat* but starts with /m/" (*mat*). Once you are around the circle, start a new round with a new word. If you have a larger group of children, you can decide to start a new round at any point. In that case, after you give the new word, roll the ball across the circle to the next child. The main thing is to give all children multiple opportunities to generate rhyming words with many rounds.

Wrap It Up

"That was fun! Plus, we thought of so many rhyming words! Like the time I said *sack*. We thought about words that ended with /ăk/ like *sack*, and we got so many words! Let's count them (put a finger up with each word you say). . . *sack, back, pack, track, Jack, crack*. That's six words!"

> ## Flex the Activity!
> You can play other games where you go around the circle generating rhyming words like a variation of the telephone game where each child whispers a rhyming word as you go around the circle. Or you can play a game called Round Robin where you say you are getting ready to do something and everyone talks about what you'll take. The catch is everything must rhyme. For example, "I'm going to the park, and I'm taking a mat." The next child in the circle might say, "I'm taking a mat and a hat." Then the next child might say, "I'm taking a mat and a hat and a cat."

ACTIVITY Rhyme Hunt

▢ Get Things Ready

This is another low maintenance game like Hot Potato. One option for starting it is to read Michael Rosen and Helen Oxbury's classic book *We're Going on a Bear Hunt.*

▢ Make an Introduction

"We're going on a rhyme hunt today. . . in our classroom! I'm going to ask you to find something in the room that rhymes with a word I say."

"I see the number four. What do I see in the classroom that rhymes with *four*? I see the floor! *Four, floor.* They both end with /or/, so they rhyme."

▢ Let's Get Some Practice

Continue with the frame: "I see a ___. What do you see in the classroom that rhymes with ___?" You might say you see a sock (for clock) or hair (for chair). Sometimes you might have more than one option like *door* or *floor* to rhyme with the number *four*.

▢ Wrap It Up

"We had a good rhyme hunt! You found so many things that rhyme like *sock-clock* and *hair-chair*."

Flex the Activity!

Children like playing rhyming games with names, too. For example, you can sing to the tune of "Skip to My Lou," "Silly Willy, Willy Willy, who should I choose. . . I choose Wella Bella" (Fitzpatrick, 2005). Or you can sing the classic song "The Name Game" that goes like this: "Sarah, Sarah, bo-barah. Bonana fanna. Fo-farah. Fee fi mo-marah, Sarah!" You can also change the beginning sound in words for things you refer to throughout the day. For example, you might say, "Let's gather around the bircle." Have children identify the real words that rhymes with these silly words.

ACTIVITY Draw a Rhyme

▢ Get Things Ready

Fitzpatrick (1997) has a fun rhyme activity called Draw a Rhyme. You can draw many things (for example, clown, monster). You'll give rhyme directions to children, and each child will need paper and crayons. You'll also need a space for your drawing that is large enough for the children to see.

▢ Make an Introduction

"Today we're going to draw a clown! We're going to draw it part-by-part together. I'm going to give a clue for the part we'll draw, and you tell me which part by rhyming!"

▢ Now for the Model

"Let me show you what I mean. Listen. When making a clown, it is *said*, always start with his big, round. . . (pause here and get responses). Yes, we start with his big, round *head*. You got it. *Said, head*. They rhyme!" Draw a big, round head and encourage children to do the same.

Let's Get Some Practice

Continue with the directions, remembering to pause at the rhyming word. "Make it really messy 'cause clowns don't *care*. On top of his head, give him red curly. . . (*hair*). When people laugh, he wants to *hear*. So, on each side, give him a great big. . . (*ear*). Now make him look very *wise* by giving him two wide-open. . . (*eyes*). And yes, of course, everyone *knows*, give him a big, fat, rounded. . . (*nose*). Now make a line as long as a *mile,* and turn it into a great big. . . (*smile*). Look at his clothes, the clown suit he is *in*. It has a ruffle, right under his. . . (*chin*). All over his suit are big, colored *spots*, so give him lots of polka. . . (*dots*). Now look, can you *believe*? He has purple stripes on each long. . . (*sleeve*). He has two hands, one left and one *right*. One's painted yellow and the other is. . . (*white*). At the bottom of his funny *suit,* you can see one big, black. . . (*boot*). And the other foot has not a *shoe,* 'cause he just painted his toenails. . . (*blue*). Now, if you listened and did everything *right*, your little clown will be a funny. . . (*sight*)."

Wrap It Up

"We all drew our clowns using our rhyming clues. We rhymed *suit* with *boot* and *mile* with *smile*. We rhymed *spots* with *dots* and *shoe* with *blue*. Our clown is a funny sight!"

Flex the Activity!

You could use this as a rhyme awareness activity by reading the directions in full, making note of the rhyme words as you go. You can also draw other things. As an example, here are the directions for drawing a monster (Fitzpatrick, 1997):

When you draw a monster, it is said. You always begin with his head. He'll be able to see when he flies, if we draw two bright eyes. To tell which way the cold wind blows, our monster will need a great big nose. Look to the north and look to the south. Now we can give our monster a mouth. Some up above and some beneath, our monster has lots of teeth. Now under this chin, let's just check. That's where we should put his neck. So, he won't be tipsy-toddy, let's give him a polka dot body. If he really, really begs, I guess we could give him legs. To make our monster nice and neat, we'll have to teach him to wipe his feet. A notice sent by air mail. We can't forget our monster's tail. He isn't fierce, he isn't hairy, but don't you think he's a little scary?

Literature Connection

While we all have our favorite classics such as *Is Your Mama a Llama?* by Deborah Guarino or *Sheep in a Jeep* by Nancy Shaw, many new rhyming books are just as fun and will introduce you and the children to new characters and authors. Try out these titles:

There's a Bear in My Chair by Ross Collins. This fun rhyming book follows a mouse who has a problem—a bear is sitting in his favorite chair and won't move. Children will love the illustrations as well as the twist at the end.

Frog on a Log? by Kes Gray and Jim Field. Cat encourages Frog to sit on a log, but he refuses. As Frog suggests a nice spot for him to sit, Cat repeatedly refuses. Children will enjoy rooting for Frog and thinking about his perfect spot!

Rhyme Crime by Jon Burgerman. This interactive story is full of silly rhymes. Children love to guess the rhyming puzzles throughout and solve the "rhyme crime" in the ending.

Toad on the Road by Stephen Shaskin. This call-and-response book brings not only rhyme play but also a big giggle with Toad's shenanigans along the way.

Bunnies on a Bus by Phillip Ardagh. Who doesn't love a group of bunnies causing mayhem? Children will delight in all the mischief this group of bunnies gets up to on the bus through Sunny Town.

Dream Flights on Arctic Nights by Brooke Hartman. You and the children will enjoy the rhyme, learn about arctic animals, and get lost in Evon Zerbetz's illustrations.

Underwear! by Jennifer Harney. Okay. Beware: This book is all about underwear! Harney gives us a glimpse into the hilarious dialogue between a bear dad and his bear cub.

Hip-Hop Lollipop by Susan Montanari. Talk about a book that will get children moving. *Hip-Hop Lollipop* is filled with rhymes to get you dancing.

Mr. Scruff by Simon James. In this rhyming book, we are introduced to a boy and a dog who seem like an unlikely pair. The fun comes not only in the rhyming but also the illustrations that highlight how some dogs look just like their owners.

After Squidnight by Jonathan Fenske. This rhyming tale follows a group of squid as they come to our houses at night to leave you some art—or maybe a big mess!

Word Awareness

We often say children move from a shallow to deep understanding of phonological awareness. As children move along their awareness of the phonological structure of language, they become quite adept at identifying rhyme and start exploring spoken words in sentences and phrases. They also begin to develop an awareness of syllables in words (Paulson, 2004). Your five-year-old children should be able to segment words in spoken sentences and syllables within words. For example, they would know "I like pizza" has three words, and *pizza* has two syllables.

You might ask yourself if you need to hold off moving to word and syllable awareness if children can't generate a word that rhymes with *cat*. In other words, do children need to master rhyme detection and generation before you move forward along the phonological continuum? The answer is no, and there are three reasons. First, research shows that mastery of rhyme, as noted previously, depends on the task. Children, for example, may be able to detect rhyme around the age of four, but it's not until kindergarten that we can expect them to generate rhyming words (Paulson, 2004). If you look for the children to master rhyme generation in preschool, you may find yourself frustrated and feel like you are spinning your wheels. Second, research has also found that a curriculum that prioritizes rhyme is not as efficient and effective as one that also emphasizes word, syllable, onset-rime, and phoneme activities. Moreover, there is no evidence to suggest a mastery approach to phonological skills is more effective than a mixed-level approach (Gillon, 2018). Third, rhyming may be an early red flag (or indicator of future reading difficulty), but it is only moderately correlated with early reading and spelling (Gillon, 2018). The phonological skill most associated with early reading and spelling is phoneme awareness. With this in mind, rhyme is a fun part of language play in early education, but other phonological skills (for example, word, syllable, onset-rime, phoneme) play a vital role in early reading and spelling.

Remember, these activities are all oral without the use of print. Each of the following activities is designed to encourage an awareness of words in spoken language. As with the rhyme activities, they are game-like and fun for young children as they refine their understanding of the phonological system. Let's get started with activities to develop word awareness.

> **Look For**
>
> You'll want to monitor children's accuracy while segmenting the words in spoken phrases and sentences. Keep a close eye on how the segment words with more than one syllable. For example, children commonly segment the sentence *I like pizza* into I – like – pi – zza, separating *pizza* into syllables.

ACTIVITY Head, Shoulders, Knees, and Toes

▢ Get Things Ready

Prepare a set of short sentences to orally present to children. To begin, you'll want your sentences to be three to five words in length and include only one-syllable words. "I like milk" or "I ride on the bus" are examples. Once the children can easily identify words in sentences with single-syllable words, begin to incorporate a two-syllable word, such as "I like pizza" or "I ride in a taxi." As a prep for the activity, you could also read aloud (and sing along!) the book *Head, Shoulders, Knees, and Toes* by Skye Silver.

▢ Make an Introduction

"Today we are going to think about words. When we talk, we are saying words. This morning when you walked in our classroom, I used the words 'good morning' to greet you and say hello. 'Good morning' is two words. Good (hold up a finger). Morning (hold up a second finger). One, two. Good. Morning. I'm going to say a sentence out loud, and we are going to say each word as we touch head, shoulders, knees, and maybe even toes! Each word gets a new touch. So, if I do that with good morning, I'd do this. Good (touch your head). Morning (touch your shoulders)."

▢ Now for the Model

Model the first sentence for the children. Touch your head with the first word, shoulders with the second, and so on. If you have more than four words, simply move back up. "Watch me. My sentence is: 'I like milk.' Watch me touch as I say each word. I (touch your head). Like (touch your shoulders). Milk (touch your knees). Three words, three touches. I (touch your head again). Like (touch your shoulders again). Milk (touch your knees again)."

Let's Get Some Practice

Continue with your oral sentences, saying each aloud and touching head, shoulders, knees, and toes with the children. First, have children repeat the sentence. After repeating, they can begin, touching their head as they say the first word. Children can do this in unison, or you can have groups of them work with different sentences. If children make mistakes, have them watch you say each word as you touch and then have them do it again with you. If you notice they are having trouble, then say shorter sentences or phrases of two to three words. You might find you need to provide guided practice as you have children echo you. For example, using the phrase "blue sky," you touch your head for "blue" and your shoulders for "sky" and then they touch for "blue" and "sky." You might also need to practice the motor movements of touching heads, shoulders, knees, and toes as you say the body part and touch as you do this together, and then say body parts for them to touch (for example, heads and shoulders) for them to practice.

Wrap It Up

"Today we thought about the words we say when we talk. We counted three words in 'I like milk.' I (touch your head). Like (touch your shoulders). Milk (touch your knees). We counted five words in 'I ride on the bus.' I (touch your head). Ride (touch your shoulders). On (touch your knees). The (touch your toes). Bus (go back up and touch your knees)."

> **Connect to a Book!**
> After reading any book, say favorite sentences to play Head, Shoulders, Knees, and Toes. For example, after reading the *The Proudest Blue* by Ibtihaj Muhammad, use sentences or phrases like "her hijab smiles at me" or "first day of school."

ACTIVITY Sentence Hopscotch

Get Things Ready

For this activity, you'll need sidewalk chalk for outside or tape for your floor. Make a hopscotch board. It's good to have played hopscotch before, so the movements of hopping and switching from one foot to two is practiced. This way the focus can be on the words. Do not add numbers to the hopscotch board. A numbered board might be confusing since our hops won't correspond to the numbers on the board.

Make an Introduction

"Today we're going to play hopscotch, but this time we'll say words in sentences as we hop. Remember, when we talk, we use words. Like I said, 'Let's play hopscotch.' That's three words. *Let's. Play. Hopscotch.* (Put up a finger as you say each word ending with three fingers.) 'Let's play hopscotch!'"

Now for the Model

"Watch me. I'm going to hop for each word in this sentence: 'She can run fast.' She (hop with one foot on square 1). Can (hop with two feet on squares 2 and 3). Run (hop with one foot on square 4). Fast (hope with two feet on squares 5 and 6). I hopped four times, once for each word. She. Can. Run. Fast."

Let's Get Some Practice

Continue providing short oral sentences for the children to hop individually. Before a child hops, have all children chorally repeat the sentence. If needed, you could work together to say each word using your fingers for a visual. Then the child can hop the sentence. Remember, you can adjust the difficulty by having fewer words, so you might want to use phrases (for example, *blue sky*). You can use only one-syllable words (for example, *I like cake*). This activity is an easy one to adjust for each child. For example, when you know a child is just beginning to understand words in spoken sentences, you might want to provide a short phrase with one-syllable words. For other children who have already formed an understanding, you can provide a sentence that includes longer words (for example, "Michael went to the party."). After each child hops, do a quick review with the group. "Cordrick just hopped 'I like cake.' He hopped three times. I. Like. Cake. That's three words."

Wrap It Up

"We hopped for words today. Remember my sentence when we started. 'She can run fast.' Let's hop in place for each word all together. She (hop). Can (hop again). Run (hop again). Fast (hop again). That was four jumps for four words. She. Can. Run. Fast."

> **Connect to a Book!**
>
> After reading *Marisol McDonald Doesn't Match* by Monica Brown, you could choose sentences and phrases such as "I don't match" or "the color of fire."

ACTIVITY Sentence Move It Up!

Get Things Ready

For each child make a paper on which is a 2 x 6 array; or make only one for the group to share. Number the top row 1–6 (see below). Collect six markers. I keep these papers in sheet protectors, but you could also use a laminated paper. This could also be drawn on your dry-erase board. You might want to think of sentences before you do this activity to make sure you have a variety of options based on children's understanding. You may also choose to use a sentence from a favorite book.

1	2	3	4	5	6

⬜ Make an Introduction

"We are going to play Move It Up today. In this game, we'll move markers for each word we hear in a sentence. Like this: 'Move it up!' That is three words. Move (hold up a finger). It (hold up a second finger). Up (hold up a third finger). Move. It. Up."

⬜ Now for the Model

"Watch me as I do it. My sentence is 'I like pizza.' Okay. I'm going to push a marker for each word as I say it. Let's say my sentence again together. Listen to me first. 'I like pizza.' Now together: 'I like pizza.' Now let's Move It Up! I (push a marker under 1). Like (push a marker under 2). Pizza (push a marker under 3). Let's see. 'I like pizza' has three words."

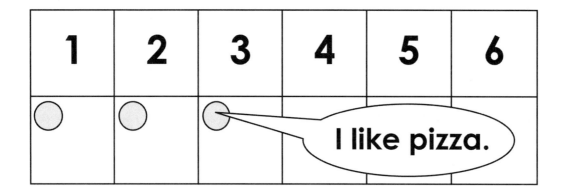

⬜ Let's Get Some Practice

Orally present children with one short sentence at a time. As with the other activities, you would choose short sentences with single-syllable words or include two-syllable words. If you are working with a larger group, you will want to do this work chorally with everyone responding together. With smaller groups, children could go individually. If children have difficulty, you can adjust the complexity of your orally presented phrase or sentence. You can also have them piggyback on your finger as you "move it up" for each word.

⬜ Wrap It Up

"We thought about the words we hear when we talk. We moved up words as we said them. Let's think back to Marisol's hair—'the color of fire.' We moved up four markers for that. The (push a marker under 1). Color (push a marker under 2). Of (push a marker under 3). Fire (push a marker under 4). The. Color. Of. Fire. Four words!"

Flex the Activity!

You can play Hot Potato to practice word awareness. To do this, you simply pass the potato as you say each word in a spoken sentence.

Syllable Awareness

You can help the children "get into the words" with syllable awareness activities where you support their growing understanding. How do you introduce the children to the concept of syllables in words? I have always found a concrete connection to syllables helpful, taking advantage of the chin drop with each syllable. I begin by explaining that all words have one or more syllables and our mouths open each time we say a syllable. All we have to do is pay attention to our mouths to find out how many syllables a word has. Then I show them how my chin drops when I open my mouth, putting my hand under my chin to demonstrate. "Try it. Say your name. I'll do mine: Latisha. As I say my name, my chin drops three times. La–tish–a. Three drops, three syllables." Children love anything that involves their names and the names of their friends. So, I often use names when I demonstrate the concept of syllables and have them start to play around with syllables. I usually have us say names in slow motion to help them connect more with how their mouths open and chins drop.

Each of these syllable activities is offered to provide more practice with syllables. Syllable activities can blend or segment syllables. As previously noted, it's easier to blend than segment syllables. To focus on blending, you can play games like I Spy or Mystery Bag. As you spy things in the room, you say them by syllable and invite children to blend to make the whole word (for example, ta–ble *table* or com–pu–ter *computer*). Or collect objects in a mystery bag (for example, basket, umbrella). Say each syllable-by-syllable and have children blend the syllables for the whole word. Pull out the object from the mystery bag to check. The activities here are all segmenting activities.

> **Connect to a Book!**
>
> Concept books are a great segue to syllable work. *Apples and Robins* by Lucie Felix can lead to shapes (for example, circle, triangle, square). *Red: A Crayon's Story* by Michael Hall can springboard to colors. *Rumble, Rumble, Grumble, Grumble* by Jennifer Shand offers sounds of storm like rumble, rustle, crash. Each of these can be the words for syllable activities. That said, any book is a great segue. For example, reading books to introduce acceptance and tolerance might include *Strictly No Elephants* by Lisa Mantchev. This book is the backdrop to a syllable sort with animal names.

ACTIVITY Busy Bumblebee

Get Things Ready

You could teach the children the chant in advance, but otherwise, there is nothing to prepare for this activity.

Make an Introduction

"We're going to play a game called Busy Bumblebee, and we'll break our names into syllables. We'll go around our circle and break everyone's name into syllables by snapping, clapping, stomping, shouting, and whispering. Remember, our mouths open up every time we say a syllable."

▢ Now for the Model

"This is how the chant goes. 'Busy, busy bumblebee, won't you say your name with me?' I'll let us know if we will clap, snap, shout, whisper, or stomp. Watch me start with my name. Latisha. Busy, busy bumblebee, won't you say your name with me? Clap it (clap, clap, clap as you say La–tish–a). Snap it (snap, snap, snap as you say La–tish–a). Shout it (shout each part). Whisper it (whisper each part). Stomp it (stomp, stomp, stomp as you say La–tish–a)."

▢ Let's Get Some Practice

Go around the circle starting off with the chant and then clap it, snap it, shout it, whisper it, and stomp it. Do this chorally so everyone is breaking the names into syllables with each child. For example, if your next child is Preston, it would go like this:

> *Busy, busy bumblebee,*
> *Won't you say your name with me?*
> *Clap it. Pres–ton (clap, clap)*
> *Snap it. Pres–ton (snap, snap)*
> *Shout it. Pres–ton (shout each part)*
> *Whisper it. Pres–ton (whisper each part)*
> *Stomp it. Pres–ton (stomp, stomp)*

▢ Wrap It Up

"We were busy, busy bumblebees! We said the syllables in our names. Let's snap out for Elijah again. Snap it. E–li–jah (snap, snap, snap). Now for Anne. Stomp it. Anne (stomp)."

ACTIVITY Syllable Snap

▢ Get Things Ready

All you need for this activity are sets of snap cubes or Unifix cubes. I've always found making sets with different colors can help make the number of syllables more visible. Most of the words you'll use (and here we'll continue with names) won't be over four syllables, so each set could have four different colored cubes.

▢ Make an Introduction

"We're going to play Syllable Snap! To play this game, we'll use these snap cubes to show how many syllables are in our names. We know all words have syllables, and names do, too! Names can have one syllable, two syllables, or more."

▢ Now for the Model

"We all have a pile of snap cubes. Watch me. I'm going to say my name. Then I'll get a cube for each syllable in my name as I say each syllable. Then I'll snap my cubes. Latisha. La (grab a cube). Tish (grab another cube). A (grab a third cube). Now, I'll snap my cubes. I have three cubes: La–tish–a (point to a cube as you say each syllable). To get ready for the next name, I'll say each syllable again as I unsnap. La (unsnap the first cube). Tish (unsnap the second cube). A (hold up the last cube)."

◼ Let's Get Some Practice

Make sure each child has a set of cubes. Move to the child next to you in the circle. Select that child next. Everyone will chorally say the child's name. You might say, "It's your turn. Tell your name to the group." For example, Lucy. "Everyone, say *Lucy*. Okay, now let's all slide one cube for each syllable we hear in *Lucy*. All together now, Lu (grab a cube) cy (grab another cube)." As each child slides down a cube and says the syllables, monitor for the right number of cubes/syllables. "Everybody snap your cubes. How many syllables are in the name Lucy? Yes, we have two cubes, Lu–cy" (point to each cube as you say the syllables). As you unsnap to return cubes to the pile, say the syllables again, unsnapping for Lu–cy. Continue around the circle until each child's name has been segmented.

◼ Wrap It Up

"We snapped so many syllables! Let's think about how many cubes we snapped for Finnigan. Say his name with me: Finnigan. Now let's say it by syllable. Finn–i–gan (grab a cube with each syllable). 1 -2 -3, three syllables. Let's say each syllable one more time. Finn–i–gan (snap the cubes together as you say each syllable)."

ACTIVITY Syllable Sort

◼ Get Things Ready

Syllable sorts can be done with objects or pictures. Whichever you choose, collect twelve to fifteen to sort ranging from one syllable to three or four (for example, cat—1, rabbit—2, kangaroo—3, alligator—4). You can keep your collection in a bag, basket, or just a pile. Set up a board for your work, and use headers with numbers 1, 2, and 3. If you are worried children may not recognize all of the numbers, you can put dots on the header cards or have keywords like *cat*, *rabbit*, and *kangaroo*. I usually use a large 11 x 16 piece of construction paper or a table mat.

◼ Make an Introduction

"We're going to sort words by how many syllables they have. To play this game, we'll choose a picture from this pile and clap out the syllables. We know all words have syllables. Words can have one syllable, two syllables, or more."

◼ Now for the Model

"Watch me. I'll go first (pick up picture card off the pile and show the picture). I have *apple*. I'm going to say it again—*apple*. Now I'm going to clap the syllables: ap–ple. Two claps, so two syllables. I'll put my apple picture under 2 since it has two syllables."

Let's Get Some Practice

Have children pick a new picture, verbalizing what's in the picture and clapping for the syllables. Then sort the pictures by the number of syllables they hear/clap in the words. For example, *zebra* and *rabbit* would be placed in the two-syllable category with *apple*.

Wrap It Up

After the sorting is finished, have children say each word, count the syllables, and reinforce why they have each picture in the categories.

Onset-Rime Awareness

Now we are talking about getting children "into the syllable." The *onset* is the first sound of a syllable, and the *rime* is the vowel and everything that follows. For example, /k/ is the onset in *cat*, and /ăt/ is the rime. You can engage children in activities that help them blend and segment words by onset-rime. To do this, you can only use single-syllable words (for example, cat /k/ /ăt/, cake /k/ /āk/, crash /kr/ /ăsh/). As with syllables, you can play I Spy or Mystery Bag where you say words by onset-rime and invite children to blend for the whole word. You would just adjust your word choice, choosing items in your room like *chair* or *rug* and collecting objects like *house*, *tub*, or *cat*. Again, notice these are all single-syllable words. You can also include activities where children segment words by onset-rime. The Mystery Bag, for example, can change to the children choosing an object and saying it by onset-rime for their friends to blend for the whole word. The activities that follow are all designed to encourage children to pay attention to the initial sounds in words—the onset.

ACTIVITY Thumbs-Up, Thumbs-Down

Get Things Ready

This game follows the same procedure as with rhyming pairs. This time we are thinking about the initial sounds in words. You'll need to collect enough pictures to have some pairs with the same initial sound and some that are not the same. You might have these picture pairs prepared: *sun-seal, man-mop, soap-moon, sink-soap, mop-mat, moon-seal*. Notice they can repeat, and we've kept it to only two different sounds, /m/ and /s/. This is an example of an introduction to thinking about initial sounds, so we are focused only on two sounds. I usually begin with these two sounds because: 1) they are distinct in both how they sound but also how they feel in the mouth, 2) they are both continuous sounds (meaning you can hold on to them. . . /mmmmm/ and /ssssss/), and 3) they are usually the first sounds taught in a letter-sound phonics sequence.

Make an Introduction

"We are going to play a game where we listen for the beginning sounds in words. We are going to listen out for the words that have the same sound at the beginning. So, I want you to think about only the first sound of the words I say. Before we start, let's name all of the pictures so that you know what each one is called."

Now for the Model

"I'll go first (get two picture cards). I have mmman (stretch out the /m/ at the beginning and hold up the picture). My other picture is mmmouse (stretch out the /m/ at the beginning and hold up the picture). Mmman, mmmouse. I hear the same sound at the beginning of these words. I hear /m/ at the beginning. Listen. Mmman, mmmouse (point to the pictures as you say each word). When we have words with the same beginning sound, let's do a thumbs-up. So, I'm putting thumbs up. Mmman, mmmouse. They both begin with /m/. Mmman, mmmouse (have the children say the words with you). Let's do another one (pick two pictures). Sssun (stretch out the /s/ as you hold up the card). Sssock (stretch out the /s/ as you hold up the card). Listen. Sssun, sssock (point to the pictures as you say each word). I hear the same sound at the beginning of sssun and sssock. They both begin with /s/. Sssun, sssock. Let's all put our thumbs up since they both begin with /s/. Sssun, sssock (have the children say the words with you).

Let's Get Some Practice

Explain that you'll put your thumbs up for words that begin with the same sound and thumbs down for words that don't have the same sound at the beginning. Continue following the same process, emphasizing the beginning sound of each word. Make sure the children repeat the words and say the beginning sounds. If children have difficulty, say "Mmmoon, sssseal. Thumbs-down. They don't begin with the same sound. Mmmoon begins with /m/ but sssseal begins with /s/. Let's say them together. Mmmoon, sssseal. Thumbs-down."

Wrap It Up

"We thought about words that begin with the same sound like mmmoon and mmmouse. They both begin with /m/. Or sssun and sssseal. They both begin with /s/."

ACTIVITY Larry the Llama

Get Things Ready

Prepare a list of animals and an adjective that starts with the same sound. For example, you might say *shy sheep* or *silly seals*. You'll also need some that don't begin with the same sound like *cute dogs*. Try to find a llama stuffed animal, puppet, or print-out.

Make an Introduction

"Larry the llama loves to laugh. You know what makes him laugh? He laughs when animals begin with the same sound as the word that describes them. So when I say an animal, you'll listen for the beginning sound to see if Larry the llama will laugh."

Now for the Model

"Listen. *Messy monkeys*. Do messy monkeys make Larry the llama laugh? Yes, messy monkeys make Larry the llama laugh because mmmessy mmmonkeys begin with the same sound. . . /m/. What makes Larry the llama laugh? Mmmessy monkeys (make sure all children chorally respond when you have two words with the same beginning sound). How about *happy turtles*? Do happy turtles make Larry the llama laugh? No, happy turtles don't make him laugh because they don't begin with the same sound. Happy starts with /h/ and turtles starts with /t/."

Let's Get Some Practice

Continue with the same procedure. Ask questions, mixing up animals and adjectives that begin with the same sound and those that don't. Make sure the children repeat the word pairs (for example, *dancing dolphins*) and have them explain if the words have the same beginning sound or not (for example, dancing dolphins both begin with /d/). Some example questions you might ask:

- Do *cute cows* make Larry the llama laugh? cute cows

- Do *tiny turtles* make Larry the llama laugh? tiny turtles

- Do *happy birds* make Larry the llama laugh? happy birds

- Do *bouncing bunnies* make Larry the llama laugh? bouncing bunnies

- Do *jumping kangaroos* make Larry the llama laugh? jumping kangaroos

- Do *racing raccoons* make Larry the llama laugh? racing raccoons

- Do *big birds* make Larry the llama laugh? big birds

- Do *small horses* make Larry the llama laugh? small horses

Wrap It Up

"We made Larry the llama laugh a lot today! He laughed with *big birds* since they both begin with /b/ and with *racing raccoons* since they both begin with /r/.

Flex the Activity!

You can play this same game with rhyming pairs. For example, you'd ask if a big pig will make Larry the llama laugh. Since big and pig rhyme Larry the llama will laugh!

ACTIVITY Mystery Bag

Get Things Ready

Prepare a group pictures of things (animals, objects, and so on) that include many that start with the same sound and some that do not. Fifteen to twenty pictures is usually enough as long as we have around ten matches to have some good practice.

Make an Introduction

"We're going to play a game with the pictures I have in my mystery bag. Your job is to figure out if the words begin with the same sound or if they begin with different sounds. First, let's name each picture so that you know what each one is called." You can name each picture by pulling one out and saying, "This is a bee. What is it?"

Now for the Model

"Let me show you how we play (choose two pictures from the bag and show them to the children). *Bee, bear.* These words begin with the same sound. Let's say them together. *Bee, bear.* They both begin with /b/. I'm going to get two more pictures. *Fork, pen.* These words don't begin with the same sound. Let's say them together. *Fork, pen.* Fork begins with /f/, but pen begins with /p/."

Let's Get Some Practice

Continue with the same procedure. Choose pictures, mixing up those that begin with the same sound and those that don't. Make sure to have children say each pair of words and explain if the words have the same beginning sound or not (for example, *fan* and *fish* both begin with /f/).

Wrap It Up

"I love picking things out of my mystery bag. Today we thought about words that begin with the same sound like *socks* and *soap*. *Socks* and *soap* both begin with /s/."

> **Look For**
>
> As the children engage in these onset-rime activities that emphasize the beginning sounds in words, you will want to monitor how quickly and accurately they identify words that begin with the same sound. You will also want to observe if they can isolate the beginning sound. In other words, you'll want to ensure they can determine *moon* and *map* begin with the same sound as well as isolate the beginning sound /m/.

Phoneme Awareness

Ultimately, we are helping the children develop an awareness of phonemes, or individual sounds in words. This level of awareness is necessary for early reading and spelling. For example, children decoding a word like *cat* will say each sound /k/ /ă/ /t/ and blend those sounds to make the word—*cat*. Young children will also want to spell words like *run*. To do this, a first step they will need to do is segment each sound they hear in the word.

Children need practice blending sounds to make whole words. Many have designed activities for this purpose (for example, Troll Talk from Adams, Foorman, Lundberg, and Beeler, 1998). These particular activities are completely oral and are designed to give young children practice with blending sounds. I like to play I Spy and Puppet Sound Blending. In both activities, I use pictures to provide support as needed. I generally pause one second between sounds. Be careful not to add a schwa to sounds, particularly stop consonants. Be careful to say /b/ rather than *buh*.

Practicing blending activities can make the transition to segmentation tasks easier. I use an activity called Say It and Move It because it's a supportive first step for young children as they begin segmentation activities. This activity is based on the work of Ball and Blachman (1991) who found phonemic awareness training in kindergarten positively influenced later reading and spelling skills. Just as you avoid saying a schwa when pronouncing individual sounds, you will want to support the children in this same effort. If they develop the practice of saying schwas (for example, saying *puh* rather than /p/), it can impact how easily they blend sounds.

Look For

As children complete these activities, you'll want to notice if they can blend words with two, three, and four sounds. You'll also want to observe whether they can segment words with two, three, or four sounds. Remember, the expectation for end of prekindergarten is isolating the beginning sound in words. It isn't until kindergarten that we expect children to segment words with three sounds.

ACTIVITY I Spy

Get Things Ready

Collect pictures representative of the words to be blended. Be thoughtful in your collection. As you are beginning with this activity, especially with young children, you should concentrate on words with two sounds and then move to words with three and four sounds. Remember, phonological activities are completely oral, so no word will be written for children to see. Here are some options:

TWO SOUNDS	THREE SOUNDS	FOUR SOUNDS
sea	cat	clap
two	bed	stuck
key	pig	flag
day	pot	clock
bee	sun	desk
hay	ship	grape
knee	play	plug
zoo	snow*	gift
toe*	tack	sleep
mow*	rock	broom
tie	clay**	nest

* Avoid adding /w/ when pronouncing long *O*; don't say /s/ /n/ /ō/ /w/.

** Avoid adding /y/ when pronouncing long *A*; don't say /k/ /l/ /ā/ /y/.

Make an Introduction

"We're going to play I Spy. I'll show you some pictures, and then I'll give you a clue for what I'm spying. But I'm going to say the words slowly, one sound at a time. Your job is to put those sounds together to make the whole word."

Now for the Model

Lay out three picture options (for example, hay, knee, tie) with one picture as your target. "I spy with my little eye: /n/ /ē/. I have to put the sounds together to find out which picture. /n/ /ē/." Remember to avoid adding schwas to sounds (for example, *nuh* instead of /n/). Once the word is provided, chorally segment and blend the word again. To make segmenting more concrete, hold up fingers as you segment. I hold up however many fingers, keeping them apart. Then when I blend, I put my fingers together. This quick motion provides a visual for separate sounds and blend for one word. You can also use a finger to thumb tap for segmenting and then swipe the thumb across fingers to motion blending.

Let's Get Some Practice

Lay out three new pictures. With each new set, say your phrase, "I spy with my little eye. . ." and then say your target word one sound at a time. Follow the same process of eliciting a response from the children and then chorally segment and blend the word. If you notice children having trouble, think back to your picture choices. Do you need to use only two-sound words rather than words with more sounds? If you were focusing on words like *gift* and *clock*, then you may need to move to *cat* and *pot* or *sea* and *toe* and avoid blends. Or do you need to use continuous sounds and avoid the harder stop sounds? For example, it is easier for children to blend /sssssē/ than /bē/.

Wrap It Up

"That was a good game of I Spy. You listened to my clues as I said a word one sound at a time. Then you blended those sounds to make the whole word. Like this /t/ /ō/. What's my word? *Toe.* That's right!"

ACTIVITY Puppet Sound Blending

Get Things Ready

Find a puppet with a mouth that you can move. I've found making a sock puppet works well, and children love them. You will want to consider how many sounds to include in your words based on children's understanding. Use the word chart with I Spy to help you generate options.

Make an Introduction

"This is my friend, Tessa. She likes to say words one part at a time. Your job is to listen to Tessa and blend the parts together to make the whole word." The children must then blend the parts together to make the whole word. Follow the same guidelines as in I Spy above. Pause one second between sounds. Avoid adding a schwa to your sounds.

Now for the Model

"Hi, Tessa! What do you want to say to my friends here? /s/ /ē/ (move your puppets mouth as you say each sound). I'm going to blend /s/ /ē/. . . see. Tessa is saying *see.*" Remember to pause one second between sounds and avoid adding a schwa to your sounds.

Let's Get Some Practice

Continue with your words, moving Tessa's mouth as you say each sound. If children have difficulty, first add the picture support detailed previously in I Spy. Put out three pictures to help support the children by giving them options. Or consider your choice of words to blend. Perhaps you need fewer sounds, or you need continuant sounds rather than stop sounds.

> ### Connect to a Book!
>
> After reading *All About Bats* by Caryn Jenner, you could have Tessa say animal names like *bat, cat, pig, fish, dog.* Or words from the book like *bat, sun, cave, pup, food.*

▢ Wrap It Up

"You all really helped Tessa today. When she said a word one sound at a time, you blended for the whole word. When she said /f/ /ē/ /t/, you blended /f/ /ē/ /t/ to make *feet*."

ACTIVITY Say It and Move It

▢ Get Things Ready

Identify ten to twelve words. Again, you'll want to decide if you want two-sound words or words with more sounds. The chart in I Spy will be a help here, too. But feel free to venture to another set of words. For example, if you are teaching the short-A sound in your phonics instruction, you might want to have the children work with a set of two- and three-sound words with /ă/, such as *at*, *map*, and *bag*. You'll need a set of tiles or snap cubes for each child. I like to have different colors in the set to emphasize that each tile or cube is a different phoneme/sound. You may also want each child to have a workspace with Elkonin boxes (Elkonin, 1971). Elkonin boxes (often called "sound boxes") are simply boxes where the children can "push" their tiles. These boxes help make the "separation" of sounds more concrete for children. Consider *chop*. By "pushing" into the boxes, you can clearly illustrate for children the three sounds: /ch/ /ŏ/ /p/.

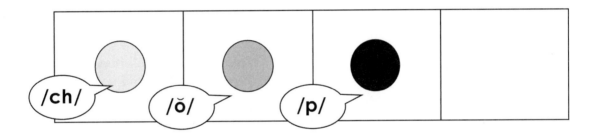

▢ Make an Introduction

"We are going to play a game today where I give you a word and your job is to say each sound in the word. When you say a sound, you will push a cube into a box. Then we can see how many sounds are in the word!"

▢ Now for the Model

"Watch me. My word is *sat*. Sat. I'm going to say each sound /s/ /ă/ /t/. I'll push a cube into a box as I say each sound. /s/ (push up a cube). . . /ă/ (push up another cube). . . /t/ (push up a third cube). 3 sounds—/s/ /ă/ /t/. . . sat."

▢ Let's Get Some Practice

Continue with the same procedure as you give the children new words to say and move. After you say a word, have them repeat it. Then say the word one sound at a time while they push a cube for each sound. After they've segmented, have them say the sounds again and then blend for the whole word. You can talk about how many sounds in the word, but do that after you've segmented and blended again. Otherwise, they may forget your target word. You can have a picture of your target word, if needed. If children have difficulty, consider your word choice. Do you need to have fewer sounds? Do you need to only include continuous sounds for the beginning sound? You can also decide to continue having them echo you. You would segment the word, move your cubes, and blend for the whole word. Then children would echo you.

☐ Wrap It Up

"We thought about the sounds we hear in words. Like in *mop*. We said each sound /m/ /ŏ/ /p/ (hold up a finger for each sound as you say them). . . mop."

> **Flex the Activity!**
>
> You can push cubes into Elkonin boxes for syllable segmenting, too. For example, you would push three cubes into three boxes as you say each syllable in *computer*. . . com–pu–ter.

ACTIVITY Cut It and Move It

☐ Get Things Ready

Identify ten to twelve words with accompanying pictures. Usually, concrete objects work well when you are using pictures (for example, coat, hat, bee). As with Say It and Move It, you'll want to decide if you want two-sound words or words with more sounds. You'll segment sounds in this activity, but instead of pushing tiles, you'll cut and then push parts of your picture.

☐ Make an Introduction

"We are going to play a game today where I show you a picture of something and your job is to say each sound of the word in the picture. We'll see how many sounds are in the word!"

Now for the Model

"Watch me and look at my picture. This is a *coat*. Coat. I'm going to say each sound /k/ /ō/ /t/. I count

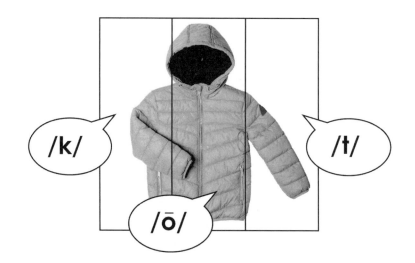

three sounds. . . /k/ /ō/ /t/ (hold up a finger per sound as you say them). I'm going to cut my picture into three pieces (cut the picture card into three pieces). Now I can push each piece as I say each sound. /k/ (push up the first piece) /ō/ (push up the second piece) /t/ (push up the third). 3 sounds: /k/ /ō/ /t/ coat."

Let's Get Some Practice

Continue with the same procedure as you give the children new words to cut and move. After you show the picture and say a word, have them repeat it. Then say the word one sound at a time while you count together the sounds. After they've segmented, cut the picture into the appropriate number of pieces (corresponding to the number of sounds). As you push each piece of the picture, have them say the sounds again and then blend for the whole word. If children have difficulty, consider your word choice. Do you need to have fewer sounds? Do you need to only include continuous sounds for the beginning sound? You can also make a choice to continue having them echo you. You would segment the word, cut into pieces and move them, and blend for the whole word. Then children echo you.

Wrap It Up

"We thought about the sounds we hear in words. Like in *coat*. We said each sound /k/ /ō/ /t/ (push the pieces of the picture). . . *coat*."

> **Flex the Activity!**
>
> You can use pictures to emphasize syllables in words. For example, you can cut a picture of a motorcycle into four pieces (mo–tor–cy–cle) or a shadow into two (sha–dow).

ACTIVITY Switch It!

Get Things Ready

Identify ten to twelve words. For this activity, you'll add or substitute individual sounds (phonemes) in simple, one-syllable words to make new words (a kindergarten standard). It is easier for children to add to the beginning or substitute a beginning sound. For example, it's easier to add /b/ to /ăt/ to make *bat*. It's also easier to change the /b/ in *bat* to /s/ to make *sat*. With this in mind, I'd suggest collecting a set of two-phoneme words (for example, *at, in, is*) to add beginning sounds to make new words like *hat, fin,* and *his*). You can focus on short vowel word families with three-phoneme words (see Short Vowel Word Family Bank). Sticking with short vowel word families will keep words short and easier for substituting activities.

SHORT A FAMILIES	SHORT I FAMILIES	SHORT O FAMILIES	SHORT U FAMILIES	SHORT E FAMILIES
-at bat, cat, hat, mat, pat, rat, sat, that	-it bit, fit, hit, kit, lit, pit, sit	-ot cot, dot, got, hot, jot, not, pot	-ut but, cut, gut, hut, nut, shut	-et bet, get, jet, let, met, pet, set, wet
-ap cap, lap, map, nap, rap, tap, zap	-ip dip, hip, lip, rip, sip, tip, zip	-op cop, hop, mop, pop, top, shop, chop	-up cup, pup	

SHORT A FAMILIES	SHORT I FAMILIES	SHORT O FAMILIES	SHORT U FAMILIES	SHORT E FAMILIES
-ag bag, rag, sag, tag, wag, zag, shag	-ig big, dig, fig, jig, pig, rig, wig	-og bog, dog, fog, hog, jog, log	-ug bug, dug, hug, jug, mug, tug	-eg leg, peg
-ad bad, dad, had, mad, pad, sad	-id hid, kid, lid, rid		-ud bud, mud	-ed bed, fed, led, wed, shed
-ack back, pack, rack, sack, tack, shack	-ick kick, lick, pick, sick, tick, chick	-ock lock, knock, rock, sock, tock, shock	-uck duck, luck, suck, tuck, yuck	-eck deck, neck, peck

You can do this activity orally, but sometimes you may find it helpful to have manipulatives to give children a concrete visual to support their thinking. You could use snapping cubes or tiles. You can also use Elkonin boxes as in Push It and Say It. I always use different colors (you'll need at least 4 colors).

Make an Introduction

"We are going to change one part of a word to make new words today. To do this, we'll have to think about the first sounds in words."

Now for the Model

"Watch and listen. My word is *hug*. /h/ /ŭ/ /g/ (push a tile into a box as you say each sound). Now I'm going to say *hug* but I'll change the /h/ (put your finger on the first tile) to /m/ (pull the tile out of the box and get another color). Watch me (say /m/ as you push up a new tile). Now I have /m/ /ŭ/ /g/. . . my new word is *mug*. Watch me do it again. Hug. /h/ /ŭ/ /g/ (push a tile into a box as you say each sound). Now I'll change /h/ to /m/. /m/ /ŭ/ /g/. . . mug."

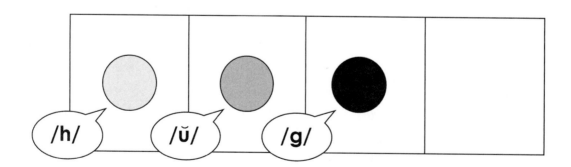

Let's Get Some Practice

Continue with the same procedure as you give the children new words. After you give them a word, have them push a tile for each sound they hear. Then tell them the sound to change (for example, *had*—change the /h/ to /d/). Have them switch the first tile and say their new sounds before they blend for the whole word. If children have difficulty, you can have them echo you. Or you could do each word chorally. If children are easily substituting the beginning sound, you can have them switch out the final sound. So, instead of changing *hug* to *mug*, you could say change the /g/ to /m/ to make *hum*.

Wrap It Up

"Today we changed the first sounds in words to make new words. Like *hug*. /h/ /ŭ/ /g/ We changed the /h/ to /m/ to make /m/ /ŭ/ /g/ to make *mug*."

Connect to a Book!

After reading *Super Satya Saves the Day* by Raakhee Mirchandani, you could talk out the problem in the story: "Super Satya's stomach felt super tight because her superhero cape was stuck at the dry cleaner so she couldn't do all of the things superheroes do." Then choose words associated with superheroes like *kind*, *fast*, *zoom*, *good*, *nice*, *bold*, *cape*, and *mask*. Notice each of these words begin with one consonant sound. This is important because it is difficult for young children to separate consonant blends like the 'cr' in *crib* or the 'st' in *stop*.

To Sum It Up

A critical component of early reading is phonological awareness. Each of the activities in this chapter are offered to support children's burgeoning phonological skills. Thinking about the continuum of phonological awareness development will help you understand children's responses to your activities as well as ways you can take a step back to provide more support or make a jump forward to provide more challenge. These phonological activities fit within a comprehensive framework that will help you lay the foundation for your developing readers and writers.

CHAPTER FOUR
Grasping the Alphabetic Code

This chapter is squarely focused on helping children grasp the alphabetic code. We'll walk through activities that support learning letter names and letter sounds, and we'll reserve letter formation for chapter 7. To begin our look at the alphabetic code, let's take a look at the early literacy standards from the Head Start Early Learning Outcome Framework and the Common Core State Standards. As you can see, prekindergarten standards range from letter names to upper- and lowercase letters to letter sounds. Kindergarten standards shift our thinking to the application of these sounds for decoding and spelling. We'll look at decoding in chapter 5 and spelling in chapter 7. This allows us to really zero in on letter names and sounds in this chapter as we work on three things:

- **Recognition:** asking a child to point to a specific letter

- **Production:** showing a letter for a child to say the name or sound

- **Fluency:** considering how quickly a child can name letters or provide sounds

HEAD START EARLY LEARNING OUTCOME FRAMEWORK—36-60 MONTHS	COMMON CORE STATE STANDARDS—KINDERGARTEN

- Points to and names some letters or characters in their names (36 months).
- Understands that written words are made up of a group of individual letters (60 months).
- Name 18 upper- and 15 lowercase letters (60 months).
- Knows the sounds associated with several letters (60 months).
	- Know and apply grade-level phonics and word analysis skills in decoding words:
	  - Demonstrate basic knowledge of one-to-one letter-sound correspondences by producing the primary sound or many of the most frequent sounds for each consonant.
	  - Associate the long and short sounds with the common spellings (graphemes) for the five major vowels.
	  - Read common high-frequency words by sight (for example, *the, of, to, you, she, my, is, are, do, does*).
	  - Distinguish between similarly spelled words by identifying the sounds of the letters that differ.

Building a child's understanding of the alphabetic code involves the recognition and naming of both uppercase and lowercase letters as well as the paired association between a letter's name and its sound. Ultimately, it's letter name *and* sound fluency that gives a child a real advantage when learning to read and write. In other words, children need to be accurate *as well as* automatic, or quick, with these tasks.

Letter Names or Letter Sounds?

Sometimes educators worry that focusing on letter names may confuse children. So, why include letter names as a critical component of alphabet knowledge? In the United States, parents prioritize letter names before children come to school (Adams, 1990; McBride-Chang, 1999). Imagine a parent telling a child how to spell "cat." They would say C–A–T, using the letter names. In some ways, letter names are the "language of literacy" (Tortorelli, 2015-16). As Adams (1990) puts it, letter names give us a concrete label for everything the children need to learn about letters. For example, their formation (including font variations), their upper- and lowercase forms, and their sounds.

Plus, early literacy curricula often prioritizes letter names first in the instructional sequence, and most kindergarten teachers report teaching letter names (Bereiter et al., 2003; Ellefson, Treiman, and Kessler, 2009; Foulin, 2005; Heroman and Jones, 2004; Justice et al., 2006). This means letter names become part of the language we use to talk about reading and writing. They become our labels for sounds—unlike sounds, letter names are actually words! Children who do not know letter names may struggle integrating the many pieces of knowledge they have about a letter without the label to hold them all together. And, some letter names are even words children already know, such as *you* as in "you are happy" or *I* as in "I am happy."

Another thing to consider: letter names and letter sounds are also related. This is called the *letter-name structure effect*. Most English letter names give us clues to their letter sounds. Consider the letter *B*. We hear its sound at the beginning of the letter name: /b/ bee. We'll call these CV letters (consonant-vowel letter names). These letters include *B* as well as *D* (dee), *J* (jay), *K* (kay), *P* (pea), *T* (tee), *V* (vee), and *Z* (zee). These letter sounds are often learned first (McBride-Chang, 1999; Treiman et al., 2008). In fact, children who already know a letter's name are more likely to also know that letter's sound (Kim et al., 2010; Huang, Tortorelli, and Invernizzi, 2014).

Now let's consider the letter *F*. We hear its sound at the end of the letter name: eff. Letters like *F* are VC letters (vowel-consonant letter names). Letters in this category include *F* as well as *L* (ell), *M* (em), *N* (en), *R* (are), *S* (ess), and *X* (eks). Children also learn these names and sounds relatively easily but usually later than CV letters (Justice et al., 2006; Huang, Tortorelli, and Invernizzi, 2014; Turnball et al., 2010). Considering all of this, we can see why it's important to assess and teach both letter names *and* letter sounds. Plus, research has shown that teaching both provides an advantage for alphabet learning (Piasta, Purpura, and Wagner, 2010).

Okay. That's only fifteen letters. What about the remaining eleven? Let's take *C* and *G*. When considering their "soft" sounds (for example, *C* as /s/ in *city* and *G* as /j/ in *gym*), they are CV letters. The issue with *C* and *G* is that they make two sounds: their soft sound and their hard sound (for example, *C* as /k/ in *cat* and *G* as /g/ in *got*). We often teach the "hard" sounds first. How about vowels? Their "long" sounds are easy since they "say their names," but we teach their "short" sounds first. These letter names give the children a clue to only one of the letters' sounds. This leads us to the final four letters. These letters have sounds that aren't connected to their names at all: *H* (aitch), *Q* (cue), *W* (double-u), and *Y* (why). Generally, these letters, or letters with inconsistent or no name-sound connections, are harder to learn as compared to CV and VC letters (Justice et al., 2006; Tortorelli, 2014).

No More Letter of the Week

To borrow the title from a useful resource—*No More Teaching a Letter a Week* from the Not This But That series (McKay and Teale, 2015)—let's think about this common practice: teaching one letter at a time over the course of a week. A suggested sequence for learning the alphabet (again, letter names and sounds) is *B, M, S, A, T, N, R, O, P, C, F, I, D, G, H, E, L, K, J, U, W, V, Y, Z, Q, X.* Please note: there isn't an established order. This sequence is based on the letters that occur more frequently in simple words that are taught first, letters that have similar sounds and are easily confused are separated, vowels are incorporated early, and the first letters taught will allow you to make simple consonant-vowel-consonant words through oral blending (for example, *mat, sat, bat*). The sequence, however, is not meant to be used in a "letter a week" approach. Rather, I usually present the sounds in sorting contrasts to teach multiple letter names and sounds during any given week. Then I cycle through them multiple times for repeated practice. You can start with two and then add another before moving to the third sorting contrast as a review plus a new vowel sound. This allows you to teach and provide recursive practice in a fraction of the time needed for a "letter a week" approach.

I acknowledge that the "letter of the week" approach has been used for many years and is a place of comfort for many of us. But let's consider three important aspects of learning, specifically literacy learning. First, we learn better through distributed practice rather than massed practice. Our learning is supported by recursive study or cycling back around to previously learned concepts. Second, learning also involves comparing and contrasting things. In other words, learning what something is as well as what it isn't. Learning one letter at a time does not take advantage of comparing and contrasting letters. And third, we know some letters are easier to learn than others; we might not need an entire week on some letters, and for others, we may need more than a week. So, we want to teach letter names and sounds, revisit them, and take advantage of name-sound connections. We want to immerse children in letters, and research has shown this to be more effective (for example, Jones, Clark, and Reutzel, 2013).

Make Letter Practice Part of Your Routine

Let's first think about ways we can fit in lots of practice throughout the day. Many of us keep collections of children's names, such as equity sticks, to call on them throughout the day. You might have yours on tongue depressors in a jar or on sentence strips collected in a basket. Use these collections to reinforce letter names and/or letter sounds. The next time you pick a child's name for an activity or job, have the child identify their name. You can also have the child spell their name aloud. Or you could simply have the child identify the first letter in their name.

You could include a picture of each child on their name card. This will allow you to use these in a variety of ways. For example, you could distribute one card to each child, making sure no one gets their own name. When a child's name is called, the child who has the card says the name and shows the card. They could then spell the name aloud, identify the first letter, or even say something positive about that child.

You can also keep sets of upper- and lowercase letters. When you are choosing children to get in line, do a job, or head to centers, you can distribute a card to each child. Make sure you have the letter match on hand. You show a card, and the child with the upper- or lowercase match shows their card and names the letter. If you've taught the letter's sound, you could also have them provide the sound.

Introducing Letters

When you think about introducing letters, you should use all components of letter learning. So, you'll use the letter's name, shape (both upper- and lowercase), sound and the mouth shape during pronunciation, and keyword. Paulson and Moats (2018) note "the more connections children are able to make for the alphabet letters they are learning, the deeper their understanding becomes." Effective instruction is also brief and explicit (Jones, Clark, and Reutzel, 2013; Paulson and Moats, 2018), lasting no more than ten minutes.

To start, you will want to have a collection of keywords you will use. These keywords may come from a curriculum or from a set you've used in the past. The bottom line is the keyword should be a common word that includes the target letter sound at the beginning and not within a blend. For example, *cat* is a fine keyword for *C*. It is a commonly known word, makes the hard *C* sound (the sound we target first) at the beginning, and does not include a blend (as, for example, *crab* or *clock* do). Keep your keywords consistent over time and across your instruction as well as displayed for quick reference in your room with pictures to illustrate each keyword. You want children to call upon them quickly and easily to assist their letter-sound development. If you don't already have a set of keywords, the following may be fine options.

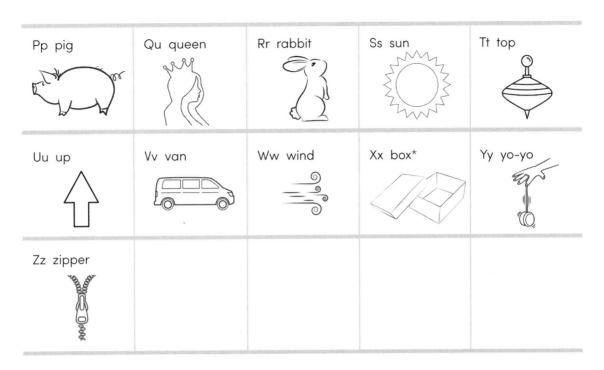

Pp pig	Qu queen	Rr rabbit	Ss sun	Tt top
Uu up	Vv van	Ww wind	Xx box*	Yy yo-yo
Zz zipper				

* *X* as /ks/ doesn't appear at the beginning of words, so the keyword has it in the final position.

Having a letter-introduction routine is often helpful. This routine will include some preparation. You'll need to ensure your proper pronunciation of the letter sound on your letter cards. As you prepare for your introduction, you should also think about the shape of your mouth and any other important aspects of letter pronunciation (for example, push of air, lips closed, tongue behind front teeth). Often you can make the sound and observe for yourself. But if you need support, a good resource is *Kid Lips Instructional Guide* from Tools 4 Reading (Dahlgren and Fierro, 2018). For example, for /d/, you open your mouth a bit, tap the tip of your tongue on the roof of your mouth behind your front teeth, and let out a little push of air.

You will need your letters on letter cards and/or displayed on an anchor chart. Use the print you are teaching children, and write both the upper- and lowercase letters. Include the picture and the written keyword on the letter card. Here's an example of a card for *S*.

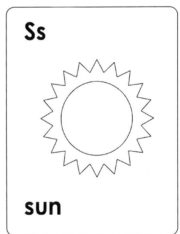

Your introduction would go something like this. You will want to create some anticipation. For example, you might have a drumroll or a "new letter chant." Then you would follow your routine. Here's a suggestion that explicitly points out the name, the sound, and the formation.

- Introduce the name and show the letter card. Have the children repeat the letter name. Say, "This is the letter *S*. Say this sentence with me. This is the letter *S*."

- Point out the uppercase *S* and say, "This is uppercase *S*. Say it with me and watch. This is uppercase *S*." As you say this, trace the uppercase *S*. Now, point to lowercase *s* and say, "This is lowercase *s*. Say it with me and watch. This is lowercase s." As you say this, trace the lowercase s. When appropriate, point out how they are the same shape. So, here you'd say, "Look everyone. Uppercase S and lowercase s look exactly the same!"

- Then introduce the sound and have the children repeat it. You might want to have a signal for when you present the sound to highlight this part of the lesson (for example, cupping your ear). Say, "The sound of S is /s/. What's the sound?" Have the children repeat. "Say this sentence with me. The sounds of S is /s/." Have the children repeat.

- Point out your keyword by saying, "I hear /s/ at the beginning of sun. Everyone say sun. Sun. Let's say it again and listen for the /s/ at the beginning. Sun."

- Skywrite the letter. Have the children watch you first as you narrate the strokes you are making to form the letter. For example, Handwriting Without Tears uses the following language: "Watch me. I'm going skywrite uppercase S. Little curve. Turn. Little curve." Have the children skywrite as you narrate the movements. Repeat with lowercase s.

- Lastly, review what you've learned. You might say, "Today we learned about the letter S. This is the uppercase S (trace S), and this is lowercase s (trace s). Letter S makes the /s/ sound. I can hear /s/ at the beginning of sun. Sun /s/." Have the children say, "S says /s/ like in sun," as they skywrite S.

My routine always includes a quick review of previously learned letters. You can do this in a variety of ways to make it fun. For example, you might shine a flashlight on a letter for the children to chant, "B says /b/ like in ball" as they skywrite. Or you might have your target letters in a mystery bag. Pull out a card and show children to cue their chant. Then again, all of the activities that follow provide ample opportunity for review and practice. So, let's get started!

Letter Names

Knowing the ABC song is a first step to learning the alphabet. However, children must go beyond the song and develop a deep knowledge of the alphabet. They must know the names and shapes of each letter. To do this, they must recognize the visual aspects of letters and learn how to form them. Not only do they need to learn the twenty-six letters, but they must also know the upper- and lowercase versions of each. This chapter takes advantage of what we know about how children learn the alphabet. We'll address both letter names and sounds since we know instruction focused on both is more effective than either alone. To start us out, we'll explore activities that boost letter name knowledge. As a prekindergarten teacher, you might focus more on letter names at first, and as a kindergarten teacher, you might shift your focus to letter sounds. Either way, you'll want to include both letter name and sound activities as part of your instructional practice.

Flex the Activity!

Many of these activities can switch between letter names and letter sounds. Or they can incorporate both. For example, Spin a Letter is presented here with letter name activities. But you could also spin, make the upper- and lowercase match, and say the letter name.

ACTIVITY **Letter Shape Sort**

Get Things Ready

You'll need a collection of magnetic letters, letter tiles, or other single-letter options. This activity uses only uppercase letters. You can collect them in a pile, in a basket, or a bag. To sort the letters, use either a t-chart labeled with "straight lines" and "curved lines" or two labeled mats. Make a drawing to provide an example with your label.

straight lines ————————	curved lines (

Make an Introduction

"Every letter has its own shape. Some letters have straight lines (make a straight line in the air). Some letters have curved lines (make a curved line in the air). Let's look at the shapes of letters and think about what kind of lines they have—straight or curved. We'll sort letters on our chart. We'll put the letters with straight lines on this side (trace the straight line or draw a straight line as a demonstration). And, we'll put the letters with curved lines on this side (trace the curved line or draw a curved line as a demonstration)."

Now for the Model

"Watch me first. Let's look at my first letter. It's the letter *H*. It has two straight lines down (trace with your finger) and one straight line across (again, trace with your finger). It has straight lines, so I'm going to put it on this side of the chart for straight lines (point to the label)."

"Now I'm going to look at one more letter. It's the letter *S*. Watch me. . . it has a curved line (trace *S* with your finger), so I'm going to put *S* on the 'curved lines' side of the chart (point to the label)."

Let's Get Some Practice

Continue with this process by having children choose a letter one at a time, say the letter name, and trace the letter. Ask if the letter has straight lines or curved lines. If children don't know the letter name, reduce options by asking, "Is that letter ___ or ___?" or using an alphabet strip for support. If children are having trouble deciding which side of the chart to place their letter, ask again if it has straight or curved lines and have them trace again. Or you trace to show them. You can also have children stand straight with their arms straight up to demonstrate a straight line and slouch over with their arms curved over (like they are making a hook) to demonstrate a curved line.

Wrap It Up

"You looked so closely at these letters today. You thought about the letters with straight lines. Let's say all of the letters with straight lines (point to each letter as you and children say the name). You also thought about letters with curved lines. Let's say all of the letters with curved lines (point to each letter as you and children say the name)."

Flex the Activity!

To look at straight lines and curved lines, you are restricted to A, C, E, F, H, I, K, L, M, N, O, S, T, U, V, W, X, Y, Z. You could add a "both" category with B, D, G, J, P, Q, R. I'd recommend focusing only on straight lines and curved lines first. Sometimes this way of grouping letters is confusing to children, especially when they are first learning letters. You can also play this with the alphabet arc (activity coming up in this section). Children will have plastic letters on their arc (matching plastic letters to the arc) and will then make piles of curvy lines, straight lines, or both. To end, children will name the letters in each group.

ACTIVITY Letter Font Sort

Get Things Ready

Collect a number of letters with different fonts on cards for the sort. To call attention to the distinctive visual features of letters, you'll want to choose fonts that emphasize these features. I've used Century Gothic, Chalkboard, Bradley, Cooper, and Ayuthaya. Different ones may lend themselves to other letters. For example, you will want versions of **g** rather than g or **a** rather than **a**. You can also adjust font by bolding the letters or adjusting their size. Use your primary font for your header cards, or the cards that will label your target categories. I usually compare two to four letters in a sort and no more. You probably already have language you use to describe these distinctive aspects of letters. For example, *Handwriting Without Tears* uses the following language for lowercase *b*: "dive down, swim up and over, then around and bump" (Learning Without Tears, 2018). With each of your font samples, you will use this same language to emphasize the main visual characteristics of the letter despite the font.

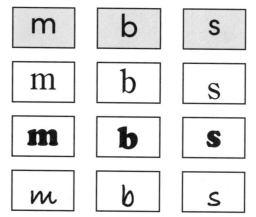

▦ Make an Introduction

"Today we'll look at letters that are written in different ways. We'll look at the letter *m*. Here you can see lowercase *m*. Start with *n*. Swim up and over. Down." (As you say these formation moves, trace the letter.) "We'll see other *m*'s written in different ways, but we know all *m*'s start with *n*, swim up and over, and then go down. Our job is to find them! We'll also look at lowercase *b*. Dive down. Swim up and over. Around bump." (As you say these formation moves, trace the letter.) "And, we'll look at lowercase *s*. Little magic *c*. Turn down. Curve around." (As you say these formation moves, trace the letter.)

▦ Now for the Model

"I'm going to choose a letter. Let me take a look (show the children your letter card). I think this is a lowercase *s*. Watch as I trace. Little magic *c*. Turn down. Curve around. I'll put this card with my other lowercase *s*."

▦ Let's Get Some Practice

Continue this process as you sort the rest of the letters. Usually, nine to twelve cards are plenty for a sort like this with young children. If children have difficulty recognizing a letter, have the child trace the letter as you say the formation language. Then pull down the header card and trace while you say the formation language.

▦ Wrap It Up

"We've thought about the shapes of letters. Today we looked at lowercase *m, b,* and *s*. Let's skywrite *m*! Start with *n*. Swim up and over. Down. Now, let's skywrite lowercase *b*. Dive down. Swim up and over. Around bump. Let's skywrite *s*. Little magic *c*. Turn down. Curve around." Note: this is *Handwriting Without Tears* language (Learning Without Tears, 2018). You can use whatever formation language you prefer.

ACTIVITY I Spy

▦ Get Things Ready

You'll need to have an alphabet chart for singing and tracking the alphabet. Many of us use charts that highlight the ABC song. To mix it up, you can sing the ABCs to different tunes. For example, the letters are listed to match the tune of the traditional ABC song on the left of the chart. On the right, they are listed to match the tune of the "Mary Had a Little Lamb." I usually vary the font of the chart, too, but only when I feel the children have a good grasp on our primary print for the classroom. I like to have individual copies for each child so they can point as we sing, but you can also have the alphabet on a big chart for the group to follow as you point or a child points. Your chart can be all uppercase, all lowercase, or include both for children to track as they sing. You may also want something the children can use for pointing such as plastic Martian fingers, hand pointers, swizzle sticks, and so on. Or they can always use their own fingers to point!

a b c d	**a b c d**
e f g	**e f g**
h i j k	**h i j**
l m n o p	**k l m**
q r s	**n o p q**
t u v	**r s t**
w x y z	**u v w x y z**

Make an Introduction

"Let's sing our ABC song. Remember to point to each letter as we sing. After we sing, we'll play I Spy and hunt for letters! So, let's sing!"

Now for the Model

"I'll go first. I spy a lowercase *h*. I'm going to sing again to help me find it." (Sing from the start, point to each letter as you say it, and stop when you say *h*). "Here it is. Lowercase *h*."

Let's Get Some Practice

Continue playing I Spy by asking children to find a handful of letters. I usually have a set of letters already identified that I want to target. These are usually letters we've been studying, letters I've noticed a number of children stumble on, or letters we've previously studied that I want to revisit. If children have difficulty finding letters, they can "sing back." This modification will allow for easier follow-up. After singing and tracking, play a quick game of I Spy. Setting your ABC chart to match the tune allows you to more easily start within the song for children to sing back.

Wrap It Up

During the wrap-up, pay close attention to any letters with which children might need more support from you, and give those one last review. For example, if children had difficulty spying lowercase *h* and *f*, you might say, "We had fun spying for letters today! Let's spy one last time for two letters. I spy lowercase *h*. Help me find it. Here is lowercase *h*. Now I spy lowercase *f*. Let's find it. Here is lowercase *f*."

Connect to a Book!

Sing with Me: The Alphabet is a book set up for singing. Not only are the letters presented on the two-page spread to the rhythm of the song, but you can even press a button and play the song. You can also read aloud other ABC books to set the stage. There are many new, fun ABC books such as *ABC Dance!* by Sabrina Moyle and *Oops, Pounce, Quick, Run!* by Mike Twohy. With any ABC book, the feature words for letters are sometimes less than desirable. For example, in *Oops, Pounce, Quick Run!*, the word associated with the letter *E* is *eye*. It works for letter naming but not for letter sounds.

ACTIVITY Letter Wall

Get Things Ready

Many, if not all, early childhood classrooms have a letter wall. Create a header card for each letter of the alphabet. Your header card should have the uppercase and lowercase letters along with your keyword for each and an accompanying picture. Make sure to place your letter wall close to where you have circle time and that it is placed so that children can interact with it. Children need it low enough to easily see each letter and low enough to reach them. Place them far enough apart so you can put words under the letters. For this activity, you'll use the children's names, so you'll need an index card with each child's name and their picture. You can put a Velcro strip under each letter and then Velcro on the back of each child's name card to make cards easy to add and remove.

Make an Introduction

"Today we'll learn about our letter wall. You can see that the letter wall has all of the letters in the alphabet. We'll learn all of these letters this year! We use these letters to make words when we read and write. Let's sing the names of the letters. We'll sing slowly so I can point to each letter as we sing it, so watch my points!" Sing the ABC song slowly and point to each letter, slowing down especially with *L, M, N, O, P*. Some children may not be familiar with the song. That's okay. You'll be singing it many, many more times throughout the year.

Now for the Model

"We're going to add our first words to the letter wall today! We're going to add our names! Each of you has your name card with your picture. Have it in front of you so you can see it. I'm going to say each letter. If your name begins with the letter I say, come up and add your name under that letter! Watch me. When I say the letter *T*, I will add my name because *T* is the first letter in my name (make sure to have your name printed so you can point to the letter at the start of your name)."

Let's Get Some Practice

Name the letters in ABC order. Have children add their name cards to the wall when you say the first letter of their name. Make sure they point to the first letter on their name card and the letter on the letter wall as they say the letter name. You could add everyone's name or add a few each day across the week. If a child doesn't know to come up when their letter is called, you can prompt them by saying, "I know someone whose name starts with *S*. Their name is /sssss/___ ." Sometimes just providing the child's name's initial sound will cue them. If this prompt doesn't provide enough support, you can have a duplicate set of the name cards so that you can hold up that child's name card. Have the children look closely at their cards to see if theirs matches.

"You all looked closely at your names and thought about the first letter in your name. Let's look at the letter wall and name all of our friends whose names start with ___ (choose a letter with many names, point to each name, and chorally say each name as you point)."

Flex the Activity!

You can also have children find their names on the letter wall after you've done this activity. Say a jingle such as, "Busy, busy bumblebee, can you find your name for me?" Call on a child and give them a pointer to find their name on the letter wall. Then ask what letter their name begins with. Later on, you can ask what sound starts their name. When they are able to easily find their own names, you can invite them to find their friends' names. "Busy, busy bumblebee, can you find Amelia's name for me?" Follow the same procedure of saying the first letter or the beginning sound.

Connect to a Book!

The nonfiction book *Bird Builds a Nest* by Martin Jenkins tells the story of a bird and how she builds her nest. After reading this book, you could highlight some key words from the story. Always use lowercase letters for the words on your word cards unless you have a proper noun. Always put the word first on the word card and then a picture (for example, clipart, drawing, and so on). Having the word first will help you line up all of the first letters under a header card and call attention to the first letter in each word. For *Bird Builds a Nest*, you might have *bird*, *worm*, *nest*, and *egg*. Pay attention to how the *B*s are lined up under the *Bb* header with *Belinda, Byron*, and *bird*. With the Velcro strips, you can remove cards to provide more room for others. For example, perhaps you read the book *Bird Builds a Nest* for a theme about animal homes. Once you've moved to a new theme, you can remove the word cards collected for that theme.

ACTIVITY Letter Families

Get Things Ready

Make a collection of letter cards with upper- and lowercase letters (one per card). Make a T-chart on chart paper or make one on the floor using painter's tape.

Make an Introduction

"Today we are going to play a game. It's called Letter Families. Let's think about families. Sometimes we look like someone in our family. For example, my uncle looks a lot like his mom— my grandmother. Do any of you look like someone in your family?" (Take a few responses.) "But we don't always look like people in our families. Sometimes we look different. Letters are like that. They can look alike, or they can look different. Let's look at uppercase letters. And then look at their lowercase matches. We'll decide if they look alike or if they look different. Let's look at uppercase *S* and lowercase *s*. They look alike. I'm going to put *Ss* on this side." (Place both letter cards at the top of the left-hand side of your T-chart.) "Now let's look at uppercase *M* and lowercase *m*. These look different, so I'll put them here." (Place both letter cards at the top of the right-hand side of your T-chart).

Now for the Model

"I'm going to get an uppercase letter. Then I'm going to look at three lowercase letters. I need to find the lowercase match and think. . . do they look alike or do they look different? Here's my first one. *O* (show uppercase *O*). Now I have these three lowercase letters. Oh, here is the lowercase *o*. (Pick up lowercase *o* and display upper- and lowercase side-by-side.) "Now I'm going to ask myself. . . do they look alike or do they look different? They look alike! So, I'm going to put them with *Ss*. . . letters that look alike."

Let's Get Some Practice

"Now it's your turn. I'm going to put down an uppercase letter and three lowercase letters. You'll find the match and ask yourselves if they look alike like *Ss* (point to the *Ss* side) or different (point to the *Mm* side)." Repeat the process with the children.

Wrap It Up

"You found uppercase letters that look like their lowercase matches and some that didn't. Let's say the names of the letters that look alike (point to each and say their names chorally). Now let's say the names of the letter that look different (point to each and say their names chorally)."

> **Connect to a Book!**
>
> There are many alphabet books. We all have our favorites such as *Chicka Chicka Boom Boom* by Bill Martin Jr. and John Archambault or *Eating the Alphabet* by Lois Ehlert. A more recent one to check out is *ABCs of Kindness* by Samantha Berger. In this book, letters are connected to acts of kindness, such as, "N for noticing when people are nice."

ACTIVITY Letter or Number?

Get Things Ready

You'll need a set of letter cards and number cards. Your letter cards can have only uppercase, only lowercase, or both. This would depend on what you are working on, but if in doubt, use uppercase since children usually know uppercase first. Your number cards should be 0–9. Shuffle your cards.

Make an Introduction

"Today we'll play a game called Letter or Number? Letters and numbers are different. We use letters to make words for reading and writing. This is a letter (hold up one of your letter cards). Who can find a letter in our classroom? (take a few responses) Numbers are different. We use numbers to count. This is a number (hold up one of your number cards). Who can find a number in our classroom? (take a few responses). Okay. Let's play the game."

Now for the Model

"Watch me first. I'm going to pick a different card (pick one and show children). I'm going to ask myself. . . is it a letter? Or is it a number? This is a letter. This is the letter *A*. I'm going to put it here and start a collection of letters."

Let's Get Some Practice

"Okay. Now it's your turn. Everyone get ready to look at the card. Then tell me if it's a letter or a number. (hold up a new card) Is this a letter or a number?" Continue with this procedure. You can have children say the letter or the number, especially if it is one you've previously taught. You can also acknowledge their response as letter or number and name it for them.

> **Connect to a Book!**
> To contrast with your ABC books, you can pick up a new counting book for your read-aloud such as *One Fox: A Counting Book Thriller!* by Kate Read and *Chicken Break* by Cate Berry. As you read, point out the numbers and reinforce we use numbers to count. Letters are for reading and writing.

Wrap It Up

"Nice work today playing our game. You could tell the difference between letters and numbers! Remember we use letters to read and write. We use numbers to count."

ACTIVITY Match 'Em Up!

Get Things Ready

You will need a collection of magnetic letters, letter tiles, or something similar. The goal for this lesson is to highlight upper- and lowercase letters that look alike or not. So, you might have a collection such as *Aa, Bb, Dd, Ee, Ff, Gg, Hh, Cc, Kk, Oo, Ss, Uu, Zz*. You'll want to sort these, so you might want two sorting mats: one for "alike" and one for "not alike." Make sure to put the words "alike" and "not alike" on your mats. You could also make a T-chart with painter's tape and label "alike" on one side and "not alike" on the other. You can keep your uppercase letters in a pile, or you could put them a mystery bag for added fun. At first, my mystery bag was a brown paper bag with a big question mark on it. Then I used a red velvet bag from a magic set. Either way, a mystery bag adds a bit of intrigue! Put the lowercase letters neatly on the table or rug, facing the children. You might want to have an alphabet strip readily available for support if needed.

Make an Introduction

"Today we're going to play Match 'Em Up! This is a fun game where we'll look at lowercase letters and decide which ones look like their uppercase partners. So, we'll decide if they look the same. If they do, we'll say they are alike. If they don't look the same, we'll say that are not alike." As you say this, point to the "alike" mat and then the "not alike" mat.

"Before we get started, let's review our letters. Say the names of our lowercase letters. I'll point and say the name. Then you say the name. Ready?" Point to one letter at a time, say the letter name, and then invite children to repeat. If you notice any hesitation or errors, repeat the letter (point, say, repeat). After you go through the lowercase letters, you will want to do the same with the uppercase letters.

Now for the Model

"Watch me. I'll go first. I'm going to choose an uppercase letter out of my mystery bag. Everyone, let's look at my uppercase letter. It's an A. Now I need to look at my lowercase letters to find its partner. Here it is. This is lowercase a. These letters are not alike. They don't have the same shape. So, I'm going to put uppercase A and lowercase a side-by-side on my 'not alike' mat."

"Now I'm going to pick a new uppercase letter from my mystery bag. This time I have uppercase O. Now I'm going to find lowercase o. These letters look alike. They are the same shape. The uppercase O is just bigger than lowercase o. So, I'm going to put uppercase O and lowercase o side-by-side on my 'alike' mat."

Let's Get Some Practice

Continue with this process having one child at a time choose a letter from the mystery bag and find the lowercase match. Discuss whether they are alike or not. If a child isn't able to name an uppercase letter, you can say, "Is this letter ___ or ___?" giving them a choice. If a child is unable to find the lowercase match, you can reduce choices again by pulling out two or three lowercase letters and say the partner is one of those letters. Or you can find the uppercase letter on an alphabet strip and look at its lowercase partner. Finally, if the decision about "alike" or "not alike" isn't easy or a placement is wrong, you can point out the shape of the letter. For example, you might say, "This letter has two straight lines down and a straight line across, but this letter has one straight line down and then a bump."

Wrap It Up

"Nice work naming uppercase letters and finding their lowercase partners! You know so much about letters. And, you thought about uppercase and lowercase partners that look alike. Let's look at our 'alike' mat (invite children to name "alike" pairs). You also thought about uppercase and lowercase partners that are 'not alike' (focus attention on the "not alike" mat and invite children to name "not alike" pairs)."

ACTIVITY Alphabet Arc Detectives

Get Things Ready

You can make your own alphabet arc similar to these from the Florida Center for Reading Research (2014).

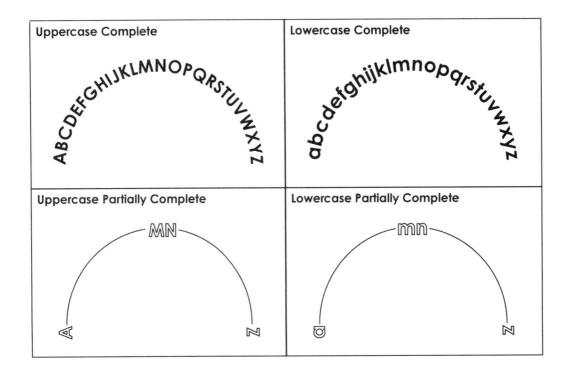

Uppercase Complete	Lowercase Complete
ABCDEFGHIJKLMNOPQRSTUVWXYZ	abcdefghijklmnopqrstuvwxyz
Uppercase Partially Complete	**Lowercase Partially Complete**
MN ... A ... N	mn ... o ... n

Your arc can be uppercase or lowercase letters, and most are meant for children to have their own individual arcs. Each child will also need a set of plastic letters (upper- or lowercase based on your arc). Start with the few letters that have been learned and work up to the full alphabet.

Make an Introduction

"We're going to be alphabet detectives. I'm going to give you a clue to find a letter on your alphabet arcs. Then you'll match the plastic letter to the letter on your arc!"

Now for the Model

"I'm going to be a detective first. Watch me. Here's my clue. Find the letter whose name is *M*. Okay. I need to find *M*. Here's my uppercase *M*, so I'll put it on my alphabet arc to make a match. Watch me run my finger along my arc until I find *M*. Here's it is. *M*." (Place the plastic letter on top of the arc letter *M*.)

Let's Get Some Practice

Continue with this process. Give the children a letter clue. "Find the letter whose name is _____ ." Make sure children say the letter name multiple times, especially when they make the arc match. Go through ten to twelve letters and choose those you've been studying as well as some from previous study for review. If a child has difficulty finding the letter, reduce their options by giving them three to five letters to choose from. If a child has difficulty finding the arc match, demonstrate how to sing to find the letter or place a plastic letter on the arc and run under the arc letters for a visual match.

Wrap It Up

"You were alphabet detectives today. Let's clean up our alphabet arcs and say the names of the letters as we put them away." Have children chorally say the letter names as they pick up the plastic letters.

Note: alphabet arcs can be filled in with uppercase or lowercase letters. Or they can be partially completed when children know many letters and completing the arc is developmentally appropriate, typically in kindergarten. Consider each of these options. I usually print these on card stock or put printouts in protective sleeves. I will say, though, the protective sleeves can sometimes be too slippery, and plastic letters can tend to move.

> **Flex the Activity!**
>
> You can play this game with letter sounds, too. For your clue, you'd say, "Find the letter that makes the /m/ sound." Or you could say, "Find the letter you hear at the beginning of the word mouse." As children find letters and make their matches, they would say, "M says /m/." As they clean up to wrap up the activity, children will say letter sounds instead of letter names. You can also flex the activity to highlight upper- and lowercase letters. With this version, you would have uppercase arcs and lowercase plastic letter sets. Children would match upper- and lowercase letters. You could give clues like "Find the letter ___" or match the first half of the arc and then the second half. I've found that matching the entire arc in one activity is too much for most early learners.

ACTIVITY Alphabet Hokey Pokey

Get Things Ready

Who doesn't love a little Hokey Pokey? Make a set of alphabet cards to make necklaces for children to wear around their necks. I've found it's better to have larger cards, so I usually cut an 8" x 11" piece of card stock in half to write or print large, bold letters on. Then I hole-punch the alphabet cards and string them to make a necklace (make sure to make it long enough for easy on and off). You can write uppercase or lowercase letters on the cards.

▢ Make an Introduction

"Today we're going to play Alphabet Hokey Pokey! We've played the Hokey Pokey before when we put our right arms in and out. Then we shake it all about! Today we'll do it with letters! Let's get in a circle."

▢ Now for the Model

"I'll show you how to play. I have the letter *A* (point to the letter you have around your neck). You put the letter *A* in. You put the letter *A* out. You put the letter *A* in, and you shake it all about! You do the Hokey Pokey, and you turn yourself around. That's what it's all about!"

▢ Let's Get Some Practice

Reveal the name of the next letter by asking, "Who has the letter *M*?" The child with the letter *M* holds up their card so the whole group can see. Tell them to follow the directions of the song with their letter *M* just like you did with *A*. All children join in singing and making the movements for Hokey Pokey. Continue with six more letters. I've found too many letters can make the fun drag a bit.

▢ Wrap It Up

"That was fun! We got to play Hokey Pokey and think about our letters. Let's go around the circle and name all of our letters!" Have children chorally name letters as you touch each child.

> ### Look For
>
> With any of these letter naming activities, your ultimate goal is both accuracy and speed. In prekindergarten, we are mainly interested in accuracy. Children aren't expected to know both upper- and lowercase letter names until the start of kindergarten. At that time, we are looking for both accuracy and speed as fluency of letter naming is predictive of future reading achievement in kindergarten. (See, for example, Dynamic Indicators of Basic Early Literacy Skills.)

My Name Letter

As an early childhood educator, you know the value of a child's name. A child's name becomes a natural focus for them. I'm reminded of the many children in my life who have exclaimed, "That's my name letter!" when they see the first letter of their names. Bloodgood (1999) included names in a category of "emotionally charged words"—words children encounter frequently early on and hold a great deal of meaning. Why else are names often the first word children attempt to write? I'm reminded of one of my own children's first written words: *Bella* (her name), *mom*, and *love*. These are emotionally charged words for sure! Each of the following activities take advantage of names.

ACTIVITY Build Your Name

▢ Get Things Ready

Label an envelope with each child's first name. Make sure to use uppercase for the first letter and lowercase for the rest. Write the child's name on a sentence strip in a similar fashion, cut the letters apart, and put the letters in the envelope. Make a set for you, too.

Make an Introduction

"Today we'll play a matching game with the letters in our names! Remember, when two things match, it means they are the same. So, you'll build your name by matching letters to the letters on the front of your envelope that are the same."

Now for the Model

"Watch me. I'll go first to show you how to match. My name is on my envelope. It says _____ (point to your name). Now I'm going to take the letters out of my envelope and lay them out so I can see them (remove the letters and lay them out). Now I'm ready to match! I'm going to pick one letter at a time and say the letter's name. Here's my first one (make sure all children can see). This is a lowercase s. Little magic c, turn down, and around (trace the letter as you say this). Let me find the lowercase s in my name on the envelope. Here it is! Lowercase s. These letters match (place the letter on top of the matching letter on the envelope)." Continue with this procedure until you've finished matching your name. Note: use whatever formation language you use in your classroom.

Let's Get Some Practice

Give the children their name envelopes. Have them follow your directions to take their letters out and lay them out in front of themselves. Then have them put their name envelopes in front of themselves so they can see them easily, and say each letter name as they make a match. You can move around and ask children questions such as, "What is the name of this letter? Is this an uppercase or a lowercase letter? What is the first letter in your name? Point and say each of the letters in your name." If children have difficulty, you can tell them the names of the letters so they can focus on the matching. You can also have the child trace the letter with you as you say the letter's formation language.

Wrap It Up

"You matched the letters in your name. To clean up, point and say each of the letters in your name and put your letters back in your envelopes."

The envelopes can be put in a center for children to build their friend's names. It is helpful to include a photograph of the child on the outside of the envelope. The children can see their friend, say their friend's name, take out the letters, and build their friend's name as they say the letter names.

> **Flex the Activity!**
>
> You can connect to names with the alphabet arc activity. Each child would need their name written on an index card (or their letter name envelope from the Build Your Name activity). Invite the children to find the first letter of their names on the arc. You'd model with your name first by saying, "My name is Tisha. The first letter in my name is *T*. I see it here (point to the first letter)—it's an uppercase *T*. Now I'll find the uppercase *T* on my alphabet arc." Children can then take turns finding the first letter of their names on the arc, saying "The first letter in my name is ___."

ACTIVITY Disappearing Name Game

Get Things Ready

Write each child's name (and your own name) on a sentence strip. You'll need a collection of plastic letters or letter tiles (upper- and lowercase letters) in a bag or basket. I usually use letter tiles because they are easier to see if you need to show letters to the group or a child. I like to use a basket because I see the letters more easily and make intentional picks. I also like to only include letters that are in the children's names. For example, if no children have the letter X, I wouldn't include an upper- or lowercase X. Or if no one in my class has a name that starts with C, then I wouldn't include an uppercase C. Each child will need a pencil or a crayon.

Make an Introduction

"We're going to play the Disappearing Name Game today! You all have a card with your name on it. I'm going to call out the names of letters from my basket. If I call a letter in your name, you will put a big X on that letter to make it disappear!"

Now for the Model

"Watch how this works. Here's my name card (with my name Tisha). I'm going to pick a letter from my basket. I have lowercase s. I'm going to look at each letter in my name and start at the beginning. Remember, I'm looking for lowercase s (point and say each letter and stop when you come to the one called). S! Lowercase s is in my name, so I'll put a big X over the lowercase s." You can also be more deliberate if needed. For example, you could point to the first letter and say, "This isn't lowercase s. It's an uppercase T." Keep choosing letters and sometimes choose one that isn't in your name. Once you've called out all letters and made your last X, say, "I made my name disappear!"

Let's Get Some Practice

Now give the children a chance to make their names disappear. Pass out their name cards and a crayon for each child. Have them listen for the letter name you call. As you pick a letter, you might say, "The letter is uppercase M. M. Put an X on uppercase M if you have one in your name." You can ask questions as you go to increase engagement such as "Who has made their first letter disappear?" If children have multiples of the same letter, they can cross them all out when the letter is called. If needed, you can show the group or an individual child a letter. For example, if a child has the called letter but hasn't placed on X on it. You can put the letter tile in front of them, say the letter name, and tell them they have that letter in their name. Once you've played this game a few times, you could let children pick the letters.

Wrap It Up

"We made letters in our names disappear! Everyone point and say the letters in your name to your knee partner."

ACTIVITY Name Song

Get Things Ready

This song goes to the tune of "Bingo." Make a name book for each child in your class. You can use these, for example, when you have a special student for the week, with your line leader, or to celebrate birthdays. Or you could keep track as you highlight a child with the name song until everyone has had a turn. These name books can be collected in a basket for children to read and sing as they point to the letters.

To make the book, fold a sentence strip in accordion style. You need at least enough folds for each letter of the child's name plus two extra. Put a picture of the child on the first square. Have the child tell you something about themselves for you to write on the second square. You'll fill in this frame: "There was a child who _____ and ___ was his/her name-o." If a child says they love pizza, you could write: "There was a child who loved cheese pizza and Amelia was her name-o." Then write each letter in the child's name on a different fold, making sure to use an uppercase letter for the first letter in the child's name and lowercase for the rest.

| | There was a child who loved cheese pizza and Amelia was her name-o | A | m | e | l | i | a |

Make an Introduction

"This week's line leader is Amelia! Let's sing a song about Amelia and look at the letters in her name."

Now for the Model

"Remember the song 'Bingo' we've been singing? (Note: the children don't need to know "Bingo." You can teach them the tune with the name song.) Listen to me sing Amelia's name song first. There was a child who loved cheese pizza and Amelia was her name-o. A – m – e l – i – a. A – m – e l – i – a. A – m – e l – i – a. And Amelia is her name-o." You may notice I put the 'e' and the 'l' together: A – m – e l – i – a. I did this so we could stay with the beat. You can do this with longer names, too. For example, Rachella would be Ra – ch – el – l – a.

Let's Get Some Practice

Have the children sing the song with you. Make sure to point to each page as you sing. I've personally found it difficult to turn pages while singing with the children, so I keep the name book flat for the introduction and then make it into a book. I also sometimes just don't make books. I make the sentence strip as described above, but instead of folding, I make a line with a marker. You can still keep a collection for children to point and sing.

Wrap It Up

"Nice job singing Amelia's name song. We sang every letter in her name. Did you see any letters in Amelia's name that are also in your name?" Take a few minutes for children to talk about their shared letters.

ACTIVITY Mystery Name Game

Get Things Ready

Use whatever method you use for calling on children. For example, you might use equity sticks, or craft sticks with children's names on them that you keep in a jar. You'll want to have your class collected around the white board or use chart paper. This game is usually most productive after children have had a bit of practice with their own names and the names of their friends.

Make an Introduction

"We are going to play a game called the Mystery Name Game. A mystery is something that we don't know. We have to figure it out! Like this: I'm thinking of a mystery animal. You have to figure it out which one I'm thinking about. I'll give you clues. It has feathers, flies, and lives in a nest. That's it! My mystery animal is a bird. We'll play today with our names."

Now for the Model

"Watch me. I'll try to figure out our first mystery name. My mystery name has five letters. I'm going to write a blank space for each letter in the name." (Make ___ ___ ___ ___ ___). "My first guess is A. That's my last letter. So, I'll write A there (write a lowercase a). Next, I'm going to guess M. There isn't an M in my mystery name, so I'm going to write M (write a lowercase m) over there. My next guess is L. Oh! There are two Ls in my mystery name (write lowercase l's on the third and fourth lines). This name is starting to look like one I know. My next guess is B. That's the first letter of my mystery name (write uppercase B on the first line). Does anyone know my mystery name? It's Bella (point to Bella's name card on the letter wall). So, I need the letter E (write on the second blank line). Let's say Bella's letters together. Let's point and say. B–e–l–l–a. Bella."

Let's Get Some Practice

Choose a name from your equity sticks. Tell the children how many letters and write that number of blank spaces. Put the name back in the jar and use the equity sticks to call on children to guess a letter. If children say a letter that has already been guessed, point to the letter (remember, you are keeping a collection of guessed letters that aren't in the name) and allow them another guess. If children can't think of a letter, encourage them to use the letter wall. If you need to limit the amount of time guessing, you can give clues. For example, you might say, "Our mystery name has nine letters, so this name is long." This would encourage them to look at the letter wall for longer names. Or you might say, "Our mystery name shares two letters with Amelia's name."

Wrap It Up

"Wow. We figured out a lot of mystery names and had fun practicing our letter names. This time Christina had our longest name. Let's point and say Christina's letters. Christina, what is the first letter in your name? C. Let's find Christina on a letter wall. Ready? Say the letters as I point." You don't always need to choose the longest name or even review a name, but it does provide a quick way to wrap up and review letters before moving on.

Classic Games

There are many classic games that lend themselves to this type of practice. I won't map out how to play these games, because they are widely known. One game you can play is Alphabet Bingo. You can have only uppercase or only lowercase letters. Or you can have them match upper- to lowercase. You can also adjust the challenge by having fewer cells on the grids or by having only a select set of letters chosen for review. The example bingo board here shows an example of matching upper- and lowercase letters but only from a set of five letters. Before beginning play, say all of the letters in the letter bag. Then have children take turns picking a letter from the bag to announce to the group as each child looks for a match. Note: Make sure to have a match in the bag for every letter on the grid. You can adjust this for letter sounds by having letters on the grid and pictures to present initial sounds (for example, a picture of a bag for *b*, a picture of tape for *t*).

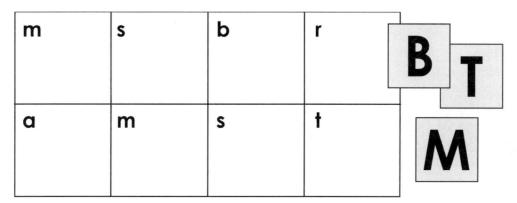

You can also play ABC Matching. This can be played with all uppercase, all lowercase, or both. I usually find that eight matches (sixteen total cards) are plenty for this game and often have fewer. To make a quick matching game, you can print out a grid on card stock (this is best so you can't see through). I usually prepopulate the grid with the letters I want to use, such as *m, s, b, r, a*. You can adjust for letter sounds easily by having letters that match to pictures with the beginning sound (for example, the letter card *m* would match with a picture of a mouse).

Another fun classic game is Hot Potato. You'll need to create another grid. I usually have a 3 x 3 or 4 x 4 grid on chart paper. It needs to be large, so fill up the chart paper (you can also make a grid outside with sidewalk chalk). Write letters in the grid, using both upper- and lowercase letters. To get the game started, you can say a jingle like, "Hot potato, hot potato. Who has the hot potato? If you have the hot potato, you are IN!" The children will pass a beanbag around the circle as you say "hot potato, hot potato" until you say "stop." The child holding the beanbag gets to toss the beanbag on the grid and name the letter the beanbag lands on. While any beanbag can work, triangular beanbags tend to land more smoothly. You can adjust to have the child say the letter sound.

a	s	A	m
n	R	B	N
r	b	M	s

Letter Sounds

Children need letter-sound knowledge to begin to decode and spell words, so you will want to provide equal, if not more, instructional time for letter sound practice. Remember, it's not just about accuracy. It's also about the children's quick production of a letter's sound, but we wouldn't be looking for automaticity until kindergarten. You know CV and VC letters are relatively easier for children to learn, so you will want to pay some extra attention to those harder-to-learn letters (for example, *H, W, Y*).

You'll want to follow a routine for letter-sound introductions. You can look back at the suggested routine earlier in this chapter. The main thing to remember is that children benefit from multiple connections to the letters they are learning, so we want to talk about letter names, letter sounds, letter formation, and keywords that start with the letter's sound. Physical movements can also help form more connections. For example, if learning the letter *M*, children can get in a crab position on the floor to mimic the shape of uppercase *M*. Or if *ball* is the keyword for *B /b/*, you could make a shape like a ball with your arms.

You'll use a similar routine with vowels. Short vowels are the most useful letters to teach first for two reasons. First, their sounds are regular. Second, they are usually represented with a single letter. This is why assessments of letter sounds target short vowels. Long vowels are taught later, so concentrate on short vowels. Some vowels are difficult to discriminate, especially *a, e, i* and especially in certain regions of the country. You will want to intersperse short vowel instruction with your consonant instruction so children can start making small words. For example, if you include *a* in a sequence of *m, t, s, r* (a common beginning set of letters in a scope and sequence), children can make words like *sat, rat, mat, at*. The following activities are offered to give children fun, game-like ways to practice letter-sound connections.

ACTIVITY Sound Sort

Get Things Ready

Choose two, three, or four letters to contrast. These sorts are done with pictures, emphasizing the initial sounds. I usually only have ten to twelve pictures total and keep them in a pile. Be careful not to use pictures with initial blends or sounds outside our target. For example, do not use a picture of *clock* for C. Early learners need to hear the sound without the complication of the blend. You also wouldn't use a picture of a *giraffe* for G, because our target sound will be hard *g* as in *girl*. Same thing for vowels. You wouldn't use a picture of an *ape* for A, because our target sound is short *a* (as in *apple*). Lastly, I don't typically use pictures of words where the vowel is followed by an *m, n,* or *r*. These letters tend to change vowel sounds. Consider these words: *ham, tank,* and *park.* The *a* in these words don't sound like the *a* in *apple.* You'll also need header cards, and these should be similar to your letter cards on your letter wall. You want to keep your keywords consistent, so children can have a consistent reference for each letter sound.

▢ Make an Introduction

"Today we'll sort pictures of things and think about their beginning sounds. We'll put all pictures with the same beginning sounds together in one group."

▢ Now for the Model

"Here is a picture of a ball. *Ball* starts with /b/. /b—b—b—awl/. You say it: /b/. *Ball* starts with /b/. The letter *B* makes the /b/ sound we hear at the beginning of ball. What sound do you hear at the beginning of *ball*? Yes, that's right. /b/. Over here is a picture of a mouse. *Mouse* starts with /m/. /mmmmmous/. You say it: /m/. *Mouse* starts with /m/. The letter *M* makes the /m/ sound we hear at the beginning of *mouse*. What sound do you hear at the beginning of *mouse*? Yes, that's right. /m/. Now, I'll take my first picture. *Bird.* /b—b—b—ərd/. I hear /b/ at the beginning of *bird. Bird—ball. Bird—mouse. Bird* and *ball* both begin with the same sound, /b/. I hear /b/ at the beginning of bbb-*bird* and bbb-*ball*. So, I'm going to put *bird* with *ball*. They both start with /b/."

▢ Let's Get Some Practice

Have children continue with the sort, inviting individual children to pick a new picture. Identify any pictures they are unsure of right away to keep the focus on the target initial sounds. Have the children name each picture as they sort. If a child has difficulty, refer them back to the keyword. You might say, "So, we have a picture of the moon. Mmmmmmoon. Does *moon* start like *ball* or *mouse*? Mmmmmoon-bbbball. Mmmmoon-Mmmmouse. I'm thinking *moon* begins with /m/ like *mouse*. Let me check with the other pictures. *Mouse, mop, man, mouse.* Yes, they all begin with /m/."

◻ **Wrap It Up**

"We thought about the beginning sounds in words today. Let's say the pictures in our first group: /b/ like at the beginning of *ball*. *Bird, bike, bell, bat*. These all begin with /b/. They all begin with the letter B. Now let's say the pictures in our next group: /m/ like at the beginning of *mouse*. *Man, moon, mop, mat*."

Sound cards (see below) are also a fun extension. These are used to help develop automaticity with letter sounds, so they are likely most appropriate for kindergarten. You can demonstrate and/or have the children practice providing the letter sounds before getting started. Then children simply "read" across each line, saying each letter sound.

Mm mouse		Ss soap		Bb ball	
m		s		b	m
s		b		m	b
m		s		s	m
b		s		m	b

Look For

As with letter naming, we are looking for children to become more accurate in their matching of like sounds at the beginning of words as well as identifying the sound at the beginning of words. Children typically pay attention to beginning sounds first (think back to the onset-rime activities in chapter 3), so we take advantage of this to help them begin to hear sounds in words. This type of sorting also helps children practice making the connection to the letter that makes a certain sound. Over time, we'll be looking for children to increase the accuracy of their responses, and especially in kindergarten, we'll be looking for them to increase the automaticity of their responses. When they are decoding and spelling, they need to call upon their letter-sound knowledge quickly and accurately.

ACTIVITY Where Is It?

▢ Get Things Ready

Decide on a collection of pictures with your target sound at the beginning or the end of the word. For example, if you are focusing on /sh/, you might have *shoe, fish, shell, shark, dish,* and *bush*. Make two cards with sh___ on one and ___sh on the other to indicate /sh/ at the beginning and /sh/ at the end. I usually do this type of sorting in a pocket chart, but you can do this on the floor in the middle of your circle or on a table. Picture cards can be in a bag, basket, or simply in a stack.

▢ Make an Introduction

"Today we're going to sort pictures and think about the sounds we hear in the words. We're listening for /sh/ today. Your job is listen and decide if you hear /sh/ at the beginning of the word or at the end. I have this card with *SH* at the beginning for us when we hear /sh/ at the beginning (put your sh___ card in your pocket chart) and this card with *SH* at the end for when we hear /sh/ at the end (put your ___sh card in your pocket chart)."

▢ Now for the Model

"Watch me first. I'm going to pick a card. Oh! I have fish. Say it with me. *Fish.* I'm going to think. . . do I hear /sh/ at the beginning, or do I hear /sh/ at the end? *Fish* (emphasize the /sh/ at the end). I hear it at the end, so I'm going to put my picture here below this card (move to the ___sh card)."

▢ Let's Get Some Practice

Pick a new card and show the children. Say the word and have children repeat. Ask: "Do you hear /sh/ at the beginning of ___, or do you hear /sh/ at the end of ___?" You can also use first/last to note the place in the word. Regardless, once the children make a decision, say "Because we hear /sh/ at the beginning of ___ (for example, *shell*), I'll put the picture of ___ here (point to the sh___ card)." If children have difficulty, emphasize the target sound in the word.

▢ Wrap It Up

"You listened so carefully today! You thought about where you heard /sh/ in words. We heard it at the beginning and at the end! How about one last word? Do you hear /sh/ at the beginning of *mash* (make a mashing motion) or at the end of *mash*? *Mash*. At the end, yes!"

> **Connect to a Book!**
>
> When targeting sounds, ABC books can sometimes be helpful, but sometimes they may lead us astray (see section on ABC books at the end of this chapter). I've found I can pull words with my target sounds out of my read-alouds. For example, with this lesson on /sh/, I would pull from the classic Sheep in a Jeep series by Nancy Shaw. Then sheep would be one of my pictures along with ship! Or *The Goose Egg* by Liz Wong could work with a study of /g/. There aren't a ton of words that begin or end with /g/ in this book, but *goose* and *egg* can be springboards into our study of /g/.

ACTIVITY Letter Sound Toss

Get Things Ready

You can have a muffin tin with alphabet cards taped to the bottoms. Or you could have a grid similar to the grid from Hot Potato (for example, large grid made on chart paper) with your target alphabet. You'll also need a beanbag. As I pointed out before, any beanbag will work, but triangular beanbags work a little better for this game.

Make an Introduction

"Today we'll play Letter Sound Toss. This is a fun game where we'll toss a beanbag and say the sounds we land on."

Now for the Model

"Watch me. I'll go first (toss the beanbag). The beanbag landed in the letter *B. B* makes the /b/ sound. Does anyone's name begin with *B*? Yes, Byron's name begins with /b/. I hear /b/ at the beginning of *Byron*. What's our keyword for *B*? I'm going to look to the letter wall to help me. *Ball. Ball* begins with /b/ just like *Byron*."

Let's Get Some Practice

Continue having the children pass the beanbag around the circle or choose children by picking from your equity sticks. When they've landed on a letter, have them say the letter name and the sound it makes. "___ says ___." Then ask if anyone's names start with that sound (if you have a child in the class with a name that matches) and the keyword that references that sound.

Wrap It Up

"Nice job playing Letter Sound Toss! This game helped us practice our letter sounds and remember our keywords for sounds. Like the letter *M. M* says /m/ like at the beginning of *mouse*."

> **Flex the Activity!**
>
> You can play this game to focus on letter names instead of sounds. Just use upper- and lowercase letters to say the letter name.

ACTIVITY Letter Hunt

Get Things Ready

This is a great game, because you have nothing to prepare!

Make an Introduction

"Every letter makes a sound. In our game, Letter Hunt, I'm going to give you a letter sound. Your job is to find the letter that makes that sound in our classroom." You could play this game during a transition (for example, walking to the library or outside for recess).

Now for the Model

"Watch me. I'll show you how to play. I'm going to find the letter that makes the /s/ sound. This means I need to find an S. Here's the letter S on the ___." Point to a letter S in your classroom. Try to not use the letter wall. Perhaps you find the letter S on a book cover or on a chart with a jingle you've been practicing.

Let's Get Some Practice

Continue with this routine as you ask children to find letters that make target sounds. You can wait for children to raise their hands or call on children using your equity sticks. If children have difficulty, tell them the letter name (for example, M says /m/ so look for the letter M). If you are planning to target a letter that you don't see readily in your classroom, then make sure to use it somewhere in a word/label. This might take some planning. For example, let's say you wanted to target /z/. Z is not a commonly used letter. You might want to play a game that day with your buzzy bee and write *buzzy bee* on your whiteboard. You could also ask children to find something in the classroom that begins with the target sound, such as *tape* for /t/ or *mirror* for /m/.

Wrap It Up

"Nice work thinking about letters and the sounds they make. You found so many letters! Amelia found /m/ here when she pointed out M, and Byron found /b/ over here when he found *B*."

ACTIVITY Dig for Sounds

Get Things Ready

Collect a set of letter cards for the sounds you'll target. You'll also need ten to twenty objects or picture cards (these will either need to be laminated or on card stock to work) that have the same initial sound as the target letters. Fill a large plastic tub with sand or dry rice. I prefer rice since it's easy for children to dig through and not very messy, relatively speaking. Bury your objects in your tub.

Make an Introduction

"Today we'll practice saying the beginning sounds of objects. You'll dig for an object buried in this tub. When you find an object, say the name of the object and its beginning sound. Then tell us the letter that makes that sound. First let's review our letter sounds for today." (Hold up the letter card and have children say, "___ says /___/.") If children quickly provide the beginning sound and letter for a found object, you can also have them provide another word that starts with the same beginning sound.

Now for the Model

"Watch me first. I'm going to slowly put my hand in the rice and gently move it around as I feel for an object. Oh! I found one! I'll pull it out slowly. This is a bell. *Bell* begins with the /b/ sound. /b/. . . bell. *B* says /b/."
Find the *B* in the set of letter cards and hold it up.

Let's Get Some Practice

Continue with this procedure, reminding the children to slowly put their hand in the rice and gently pull out an object. These reminders will be key to keeping the mess at a minimum! Prompt as needed with questions like "What's the beginning sound in ___?" or "What letter makes /___/?" or "Show us the letter that makes /___/." Play until each child has at least two opportunities to pull out objects.

> ## Connect to a Book!
>
> We don't always need an alphabet book when we are talking about letters and the sounds they make. Mac Barnett's *Sam and Dave Dig a Hole*, Kevin McCloskey's *We Dig Worms!*, and Kate Messner's *Up in the Garden and Down in the Dirt* are good options to connect to digging for things. You can still connect to sounds, too! For example, *Up in the Garden and Down in the Dirt* includes things like boots and bugs that you can pull in for a discussion of /b/ at the beginning of words.

Wrap It Up

"We practiced our letter sounds and thought about the beginning sounds in words." Allow two to three children to say their favorite objects and their beginning sounds.

ACTIVITY Jumping Jacks

▢ Get Things Ready

You'll make sixty index cards for this game. I usually use small index cards. Print uppercase and lowercase letters on cards. This will leave you with eight cards to mark as your "jumping jacks" cards. I usually put a picture of children doing jumping jacks. You don't need all sixty cards for the game. You'll want to choose only those letters you want children to practice. Mix your cards up and put them in a basket or box facedown.

▢ Make an Introduction

"Let's play Jumping Jacks! In this game, you'll name letters and say their sounds. I have some cards that look like this (show your jumping jacks card). When we get one of these cards, we'll all do jumping jacks! Let's go through the letter cards and practice first." Show one card at a time and have the children say, "___ says /___/."

▢ Now for the Model

"Here's how we'll play. We'll take turns pulling a letter card out of the box. I'll go first (pull out a card and show everyone). I have the letter A. A says /ă/. What's our keyword for /ă/? I know! *Apple*. *Apple* starts with the letter A. . . /ă/. Now, I'll pull another card. Oh! It's a jumping jacks card! Ready? Let's all do jumping jacks!"

▢ Let's Get Some Practice

Have children get one card at a time from the box. Have children show their card to the group and say, "___ says /___/." You can ask children to provide the keyword or another word that begins with the same sound. If a jumping jacks card is drawn, then everyone stands and does jumping jacks.

▢ Wrap It Up

"We practiced our letter sounds today! Let's go through our letters one more time." Show the letter cards one at a time and have the children say, "___ says /___/."

> ### Flex the Activity!
>
> You can play this game with letter names, too. Just adjust to say the letter name when you pull a card. You can also include upper- and lowercase for children to say uppercase *A* or lowercase *s*, for example.

ACTIVITY Letter Hunt

Get Things Ready

You can go on Letter Hunts in a variety of ways. Children can hunt for letters in the classroom. They can hunt for letters on a page of a read-aloud. Or they can hunt for letters in a shared jingle. To illustrate here, I'll use "Busy, Busy Bumblebee." Write out on chart paper: "Busy, busy bumblebee. Won't you say your name for me?" Have a special pointer on hand or highlighting tape, Wikki Stix, view finders, and so on.

Make an Introduction

"Today we're going to find letters and think about the sounds they make. We'll listen for letter sounds in the words we read."

Now for the Model

"Listen and watch. Busy, busy bumblebee. Won't you say your name for me?" Point to each word as you read aloud. "I'm going to look for a *B*, and I see one right away. I'm going to circle my letter *B*. *B* says /b/" (stick a circular Wikki Stix around the first *B*).

Let's Get Some Practice

Continue finding target letters, inviting one child at a time to the chart paper. As they circle their found letter, have them say, "___ says /___/." You can make this fun by tallying every time you find target letters to see which one wins.

Wrap It Up

"We found so many letters in our busy bumblebee reading. We can hear the sounds in the words! And, let's look. Which letter won? *B* won! We had five *B*s. Look at the word *bumblebee*. That word has three *B*s! What's the sound for *B*? /b/. What's our keyword for /b/? *Ball*."

ACTIVITY Fill It In!

Get Things Ready

Make a 4 x 4 grid and fill in each square with a target letter. You could have sixteen different letters or just a few that you put down multiple times. Make a set of picture cards with the same beginning sounds of your target letters. Just make sure that you have a picture for each letter. You can collect the pictures in a bag or a basket.

Make an Introduction

"We're going to play an alphabet game today called Fill It In! See the letters on our grid. Let's go through and say all of the letter names and their sounds (point to each letter as children say "___ says /___/"). We'll pick a picture card from our bag and think about its beginning sound. Then put the picture on the letter that makes that beginning sound. Our goal is to fill in our grid."

Now for the Model

"Watch me. I'm going to take a picture card from my bag. It's a bike. *Bike. Bike* begins with /b/. I know *B* says /b/. So, I'm going to put my picture of a bike on a *B*."

a	m	s	t
b	r	g	h
f	n	i	p
o	l	g	d

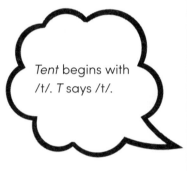

Tent begins with /t/. *T* says /t/.

Let's Get Some Practice

Have children take turns choosing a picture card. They should show the picture to the group, say the word, say the sound the word begins with, and say the letter. For example, if a child gets soap, they'd say, "*Soap.* /s/. *S* says /s/." Continue until the grid is full. If a child has difficulty saying the word's beginning sound, say "*Soap* begins with /s/. What's the beginning sound in *soap*?" If a child has difficulty identifying the letter that makes the beginning sound, then direct them to your letter wall for help. Or give them choices (for example, Which letter says /s/? *M* or *S*?).

Wrap It Up

"Nice job matching beginning sounds to the letters that make that sound. Let's go through our letters one more time!" Make sure you've removed the pictures, point to the pictures, and have the children say, "___ says ___."

Flex the Activity!

As with many of these activities, you can play this focusing on letter names, too. Instead of picture cards, have uppercase letters. A child would pick a card and identify the uppercase letter and then put the letter card on top of the lowercase match.

ACTIVITY Picture Match and Write!

Get Things Ready

Create a set of cards that have letters that have been taught and a matching picture card. I like to make them small enough so that children can have a collection that they glue on a paper and write the letter. For example, you might have children work on a page that looks like this (the top line is filled out as an example). If you play this like, you'll need to have a set of cards for each child.

Match it!		Write it!
2+2	a	**a**

Make an Introduction

"Today we'll play a matching game. You'll find the letter and beginning sound match. Then you'll write the letter that makes that sound." You can play this like Concentration with the cards facing down. Or you can have the cards all face up for children to make matches.

Now for the Model

"Let's look at the cards. I'm going to pick a picture. I'm going to pick *add*. *Add* begins with /a/. *A* says /a/, so I need to find lowercase *a*. Now I'm going to glue these on my paper. First, I'll glue down *add* and then the lowercase *a*. Then I'll write lowercase *a*. Watch me write *a*: magic *c*, up, bump, back down bump."

Let's Get Some Practice

Support children as they make their matches and write letters. If children have difficulty making a match, help them isolate the beginning sound of their picture card. If they have difficulty matching the sound to a letter, you can say, "*R* says /r/. What does *R* say?" If children have difficulty forming the letter, have them skywrite with you as you use formation language.

▢ Wrap It Up

"Wow. We matched the beginning sounds of pictures to the letters that make that sound. And, we wrote that letter! We are thinking a lot about the letters that make up words."

ACTIVITY See You Later, Alligator!

▢ Get Things Ready

This is a game often played to practice rhyming. It's sometimes called Odd Man Out or Odd One Out (see chapter 3). We can adjust it for a great beginning sound game. Prepare a set of pictures to focus on beginning sounds. You'll want to collect these in sets of three—two pictures with the same beginning sound and one with a different beginning sound (for example, *bug, boot, sad*). The children will also need individual dry-erase boards, markers, and erasers. I like the small dry-erase boards with handles so children can share easily.

▢ Make an Introduction

"Today we are going to play See You Later, Alligator! In this game, we'll look at three pictures. Two of the pictures begin with the same sound. Then we'll identify the picture that doesn't match—see you later, alligator!"

▢ Now for the Model

"Watch me. I'll go first. Here are my pictures: *bug, sad, boot*. First, I'm going to find the two that begin with the same sound. *Bug. Sad. Boot*. I know—*bug, boot*. That means I'm going to say, 'See you later, alligator!' to *sad*. Say it with me: See you later, alligator! *Bug* and *boot* start with /b/. What letter makes /b/? *B*. Yes! Now I'm going to write lowercase *b* on my dry-erase board. You all do it with me. Dive down. Swim up and over. Around bump. Everyone, show your *b*! *B* says /b/."

▢ Let's Get Some Practice

Show the next set of pictures. Lay them out so all children can see you mixing up the order. Look at the pictures and ask, "Which two have the same beginning sound?" Once you have your answer, pull them to the side together and say "See you later, alligator!" to the odd one out. Then ask what is the beginning sound as you say both words again as well as what letter makes that sound. Have children isolate the beginning sound (for example, *bug* and *boot* start with /b/) and identify the corresponding letter (for example, *B* says /b/). Then have children write the letter on their dry-erase boards as you say formation language and demonstrate on your own board. As children show their written letters, say "___ says /___/." If children have difficulty making a match, emphasize the beginning sounds as you name the pictures. You can also reduce the number of choices and ask, for example, "Do *bug* and *sad* begin with the same sound? Or do *bug* and *boot*? *Bug, sad. Bug, boot*." If children have difficulty identifying the corresponding letter, you can refer them to the letter wall or you can tell them and have them repeat. "*B* says /b/. What letter says /b/? *B*." You can take out the writing step if that is too much for children to handle at one time or it's taking too much time. Or you can model writing for all children to see, and then everyone skywrites.

Wrap It Up

"We said 'See you later, alligator!' to some words. We really thought about the sounds at the beginning of words and the letters that make those sounds. Here's a match we made. *Moon, man*. What's the beginning sound? /m/. . . yes! What letter makes that sound? *M* says /m/. If I'm writing *moon*, I know I need to start with *M*."

Look For

The Look For box in the "Sound Sort" activity (on page 108) holds true here (and with all of these activities really). As children are playing Odd One Out, look for their increasing accuracy matching pictures with the same beginning sound, isolating that sound, identifying the letter that represents that sound, and writing the letter.

ACTIVITY Spin a Letter

Get Things Ready

Spin a Letter is a fun game! You can make spinners in a couple of ways. You can use spinners and brad fasteners, or you can use a large paper clip instead of a spinner. I usually use a pencil and a large paper clip. I will say, though, the pencil/paper-clip method requires some good fine motor skills and is usually more successful in kindergarten (even then, not with all children). I make a large spinner (so children can easily see it when we do this as a group) out of card stock that I laminate. Lamination helps with easier spinning! Your spinner should have six or eight spaces. Label each space with one of your target letters. For example, you might have *m, r, s, t, a, b, g, o*. You could have uppercase, lowercase, or both. When I'm reviewing a number of letter sounds, this means I'm usually trying to review lowercase letters, too. So, I usually use lowercase for this game. You'll also need a collection of pictures with beginning sounds that match your letters (three or four pictures per letter depending on how many spaces you have on your spinner). I usually like to have children write with this game, so I'd also have paper, pencils, and dry-erase kits for each child.

Make an Introduction

"Today we're going to play Spin a Letter! You get to spin for a letter, think about its sound, and then find a picture that starts with that sound! Let's practice our letters first (show the spinner). Let's point and say the sounds (as you point to a letter, you and children will say, "___ says ___"). Now let's look at our pictures. Watch me. I'll say them as I lay them out (name each picture as you lay them out for all children to see).

Now for the Model

"Watch me first. I'm going to spin and see what letter I land on. I landed on *r! R* says /r/. Now I'm going to *look for* a picture that begins with /r/. (Start pointing to and naming pictures, emphasizing the beginning sounds.) *Moon. Apple. Sun. Rug. Rug!* The first sound I hear in *rug* is /r/. I'm going to turn that picture over. Now I'm going to write a lowercase *r*. Dive down. Swim up and over."

Let's Get Some Practice

Continue with the procedure and have children take turns spinning. Once they land on a letter, ask them to name the letter and sound. Then invite them to find a picture with that beginning sound. If a child has difficulty, reduce the number of choices. Show them two or three pictures, name them, and ask which one begins with their sound (for example, "Your sound is /m/. *Moon, Sun*. Which one begins with /m/?). As a last step, have all children write the letter while you support with formation language and a model. You can take out this last step, have the children watch you write the letter, or skywrite the letter.

Wrap It Up

"Nice job being so responsible with our spinning game today! Plus, you practiced your letter sounds. Let's point and say the sounds on our spinner (point to each letter as you chorally say the sounds as a group: ___ says /___/)."

ACTIVITY Silly Sound Snake

Get Things Ready

You'll need a puppet for this activity. As an early childhood educator, you likely have a few from which to choose! But just in case, a face drawn on a sock also works! In fact, I think my children loved my sock puppet more than any other! I called him Silly Sound Snake (a name borrowed from a colleague—thanks again, Nancy!). Have a large letter card prepared (or you can just write on your dry-erase board) with your target letter/sound (both upper- and lowercase). You could also move your letter card from the letter wall front and center if your letter wall is set up for easy mobility. There are a few ways you can play this game. You could make a list of words that begin with your target sound and some that don't. You could collect a set of pictures. Or you could have children find things in your classroom that begin with your target sound.

Make an Introduction

"Silly Sound Snake is with us today! Everyone say hello! He loves a pat on the head. Who wants to gently pat his head? Silly Sound Snake told me that today he feels very picky. This means he only likes things a certain way. Today he only likes words that begin with this sound. . . /s/. What letter makes /s/? S. Yes, let's find S on our letter wall. Here it is! (Pull down your S letter card and place it in the middle of the group). Here's uppercase S and lowercase s. S says /s/ like at the beginning of sun. Say it with me, S says /s/. S says /s/. We need to find words that start with /s/ to make Silly Sound Snake happy!"

Now for the Model

"I'll go first. I have a pile of picture cards here. I'm going to pick one. I have tape. Does tape start with /s/? No. Tape starts with /t/. Oh no! (Make Silly Sound Snake drop his head like he's sad.) Don't worry, Silly Sound Snake. I'm going to hide tape over here. We'll find a word that begins with /s/. I'll pick another picture card. Sock. Does sock start with /s/. Yes! /s/ sock. Let's put sock in our /s/ collection for Silly Sound Snake. Oh look! He looks so happy!" (Have Silly Sound Snake nod his head.)

Let's Get Some Practice

Continue with each child choosing a picture card. Have them hold it up for the group to see and say the picture. Ask if the word begins with /s/ (for example, "Does man begin with /s/?"). If a child has difficulty, refer to your letter card and your keyword sun and say, "Sun begins with /s/. Does man begin like sun? Man, sun. No. Man begins with /m/." Hide the cards from Silly Sound Snake that don't begin with your target letter and proudly display for the group your collection of pictures that begin with /s/.

Wrap It Up

"We made Silly Sound Snake so happy today. Let's point and say all of our pictures that begin with /s/ (point to each picture as you chorally say each one as a group). Everyone, what letter says /s/? S. You got it. Let's skywrite S. Ready? Little magic c. Turn down. Curve around."

> ### Flex the Activity!
>
> You can play this game saying Silly Sound Snake only likes uppercase letters or letters with curved lines, for example. You can also up the ante of this game. For example, Silly Sound Snake might like two or three letter sounds that day, and you could collect pictures and sort them by their beginning sounds. Or you could say Silly Sound Snake only wants pictures that have the target sound at the end of the word (for example, /g/ at the end like big, tag, log rather than at the beginning like gum, gate, girl).

ACTIVITY ABC Book

Get Things Ready

Get twenty-eight sheets of construction paper, one page for each letter of the alphabet and two for the front and back covers. Write the upper- and lowercase letters on each page. Hole-punch the pages and use brad fasteners to make a book. Collect pictures that will be good examples of the initial sounds. Always include your class keywords in the collection. Remember, we are targeting short vowels and hard *c* and *g* (/k/ and /g/). Also, be careful. You don't want to choose words like *chop* and *chocolate* for *C* since their initial sounds are /ch/ and not /k/. You might also want to steer clear of words with beginning blends because it is sometimes difficult for children to hear the initial sound in a blend (for example, *crib, clap*). You can make a cover that says "Our Class Alphabet Book" and have children write their names on it and the back cover if you need the space. You'll make this book over multiple days and weeks as you and the children learn new letters.

Make an Introduction

"We're going to start building our class alphabet book today! Each letter has a page. We'll collect pictures and think about their beginning sounds."

Now for the Model

"Today we'll start with this page (turn to the *M* pages of the book and point to *M*). This is the letter *M*. What letter is this? (make sure the children chorally respond) The letter *M* says /m/. What sound does *M* make? (again, make sure children chorally respond) We are going to find pictures that begin with /m/. I can look at our letter wall and see *mouse* on our letter *M* (point this out). *Mouse* begins with /m/. Look, I have a picture of a mouse. I'm going to glue it on our *M* page." You'll want to have a collection of pictures that begin with /m/ and others that don't (for example, *soap, tent, itchy*). Choose a new picture. "I'm going to pick a new picture. My new picture is soap. Does *soap* begin with /m/ like *mouse. Soap. Mouse.* No, it doesn't. I hear /s/ at the beginning of *soap*. I'm going to put soap over here, because it doesn't go on our *M* page."

Let's Get Some Practice

Continue by having children pick a new picture one at a time. Have each child show the card to the group, say the name of the picture, and say the beginning sound. Then they'll decide if it starts with /m/ like *mouse* or not. If it does, then the children will glue it on the *M* page. You can keep the other pictures because they'll be used for other pages (for example, *soap* for *S*, *tent* for *T*, *itchy* for *I*). If a child has difficulty, you can help them say the keyword and the picture word to compare. You can also say the beginning sound and have them repeat (for example, *tent* starts with /t/. . . what does *tent* start with?). Continue until all of your /m/ pictures are glued.

Wrap It Up

"Nice job thinking about words that begin with /m/. Let's review all of our /m/ pictures on our *M* page." Point to each picture as the children chorally name them. Then review *M* says /m/. This book can go in your class library for children to read.

Connect to a Book!

Alphabet books are a mainstay in early childhood classrooms, and they can play an important role in building children's alphabet knowledge. As you are reading, stop occasionally, point to, and talk about some of the letters in the book. Point to the letter, name it, and have the children repeat the name. Talk about letter features (for example, this letter has curved lines) and have children skywrite the letter as you use formation language. You can call attention to the pictures that begin with the letters but beware. Sometimes alphabet books have the perfect picture matches such as *octopus* in *Alphablock* by Christopher Franceschelli or *Beep! Boop!* in *R Is for Robot* by Adam Watkins. But sometimes the pictures aren't good matches at all. For example, *Drip! Drop!* in *R Is for Robot*; the 'dr' sounds more like /j/. Or *cereal* in *A Busy Creature's Day Eating* by Mo Willems has a *C* says /s/ rather than the /k/ hard *C* that is our target during early literacy instruction.

We all have our favorite alphabet books. I've always loved *Dr. Seuss's ABC*. Other favorites are *Alphabet Under Construction* by Denise Fleming, *The Letters Are Lost* by Lisa Campbell Ernst, and *Eating the Alphabet* by Lois Ehlert. Here are some other options you can check out.

- *A Busy Creature's Day Eating* by Mo Willems

- *AB See* by Elizabeth Doyle

- *Alphablock* by Christopher Franceschelli

- *Apple Pie ABC* by Alison Murray

- *B Is for Bulldozer* by June Sobel

- *Creature ABC* by Andrew Zuckerman

- *Feelings to Share from A to Z* by Todd and Peggy Snow

- *For the Love of Dogs* by Allison Weiss Entrekin

- *K Is for Kitten* by Niki Clark Leopold

- *LMNO Peas* by Keith Baker

- *R Is for Robot* by Adam Watkins

- *Superhero ABC* by Bob McLeod

- *The Alphabet's Alphabet* by Chris Harris

- *The Little Red Cat Who Ran Away and Learned His ABCs* by Patrick McConnell

- *Z is for Moose* by Kelly Bingham

To Sum It Up

Alphabet learning is a cornerstone of early literacy instruction. In the prekindergarten years, letter-name knowledge is a strong predictor of future reading success while letter-sound knowledge begins to take precedence in kindergarten. The activities in this chapter are meant to support children's growing alphabet knowledge from letter names to letter sounds. We'll talk about applying our letter-sound knowledge to reading in chapter 5 and applying this knowledge to writing in chapter 7. Helping children increase their accuracy and speed of recognizing letters and their sounds will support them when they read and write. You can see how these chapters are intertwined and how these activities play one part in the bigger picture of early literacy instruction.

5 CHAPTER FIVE
Encouraging Foundational Fluency and Word Recognition

This chapter outlines literacy skills leading to word recognition and foundational fluency for early readers and writers. Children in your prekindergarten and kindergarten classrooms are working to build their print awareness. As they begin to learn to read, they are working to build a bank of known words through activities that provide opportunities to read and write decodable words (for example, *cat, bat, that*) as well as highly frequent words (for example, *she, was, in*). This work with isolated words is complemented by various types of repeated reading practice in books, poems, and rhymes. Early literacy standards from the Head Start Early Learning Outcome Framework and the Common Core State Standards reflect these foundational fluency and word recognition skills.

HEAD START EARLY LEARNING OUTCOME FRAMEWORK — 36–60 MONTHS	COMMON CORE STATE STANDARDS — KINDERGARTEN
<ul><li>Repeats simple familiar rhymes or sings favorite songs (36 months).</li><li>Holds book, turns pages, and pretends to read (36 months).</li><li>Points to and names some letters or characters in their names (36 months).</li><li>Understands that print is organized differently for different purposes, such as a note, list, or storybook (60 months).</li><li>Understands that written words are made up of a group of individual letters (60 months).</li><li>Begins to point to single-syllable words while reading simple, memorized texts (60 months).</li><li>Identifies book parts and features, such as the front, back, title, and author (60 months).</li></ul>	<ul><li>Demonstrate understanding of the organization and basic features of print:<ul><li>Follow words from left to right, top to bottom, and page by page.</li><li>Recognize that spoken words are represented in written language by specific sequences of letters.</li><li>Understand that words are separated by spaces in print.</li><li>Know and apply grade-level phonics and word analysis skills in decoding words.</li><li>Read common high-frequency words by sight (for example, *the, of, to, you, she, my, is, are, do, does*).</li><li>Read emergent-reader texts with purpose and understanding.</li></ul></li></ul>

For our earliest readers, our prekindergartners, let's think about a firm foundation to build upon. As an early childhood educator, you create print-rich classrooms with books, charts, labels, letter walls, and more. You point out how you read on the left page before the right when you are reading aloud, you demonstrate directionality as you move your pointer left to right while you track a jingle on chart paper, and you point out specific letters that start words on your labels throughout the classroom. These are all examples of promoting print awareness, sometimes called concepts about print. These early literacy experiences help lay the foundation for later literacy success (Piasta, Justice, McGinty, and Kaderavek, 2012).

In chapters 3 and 4, we explored ways you can help children build phonological awareness and alphabet knowledge. You can think of how phonological awareness and alphabet knowledge play complementary roles in promoting early literacy. Together, phonological awareness and alphabet knowledge "intertwine to allow children to comprehend the basic idea of the alphabetic principle, learn the regularities of the associations between sounds and letters, and apply these understandings to the process of phonemic decoding and 'sound out' words in print" (Phillips and Piasta, 2013). The alphabetic principle is the understanding that letters or letter combinations correspond to individual sounds in words. The ability to apply these letter-sound correspondences to familiar and unfamiliar words is a crucial foundational skill of reading. This allows our early readers to begin to build their word recognition—a foundational component of reading fluency.

Another key part of foundational fluency work is repeated readings, reading a book or text more than once. This practice has long been recommended for reading aloud to children (for example, US Department of Education Early Childhood–Head Start Task Force, 2002). Repeated reading is also a common practice once children are beginning to read on their own (for example, Rasinski and Samuels, 2011). Repeated readings of the same book or text have many potential benefits such as vocabulary learning and foundational fluency skill development. For example, familiarity with a story from repeated reading can help a child shift their attention from the storyline to the features of a book, such as following print from the left page to the right page. As children begin to read, repeated reading can help children read words accurately and increase their automaticity. Children need to not only hear books repeatedly but also have a variety of opportunities to regularly practice foundational fluency skills.

Print Awareness

Let's start at the beginning with print awareness. Print is everywhere and a common part of our everyday lives. Even though print is everywhere, we need to explicitly point it out—its organization and its many purposes. Young children begin to understand how print works before they learn to read and write; it is their "earliest introduction to literacy" (Honig, Diamond, and Gutlohn, 2018). Highlighting print in your classroom supports children's early literacy skills while it also heightens their motivation to attend to print (Neumann, Hood, and Ford, 2013). We can think about print awareness in three ways: functions of print, conventions of print, and book conventions.

You can think about the functions of print as understanding that print carries meaning. Our speech corresponds to the print on the page, word for word. We use print for different purposes. For example, we might write a letter to thank someone, we might read a book for entertainment, or we might have a list for the grocery store. Children begin to engage with the purpose of print through environmental print: the signs and logos they see every day all around them (for example, a red octagon that says "stop" or the yellow Cheerios box). At first, children use colors, shapes, and context clues (for example, driving in the car when I see the stop sign on the side of the road) to identify environmental print rather than the print itself. In other words, they see *Cheerios* on the cereal box, and they say, "Cheerios." But if we wrote *Cheerios* on a piece of paper, they wouldn't recognize it. As Johnston et al. (2015) noted, "environmental print is concrete and familiar to young children and can be used to develop concepts about print beginning with exposure and explanation." We utilize this awareness of environmental print every day in our classrooms with labels throughout our class.

Conventions of print highlight characteristics about the print itself. You can think about this with some key concepts. Printed words are made up of letters, and sentences are made up of words. Words are separated by spaces. Sentences start with uppercase letters and end with some form of punctuation. We read a line of print from left to right with a return sweep to the next line. We read print from the top left of the page to the bottom right. When we get to the bottom of one page, we move to the next page.

Book conventions are the parts of a book and the broad navigation of a book. Our books have a front and back cover. They are held right side up. They have a title page that includes the title, the author, and sometimes an illustrator. Books have pages, and we read the left page before we read the right page. We move from the first pages of a book to the last pages, moving from the front to the back.

The activities in this section cross all three of these ways of thinking about print. For example, we'll think about letters in words and words in sentences as part of conventions of print. We'll think about navigating a book from the front to the back to emphasize book awareness. All the while, we'll connect to the meaning of print to highlight the functions of print. We'll start with a description of a print awareness focused read-aloud.

Read Aloud to Promote Print Awareness

Reading books to children provides an ideal backdrop to highlighting elements of print awareness. To begin, choose a favorite big book. You need something with large print for this activity, so it is clearly seen by children. Your main goal here is for children to engage with the reading experience with you and interact with the book. You'll also want a large-scale pointer.

Preview your book to have predetermined stopping points to target features related to functions of print, conventions of print, and/or book conventions. Here are some things you may want to highlight across these categories and questions you can pose to children:

Functions of Print	<ul><li>Purpose of this book or author's purpose (for example, to inform)</li><li>Purpose of print in illustration (for example, part of list or sign)</li></ul>	<ul><li>Why do you think the author wrote this book?</li><li>What did you learn from this book? (This question may not work with all books.)</li><li>How does this book make you feel?</li><li>What is happening in this picture? (Point to a function of print in the illustration such as a list or sign.)</li></ul>
Conventions of Print	<ul><li>Letters in a word</li><li>Uppercase vs. lowercase letters</li><li>Word in a sentence</li><li>Big words vs. little words</li><li>Punctuation</li><li>Directionality (left to right) with return sweep</li><li>Start at the top of the page and move to the bottom</li></ul>	<ul><li>Where are the words on the page?</li><li>Point to where I start to read.</li><li>Move your finger to show me which way to go when I read.</li><li>At the end of a line, ask, "Where would I read now?"</li><li>Point to a letter on this page. What letter is that?</li><li>Point to an uppercase letter. What letter is that?</li><li>Point to a word on this page.</li><li>While pointing to a punctuation mark, ask, "What is this called?"</li><li>Find a question mark on this page.</li><li>How many words are in the title? How many words are in this sentence?</li><li>Point to and count the words in the title.</li></ul>
Book Conventions	<ul><li>Title, author, illustrator</li><li>Hold book right side up</li><li>Front and back cover</li><li>Read left page and move to right</li></ul>	<ul><li>What is this called? (point to the title)</li><li>What does the author do?</li><li>Who drew the pictures?</li><li>Show me how to hold the book.</li><li>Which page do I start on?</li><li>I just finished this page. Where do I go next?</li></ul>

There are some guidelines about reading aloud to the children when you want to focus on print awareness. Generally speaking, you want to read the book and highlight functions of print with a first read. Then reread to focus in on conventions of print and book conventions. In other words, I generally read the first time to engage with the story and then a second and/or third time to engage with print-specific concepts. You also want to limit your predetermined stops to three or four per reading. This allows you and children to enjoy the reread without too many interruptions. The bottom line is that, while we are trying to foster print awareness, the main purpose of reading is making meaning. The following activities help you focus on specific elements of print awareness.

ACTIVITY **Punctuation Introduction**

Get Things Ready

Choose a book with plenty of opportunities to point out different forms of punctuation. When I'm introducing this idea, I usually like to have two for a comparison. For example, *How Big is Zagnodd?* by Sandra Boynton has large print, one line per page, and asks a question with a strong response. For example, "How long is Buknok? So long!" Or *Catch That Chicken!* by Atinuke has places for you to point out periods and exclamation points. You can also create your own short, simple sentences. I usually like to connect our reading to something we are learning in our classroom. For example, you might be gathering data to create a graph in math, so you ask about children's favorite fruit. You pose questions such as, "Who likes apples? Who likes bananas? Who likes oranges?" As children respond, you create sentences such as, "Keyshawn, Isabella, and Finn like apples." This allows you to explore periods and question marks as ending punctuation. For this activity, I'm using *Catch That Chicken!* by Atinuke for my model and the classic rhyme, *Five Little Monkeys Jumping on the Bed* by Eileen Christelow for our practice. We've read this book and recited the rhyme. Whatever text you are using, pull out a handful of sentences and write them without punctuation on sentence strips. Make enough period and exclamation-point cards for each of your sentences. You're going to sort sentences by their punctuation. So, make two header cards: a face with no expression with a period next to it and a face with lots of expression with an exclamation point next to it. One last note here: you might want to have pictures to go along with each of your sentences to remind children what the sentences say.

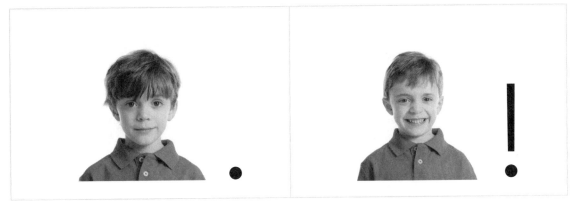

Make an Introduction

"Have you noticed how my voice changes when I read to you? Sometimes I read with a very excited voice, and other times I read with my regular voice. For example, this morning when I was reading *Catch That Chicken!*, I read 'Lami loves chickens' with my regular voice. Lami loves chickens. But I read 'Catch that chicken' with my excited voice. Catch that chicken! When I'm reading, I know when to change my voice because the author uses symbols called punctuation marks. The punctuation marks tell me how to say the words when I read."

Now for the Model

"See my regular face here." (Point to your period + face card.) "I'm going to write, 'Lami loves chickens.' See this?" (Point to the period.) "This is a punctuation mark called a *period*." (Put your sentence under the period + face card.) "Now look at my excited face." (Point to your exclamation point + face.) "I'm going to write, 'Catch that chicken!' See this?" (Point to the exclamation point.) "This is a punctuation mark, too. It's called an *exclamation point*. When I see an exclamation point, I know the author is telling me something with a lot of feeling." (Put this sentence under the exclamation point + face card.) "We're going to think about these two kinds of punctuation marks today. A period that tells me to read in my regular voice, and an exclamation point that tells me to read with my excited voice." Make sure to point out why you used your regular voice or your excited voice with your target sentences.

Let's Get Some Practice

Continue by showing your sentence strips one at a time. For *Five Little Monkeys Jumping on the Bed*, I've chosen these sentences* (so I have four cards with periods and three with exclamation points):

- Five little monkeys put on their pajamas.
- Five little monkeys brushed their teeth.
- Five little monkeys jumped on the bed!
- One fell off and bumped his head.
- No more monkeys jumping on the bed!
- So five little monkeys fell fast asleep.
- Now I can go to bed!

* Note: I've included the punctuation marks here but I wouldn't on my sentence strip.

Read each sentence with either your regular voice or your excited voice based on the sentence. After you read it once, have children say it with you a second time and note if you are using a regular voice or an excited voice. Talk about the way you read the sentence and choose your punctuation mark to add to the end of the sentence. Lastly, place the sentence under the corresponding header card: period + regular face or exclamation point + excited face. Make sure to talk about why a sentence is said with a certain feeling. For example, you might say, "The doctor is upset when the monkeys keep jumping on the bed. So, he says, 'No more monkeys jumping on the bed!'" (Make sure to read with excitement, perhaps exaggerated to make your point.)

Wrap It Up

"We learned about punctuation marks today. We use periods when we read with a regular voice and exclamation points when we read with an excited voice." (Point to the header cards to highlight the period and the exclamation point.) "Let's look for them when we are reading. And, you can use them when you are writing!"

> **Flex the Activity!**
>
> After an introduction to and practice with punctuation, you can have the children hunt for punctuation in the books you are reading. After reading *Do You Like My Bike?* by Norm Feuti, children can hunt for the punctuation marks as you talk about questions with question marks, statements of strong feeling with exclamation points, and sentences ending in periods. You can also create short, simple sentences that highlight the children. For example, "Does Keyshawn like pizza? Isabella loves pizza!"

ACTIVITY Picture, Letter, or Word?

Get Things Ready

This activity is a variation of a game called Slap Jack. All you'll need are cards with pictures, single letters (don't use *A* or *I* since these can be considered words), or words. I like to include some names in the word set because the children always love seeing their names or their friends' names. Remember, this is about word awareness not word reading. You are only expecting them to learn that words are collections of letters; they may begin to learn some words such as their names, a friend's name, or a common word like *the*.

Make an Introduction

"Our classroom has so many things hanging on the wall. We can see pictures, letters, and words. (Point to examples as you talk.) We'll play a game today to help us think about the difference between a picture, a letter, and a word. In this game, we'll slap pictures with pictures, letters, or words."

Now for the Model

"I'll say letter, word, or picture. When it's your turn, you'll look at all of the cards I've laid out and fine one with a letter, word, or picture. When you find it, you'll slap the card and say, 'Slap Jack!' Watch me. I'll show you how it goes. I'm going to slap a word. First, I have to look at my cards and find a word." (Lay out three to five cards but only one with a word.) "Oh, here's one. That's the word *my*." (Point to the *my* card.) "I'm going to slap it—slap jack!" (Put your hand on the *my* card as you say slap jack.) Now it's your turn. Get ready!"

Let's Get Some Practice

Call on one child at a time. You can play this game with more children, but it can get chaotic with multiple people trying to "slap" the word first. To encourage participation of all children, you can tell the group what you want to "slap" first and then call on a child. You might say, "Okay, everyone. Let's 'slap' a letter. Look at the cards and find a letter. Maria—you're up first. Slap the letter!" As you play, keep a collection of pictures, letters, and words that children "slap."

Wrap It Up

"Great job finding pictures, letters, and words. Let's look at all of the pictures we found." (As you show each picture, say it and have the children repeat.) "Now let's name our letters." (Show each letter, name it, and have children repeat.) "And, now let's look at our words." (Show the words, read them, and have children repeat.) "In our books, we'll see pictures. But we'll also see letters. We put letters together to make words."

> **Look For**
>
> Across all of these activities designed to help children build their awareness of a word, you will be looking to see them increase not only their accuracy of discriminating between a letter and a word but also how quickly they can make this distinction.

ACTIVITY Letter or Word?

Get Things Ready

Make a set of cards with single letters (don't use *A* or *I* since these can also be words). You'll want an equal number of each; I usually play with a deck large enough so each child has eight to ten cards. Make a die with three sides that say "letter" and three sides that say "word." You can also make a cube; I googled "cube template," printed one on card stock, and wrote *letter* and *word* before I folded and glued to make my cube.

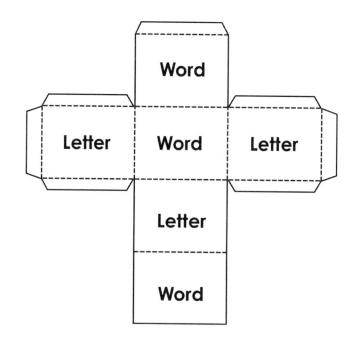

Make an Introduction

"We're going to play a game called Letter or Word? In this game, you'll roll a cube and see if you need to find a letter or a word. Let's remind ourselves of our letters by singing our ABC song." (Sing the ABC song as you point to letters either on an alphabet strip or a letter wall.) "Remember, we put letters together to make words. My name is a word. Look at my name, Tisha. How many letters are in my name? Yes! My name has five letters! Let's point and say my letters. *T-i-s-h-a.*"

Now for the Model

"Watch me. I'll go first. I'm going to lay out my cards. (Put your cards face up in front of you.) Now I'm going to roll my cube—I've landed on *word*. I need to pick up a card with a word on it. I'm going to pick this card. I know this card has a word on it because it has more than one letter. The letters go together to make a word. This is the word *is,* like in this sentence: 'My name is Tisha.' Is. I'm going to put it in a pile for all of my words."

"Now I'm going to roll my cube again. I've landed on *letter*. Now I need to find a letter. I'm going to pick this card with the uppercase *M*. I'll put it in a different pile for all of my letters."

Let's Get Some Practice

Have children sit in a circle and distribute their card sets. Make sure they have an equal number of letters and words in their set. I usually have eight to ten cards, so a mix of four to five each. Have each child lay their cards out faceup so they can see them all. I usually have them working on a mat (for example, a large piece of construction paper that I've laminated or a placemat). Then go around the circle, giving each child a chance to roll the cube. Keep going around until each child has had at least five or six rolls. Encourage them to keep their letters and words in separate piles. If children have difficulty, reduce their choice by picking one letter and one word.

Wrap It Up

"We see letters around us all of the time. And we know letters go together to make words. We found letters today, and we found words. Everyone, go to your word pile and give me one word. Now go to your letter pile and give me one letter. I'm going to say our letters. Say them after me." (Show each letter card, say the letter name, and have the children chorally repeat). "Now, I'm going to read our words. Say them after me." (Show each word card, read the word aloud, and have the children chorally repeat.) "We know these are words because they have two or more letters together."

> **Connect to a Book!**
>
> Any book is a good book to use as a springboard for this activity. For example, after reading *Old Rock (Is Not Boring)* by Deb Pilutti, you can use some of the words from the book such as *rock, hummingbird,* and *beetle*. Or after reading *Fry Bread* by Kevin Noble Maillard, you could include words such as *bread, dough,* and *round*.

ACTIVITY Nursery Rhyme Name Change

Get Things Ready

Write the words of a familiar nursery rhyme on sentence strips to go in your pocket chart. Make sure to have at least two lines, if not more. For example, with "Jack and Jill," I use four sentence strips:

Jack and Jill went up the hill

to fetch a pail of water.

Jack fell down and broke his crown,

and Jill came tumbling after.

Prepare two name cards for each child and a word card with *her*. You'll want to have already taught the nursery rhyme to the children They should be able to recite the rhyme with some degree of accuracy given your support. Lastly, a fun pointer is always a must! I like a large-scale pointer for pointing to words in a pocket chart to exaggerate the words.

Make an Introduction

"Today we're going to read a rhyme together. It's one you already know! Remember "Jack and Jill"? Let's say it together!

> *Jack and Jill went up the hill*
> *to fetch a pail of water.*
> *Jack fell down and broke his crown,*
> *and Jill came tumbling after.*

What does it mean to 'fetch a pail of water'? Yes. A bucket of water. That's right. They were going up the hill to get a bucket of water. Let's say the rhyme one more time. This time, let's whisper it!" (Say the rhyme chorally as you all whisper.) "Now let's look at the words in this rhyme."

Now for the Model

"We're going to read the words in the rhyme together. Remember, when we read, we start at the left and move this way. (Demonstrate by pointing to the first word, *Jack*, and then moving your finger to the right.) 'Jack and Jill went up the hill.' (Model reading and pointing to each word.) When I get to the end of this line, I go back to the left and start again. (Model by pointing to the last word on the line and sweep back to the left to point to the first word on the next line.) 'To fetch a pail of water.' (Model reading as you point to each word and stop at the last word.) Where do I go next? That's right. I need to go to the first word of the next line." Continue as you and the children chorally read while you point to each word. When you finish a line, emphasize the movement to the next line.

Let's Get Some Practice

"We're going to change some of the words in the rhyme. We're going to use your names! You get to be in the rhyme!" Choose two children's names to substitute. Hold them up for the group to identify and then simply put them over the words *Jack* and *Jill* in your pocket chart. You'll also put the *her* card in as needed. Choose a child to use the pointer and point to the words as the children chorally read the rhyme with their friends' names.

Keyshawn and Angelina went up the hill

to fetch a pail of water.

Keyshawn fell down and broke his crown,

and Angelina came tumbling after.

Continue until you've had a few children take a turn pointing as the group chorally reads. If a child has difficulty, hold the pointer with the child to guide the pointing. You can also point out the difference between a letter and a word as well as how names start with capital letters.

Wrap It Up

"We read each word in the rhyme! And, we had fun reading 'Jack and Jill' with our friends' names!"

> **Connect to a Book!**
>
> After reading *See the Cat: Three Stories About a Dog* by David LaRochelle, you could take sentences from the book such as 'See the dog run and jump' and switch out *dog* for children in your class. 'See Keyshawn run and jump.'

ACTIVITY Word Train

Get Things Ready

You'll need four train car picture cards per child (and you!): three for the words *my*, *name*, and *is* plus one for the child's name (notice the period at the end of the name). I simply googled "train car black line drawing" to get mine and cut the cars apart. You can put these in a pocket chart or lay them on the floor. Whatever works for you. I've found this activity can run long, so I sometimes break it across two sessions (right after they write their name cars).

Make an Introduction

"Today we're going to look at the letters that make up words. And, we'll look at words we put together to make sentences. Let's talk about letters in words first. We use letters to make words. Look at this: here's the letter M." (Write the letter M on your dry-erase board, or you could have it written on a sticky note or on a letter tile.) "It's an uppercase M because this is the first word in our sentence. Now look at this: here's the letter y." (Write the letter y on your dry-erase board.) "If we put the letters M and y together, they make the word my." (Put your train car with My in your pocket chart.) "See our first train car, the engine? It has the word My written on it. M-y (Point to M and y.) My."

Now for the Model

"Let's talk more about letters and words. Okay, let's look at my next word. (Put your name train car in your pocket chart.) It's the word name. What word is it? (Have children chorally respond.) Letters make up words. What are the letters in the word name? Point and say them with me. (Point to each letter as you chorally say each letter.) N-a-m-e. The letters n-a-m-e make the word name. (Put your name car beside the My car.)

See how our first train car, My, connects to our next one, name? This is how we build a sentence—with words. We put letters together to make a word like my, (Point to M and y and then sweep under my.) and we put words together to make a sentence. We have two train cars, so that means we have two words—My name. (Point to each word as you say it.) Read it with me. My name. (Point to each word as you chorally read.)

Here's another word. (Put your is train car in your pocket chart.) It's the word is. What word is it? (Have children chorally respond.) Remember, letters make up words. Point and say the letters with me. (Point to each letter as you chorally say each letter.) Let's add this word to our sentence. (Put your is car beside the name car.) We have three train cars now, so we have three words. My name is. (Point to each train car as you read each word.) Read them with me. My name is. (Point again as you read each word.)

I need one more word to make this a sentence. I know the letters in my name. I'm going to write my name on this train car. (Say each name as you write each letter. Make a note of your first letter as uppercase and the rest lowercase.) This is my name: Tisha. (Put your name car at the end of your sentence.) Now I have a sentence! My name is Tisha. (Point to each word as you read.)

Let's Get Some Practice

Give each child a name train car. "You are going to build your own sentence! First, write your name on a train car. Remember, your name starts with an uppercase letter." Support the children as they write their names; you may have children who need a name card to reference, a name for tracing, or hand-over-hand support with forming a particular letter. After everyone has their name train car ready, pass out the My, name, and is train cars, one set per child. Take your train cars out of your pocket chart so you can model as you rebuild your sentence one word at a time. "Let's build our sentences! Remember, our sentence is made up of words. Our first word is my, so I'm going to put the My train car at the beginning of my sentence. What's the word? My. Everyone, get your train car with My. Put it at the beginning of your sentence."

Continue with this process as you build the rest of your sentence. You might want to have work mats for the children to build their sentences on, or you could have sentence strips for them all to build on. As you work, reinforce the concepts that letters make words and words make sentences. I usually like to have the children glue their train cards down (or tape them together) so I can display them.

Wrap It Up

"We built sentences today! Remember, letters make up words. Let's look at *My.* What letters are in the word *My? M-y.* Yes! We put words together to make sentences. Let's read the words in our sentences. Point and read with me. (Have everyone either read your model sentence or point and read their own.) How many words are in our sentence? Let's count. 1-2-3-4. (Point to each word as you count.) *My name is Tisha.* Nice job thinking about letters in words and words in sentences!"

> ### Connect to a Book!
> *Alma and How She Got Her Name* by Juana Martinez-Neal is a perfect companion to this activity. You could read this book to springboard to the activity as it is written above. You could also use a different sentence frame to connect to the book. Instead of *My name is* ____, you could use ____ *is a long name* or ____ *is a short name.* For example, you might use *Josh is a short name.* And, you might use *Melisandre is a long name.* Making a decision between long and short could connect to syllable awareness— names with one syllable are short, and names with more than one syllable are long.

ACTIVITY Counting Words

Get Things Ready

Write short sentences on sentence strips. Sentences can come from a recently read book, a fun rhyme you've all learned, or a shared experience. I usually have six to eight sentences prepared for this activity.

- After reading *Bo the Brave* by Bethan Woollvin, you might have the following sentences:
  - Can I come with you?
  - You must stay home.
  - I'm smart and brave and strong.
- After learning the rhyme "Jack and Jill," you might have:
  - Jack and Jill went up the hill.
  - Jack fell down.
  - Jill came tumbling after.
- After a nature hunt around your school, you might write the following sentences from your shared experience:
  - We saw moss on a rock.

- We heard birds chirping.

- We felt the wind blow.

Notice most of these sentences have one-syllable words. Just as with oral word awareness in chapter 3, increasing the number of syllables in a word simultaneously increases the difficulty of the task. It's easier for children to identify one-syllable words in sentences. Notice, too, that the sentences with two-syllable words end with those words. Otherwise, children might get off track in the middle of a sentence and have difficulty self-correcting. You'll also need counting chips or sticky notes. Each child will need enough chips to account for the number of words in your longest sentence; I usually keep my sentences to six words or less. Otherwise, they are too difficult to remember, and we lose the focus of our activity—written words in sentences.

Make an Introduction

"Remember, we put words together to make sentences. Like this sentence: *My name is Tisha.* (Put a finger up as you say each word.) That sentence has four words. (Say this as you keep your four fingers up.) Today we are going to count words in sentences."

Now for the Model

"Watch me. Here's my first sentence: We saw moss on a rock. (Don't show the sentence strip yet—just say the sentence aloud and place the sentence strip face down in front of you.) Say it with me. We saw moss on a rock. (Chorally say the sentence.) Now I'm going to say the sentence again and lay a chip down each time I saw a word. We. Saw. Moss. On. A. Rock. (Put a chip down each time you say a word.) How many words? 1-2-3-4-5-6. I have six chips, so six words. (Turn the sentence strip over.) Now I'm going to put my chips on top of each word as I read the sentence. *We. Saw. Moss. On. A. Rock.* (Place a chip on each word as you say it.)

Let's Get Some Practice

Continue with this process. Say a sentence aloud. Have children chorally repeat the sentence. Then have children say the sentence to themselves again as they put a chip down for each word. Turn the sentence strip over for the group. Invite one child to place their chips on the words on the sentence strip as they read aloud. Check as a group as you say the sentence again, pointing to the chips/words. You can differentiate by giving some children shorter sentences with only one-syllable words and others longer sentences and/or sentences with two-syllable words (or more). If a child puts chips on letters, remind them that letters make up our words, and we are counting words in sentences.

Wrap It Up

"Nice work counting words in sentences today! Let's count our longest sentence again. *We saw green leaves on trees.* Say it with me as I put a chip down for each word. (Show the sentence strip and put a chip down as you say each word.) This sentence has six words!

Flex the Activity!

With any of these activities, you can call attention to individual words like in Point and Read Text activity. You can do this in a variety of ways. Here are a few ideas:

- Pull out one word and read it to the children. Then engage in a conversation about the word. For example, pull out the word *moss* and say, "This is the word *moss*. Let's point and say the letters in this word. *M-O-S-S. Moss.* What's this word? *Moss.* I hear /m/ at the beginning of *moss*. *M* says /m/, so I see an *M* at the beginning. What's this word? *Moss.*"

- Point to a word and ask, "What word is this?" Point and read from the first word of the sentence to identify the word. For example, point to *moss* in your sentence *We saw moss on a rock*. Then start with *we* and 'read back in.' "We saw moss. . . moss. . . that word is *moss.*"

- Encourage children to hunt for a word. With the sentence *We saw moss on a rock*, you might say, "Everyone, find the word *moss*. I hear /m/ at the beginning of *moss*. (Exaggerate the initial /m/ as you say *moss*). Think about the letter for /m/. *Moss* will start with that letter."

ACTIVITY Be the Word

Get Things Ready

Write sentences on sentence strips. These sentences can come from a recently read book or from a shared experience that you create sentences about. For example, let's say you recently went on a letter hunt around your school. You might have sentences such as *We walked down the hall. We visited Ms. Smith's office. We saw a green exit sign*. You can increase or decrease difficulty by considering one-syllable words or words with more syllables (see previous activity—Counting Words). You'll want to have a pair of scissors handy.

Make an Introduction

"We know that sentences are made up of words. We're going to cut apart a sentence into its words. And then we'll be the words in our sentences!"

Now for the Model

"Okay. I'm going to read our first sentence. Remember we start here on the left and read to the right. (Point to your first word and then sweep to the right.) *We walked down the hall.* (Hold up the sentence strip and point to each word as you read.) This sentence has five words. *We. Walked. Down. The. Hall.*

> We walked down the hall.

I'm going to cut the sentence apart into words. There is a space between words, so I know that's where I cut my words apart. (Cut between each word.) Now let's look at our sentence cut apart into five words: *We walked down the hall.* (Push words forward as you say them.) Now

I'm going to give five of you a word from our sentence. You are going to line up in order to make our sentence. (Give out the five words and support children lining up. Help them use letter sounds to help figure out their words. For example, help the child with *down* connect with the initial 'd' with /d/ for *down*.)

We	walked	down	the	hall.

"Now read your word out loud to make our sentence. (Have each child say their word.) Let's all read the sentence together!" (Chorally read the sentence. You can move from one child to the next as you read each word.)

Let's Get Some Practice

Continue with this process one sentence at a time. Point and read each sentence on your sentence strips. Count the words and emphasize how many words in each sentence. Invite children to cut sentences apart into words and remind them of the spaces between the words to support cutting. Distribute words and have children line up in front of the group, get in order, and read their words to make the sentence. Finally, have the group chorally read the sentence.

Wrap It Up

"You did a great job reading our sentences today. You cut apart words in each sentence and thought about how many words there were. Let's look at our longest sentence today. *We saw a green exit sign.* How many words? We. Saw. A. Green. Exit. Sign. Six words!"

Flex the Activity!

You can do this activity with one shared sentence to provide more support. You'd have your shared sentence (for example, *We walked down the hall.*) on a sentence strip. Read and point the sentence strip, cut it apart word-by-word, and rebuild the sentence to read and point again. Give each child a baggie with the words already cut. Leave your rebuilt sentence out so children can use it as a reference. Make sure to note how sentences begin with capital letters and end with punctuation.

ACTIVITY Point and Read Text

Get Things Ready

Choose a jingle, co-constructed story of a shared experience, short selection from a read-aloud, and so on. For this activity, you will work with a short text rather than individual sentences. Write sentences on chart paper. I like to keep a small collection of these, either at a learning center or in a reading folder. If you keep a collection in a reading folder, you'll want to make a copy for each child.

These short texts can be from a jingle they've learned like "Apples, apples in the tree. Big red apples just for me." Or a co-constructed book about playing on a playground (for example, "I can swing. I can slide. I can run. I can hide."). You can also choose a nursery rhyme, a refrain from a read-aloud, etc. The bottom line is the text is familiar so children can coordinate their speech to print match as they develop word awareness in print. You can think about the following when choosing a text for this activity.

Apples, Apples

Apples, apples in the tree.

Big red apples just for me.

Length of overall text	Should be short and have few lines per page if using a book
Length of sentences	Should not have too many words in a sentence (three to six is a good, safe bet)
Ease of remembering	Should be quick and easy to remember
Number of single-syllable words	Children just beginning benefit most from sentences with single-syllable words
Number of multisyllabic words	As children develop their awareness, bring in multisyllabic words
Position of multisyllabic words	At first, having multisyllabic words at the end of the line is more supportive

Make an Introduction

"Today we're going to read our jingle 'Apples, Apples.' You'll each have your copy to practice. We'll put it in our reading folders!"

Now for the Model

"Watch me read and point to each word. *Apples, apples in the tree.* (Point to each word as you read.) I'm at the end of the line, so I have to move to the next line. (Return sweep to point and read the next line.) *Apples, apples just for me.* Now say it with me as I point to each word. (Keep this slow and make sure to orient your text so that it is right side up for the children.) What is this word? (Point to a word in the text—here I'll point to *me*.) I know this word starts with /m/. It must be *me*. Let me check. *Apples, apples just for me.* (Point and read.) Here I see an *M* and I hear /m/ at the beginning of *me*. That word is *me*!"

Let's Get Some Practice

Distribute personal copies of the rhyme to children. You will model reading, tracking the words on the page, and then have the children point and chorally read. Call attention to individual words and begin your early decoding strategy instruction even with prereaders. The main decoding focus for your prereaders is using the beginning sound. After the children point and read, have them identify words within a line of text. During this activity, you will model, provide guided practice, and reinforce using the initial sound to identify words. If you find the children struggling to point and read text, try the following supports and modifications:

- Let them "piggyback" your finger. To do this, a child will put their finger on top of yours as you take the lead pointing while you both read aloud.

- Have a variety of pointers on hand. These pointers not only provide motivation, but they also help exaggerate the act of pointing. Drink stirrers are good options because they're small enough to use with many text types.

- Consider your text choice. You may possibly need a shorter text with only single-syllable words in short, simple sentences.

Wrap It Up

"Nice job reading 'Apples, Apples' today! We thought about the words in our jingle."

> ### Connect to a Book!
> Concept picture books are good options for these word awareness activities. Your text can come straight from the book or be inspired by the book. For example, after reading *Circle, Square, Moose* by Kelly Bingham, you might have: "This one is a circle. That one is a square. Hey! Don't eat that!" But really, any book you've read aloud is a good option. For example, when reading Josh Funk's *Lady Pancake and Sir French Toast*, children can read and point, "The last drop is mine! Not if I get there first!" Books with refrains are especially good options as you invite children to point and read the refrain, such as "Hats are not for cats at all!" from *Hats Are Not for Cats* by Jacqueline Raynor.

Print Referencing While Reading Aloud

Before moving to activities to build word recognition, I'd like to mention a particular read-aloud approach. Print referencing is a well-studied approach to reading aloud with children (for example, Justice and Ezell, 2004). Using this approach includes making verbal and nonverbal references to print. For example, you may explicitly point out an uppercase letter as a verbal reference: "Oh look. I see an uppercase *S* at the beginning of this word." Or you might point to each word as a nonverbal reference as you read aloud a sentence. Using both verbal and nonverbal references not only calls attention to print but has been shown to facilitate children's print awareness over repeated read-alouds (Justice, Pullen, and Pence, 2008; Justice et al., 2009).

Print referencing has two main goals: to create interest and awareness of print in books and to provide explicit instruction in the forms and functions of print in a meaningful context—reading books aloud. To meet these goals, print referencing targets certain elements about print. One target is conventions of print and book conventions, such as the title of the book and direction of print. A second target is alphabet knowledge, such as names of letters or differentiating letters from words. A third target is words, such as pointing and reading a sentence to practice awareness of the written word in text. For example, in the *Sit Together and Read* (STAR) program, each book is read twice with different verbal and nonverbal references across these targets. STAR lessons are all available for free download online out of Ohio State University.

Building Word Recognition

Early literacy standards include building word recognition, as do publications that synthesize current research. For example, the Institute of Educational Sciences published *Foundational Skills to Support Reading for Understanding in Kindergarten Through 3rd Grade* (2016). One of the recommendations is to "teach students to decode words, analyze word parts, and write and recognize words." This includes teaching children to blend letter sounds from left to right in order to accurately pronounce the word, as well as having them read decodable words in isolation and in text. We also need to teach regular and irregular words that are frequently encountered in text so the children can easily recognize them. With this in mind, the following activities will address decoding, analyzing, and reading words in isolation and in context.

The bottom line is we want the children to read regular words or fully decodable words such as *cat* and *big* once they've learned a few letter-sound correspondences. To begin this work, our early readers need supportive opportunities to "sound out" words. While blending these sounds, we want to encourage children to "hold" the sounds, or not to pause between sounds as they say the sounds in words to decode. You'll notice that once they become more accustomed to blending, they'll begin to do the work of blending in their heads without saying the sounds aloud.

We can support early blending attempts with our word choices. Remember, all sounds are either continuous or stop sounds, meaning you can hold on to some sounds (for example, /ă/ and /s/) and others you can't, because they are quick puffs of air (for example, /b/ and /k/). Most children find it easier to blend continuous sounds at first. The following is a recommended blending sequence from easiest to hardest (Surles, n.d.):

- CVC words with all continuous sounds—*run, rim*

- CVC words that start with a continuous sound and end with a stop—*sat, lot*

- CVC words that start with a stop sound and end with either—*gum, bed*

- CCVC words that start with a blend that includes a continuous or stop sound— *snap, step*

Our early readers also need opportunities to analyze words. This close examination of words and their component sounds further develops the alphabetic principle. Once children understand the alphabetic principle, they can apply what they know about letters and sounds to decode printed words. This, in turn, allows them to read a large number of words, even words they've never seen before.

As children learn more letter sounds and start to call up these sound matches with ease, they'll become more successful decoders. This is when word recognition starts to blossom. You'll notice children start to build a bank of words they can read without hesitation or the need to decode.

Blending to Decode

Children need practice blending sounds to make whole words. When children decode an unknown word, they must use the letters they see in a word and retrieve the sound associated with that letter. Then they say the sounds and hold them in memory as they blend all sounds together to come up with a recognizable word. This is a major feat for a young reader; in fact, blending has been called the "heart and soul" of our phonics instruction in schools.

There are two main techniques used for blending: sound-by-sound blending and continuous blending. These are described in the activities in this section. Sound-by-sound blending is considered a more supportive technique. A common thread across both is you hold the sounds rather than say each sound and pause between. Teaching children to "hold on to" sounds facilitates blending. Rather than saying, muh–ă–tuh, they would say /mmmăăăt/. Also, across both techniques, we can adjust the ease of decoding by including continuous sounds at the beginning of words. Remember, continuous sounds are sounds you can hold like /mmmmm/ and /ăăăăă/ as opposed to /b/ and /t/, and one-syllable words beginning with continuous sounds (for example, *map* and *at*) are relatively easier for children to blend.

ACTIVITY **Read Smoothly!**

Get Things Ready

Collect around six words that incorporate the letter sounds you've studied. You'll need to have studied at least five or six letter sounds. I include words that begin with continuous sounds as we are learning how to blend. For illustrative purposes, let's say you've introduced *a, m, p, s, t,* and *d*, so my words could be *map, mat, mad, sat, sap,* and *sad*.

Make an Introduction

"Today we're going to blend words sound-by-sound. I'll go first."

Now for the Model

Write the first letter of your first word on the dry-erase board—*m*. "Sound? /mmm/. (Say /m/ as you are pointing to *m*. Write the second letter. For this example, I'll write *a*.) Sound? /ăăă/. (Say /ă/ as you are pointing to *a*.) Blend. /mmmăăă/. (Say this as you scoop your finger under the *m* and *a*. Then print the letter *t*.) Sound? /t/. (Say /t/ as you are point to *t*). Blend. /mmmăăăt/. (Scoop your finger under the whole word as you slowly blend the sounds without a break.) Now watch as I read the whole word smoothly. *Mat.* (Say *mat* as you quickly sweep your finger under the whole word.) A mat is like a rug. People wipe their feet on it."

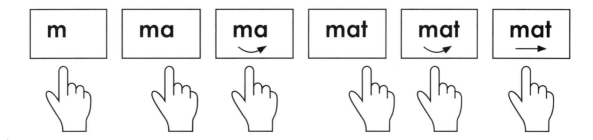

Let's Get Some Practice

Continue with this process as you support children's decoding of the remaining words. If children have difficulty, model with the word and have them repeat after you.

Wrap It Up

"Nice job blending words and then reading them smoothly! You can try this out when you are reading and come to a word you don't know."

Look For

With any of the blending activities, you are looking for the children to be able to accurately say the letter sounds, hold on to the sounds (say the sounds slowly without a break), and then say the word smoothly (or accurately read the word). As the standards point out, children should be able to apply grade-level phonics and word-analysis skills in decoding words by the end of kindergarten. In most states and education districts, decoding CVC, or perhaps CCVC, words is considered "grade-level."

ACTIVITY Follow the Eye

Get Things Ready

Make some googly eyes! I make these with craft sticks, small googly eyes, and glue. Nowadays you can get peel-and-stick googly eyes. (You don't have to have store-bought googly eyes; you could just draw an eye on paper—or cut from foam sheets—and glue that on the end of a craft stick.) If you're planning this activity for the whole group, you might want to use a large craft stick (or a ruler) and a big googly eye. Make a list of words for your work—this is a blending activity. This activity uses the continuous blending technique. Keep two things in mind: the words need to include only the sounds you've previously taught, and continuous sounds at the beginning of words support children's early blending attempts. Once children can easily blend continuous sounds at the beginning, you can incorporate stop sounds (for example, /t/). I like to write my words one at a time on a dry-erase board, but you can also list them out on chart paper or on a sentence strip with plenty of space between them.

Make an Introduction

"Let's practice reading words smoothly. But first, let's practice the sounds we'll see today. (Show letter cards with the letters used in the words you've chosen for a quick review.) We'll say the sounds in a word and then say the word smoothly. We'll use my googly eye to help!" Children love the googly eye reveal!

Now for the Model

Write *mat* on a dry-erase board large enough so everyone can easily see it. "Let's look at my first word. I need to say the sounds slowly as I stretch the word. As long as my eye is on the letter, I'm going to say the sound. I'll keep saying the sound until my googly eye goes to the next letter. So, I won't stop saying the sound until I move my googly eye. Then I'll read the word smoothly. Watch me. /mmmăăăt/." Slowly move your googly eye under the letters as you hold onto the sounds.

"Now I'll say it smoothly. Mat. /mmmăăăt/." Demonstrate with your googly eye again. "Mat." Note: when you use words that begin with stop sounds, such as *tap*, you'll explain that sometimes your googly eye moves quickly since you need to move quickly to the /ă/ while blending.

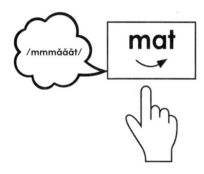 

Let's Get Some Practice

Continue with this procedure as you read additional words. You could chorally read words, starting with slow blending and the smooth reading. Or you can have children do this individually if you are working with a smaller group. I often find I need to remind children to "hold on to" the sound while the eye is under it.

Wrap It Up

"You are readers! You kept your eyes on the letters as you said the sounds slowly with our googly eyes. Then you read the words smoothly."

ACTIVITY Blending Bigger Words

Get Things Ready

Generate about four to six sentences that have letter sounds you've previously taught; write them on sentences strips. This is another blending activity, but this time, you'll support the children blending words with beginning blends (for example, *FL* in *flip* and *CR* in *crab*). This means we are working with consonant-consonant-vowel-consonant (CCVC) words. Keep your sentences relatively short (somewhere around four to six words); the purpose of having sentences is to make the task more authentic. I like to include names of the children and underline my CCVC words. For example, Isabella can flip and spin. (CCVC words are *flip* and *spin*.) I've included two target words in my sentence. But you can keep the sentences short with only one target word: Isabella can spin. You might end up with the following sentence strips.

Isabella can <u>spin</u>.	Timothy can <u>flip</u>.
Can Keyshawn <u>skip</u>?	Did Maria <u>trip</u>?
<u>Grab</u> it, Auggie!	<u>Stop</u> it, Susannah!

Or you might want longer sentences for more challenge.

Isabella can <u>flip</u> and <u>spin</u>.	Can Susannah <u>stop</u> that <u>slug</u>?
Can Keyshawn <u>skip</u> and not <u>trip</u>?	Timothy has a <u>frog</u> and a <u>crab</u>.
Maria will <u>grab</u> that <u>flag</u>.	Do not <u>drop</u> the <u>clam</u>, Auggie!

The sentences can be silly and often are, but children will love their silliness and feel proud they can read them. Once you have a set of sentences frames, you can switch names in and out. Children can take their sentence and draw a picture, and the collection can be a reading resource for later (for example, in a learning center).

Make an Introduction

"I wrote some silly sentences for us to read today, but first we'll look at some words in the sentences. Let's say them slowly and read them smoothly!"

Now for the Model

"Here's my first word. (Show the word *flip*.) I need to say the sounds slowly as I stretch the word. As long as my finger is on the letter, I'm going to say the sound. I'll keep saying the sound until my finger goes to the next letter. So, I won't stop saying the sound until I move my finger. Then I'll read the word smoothly. Watch me. /fffllliiiip/. (Slowly move your finger under the letters as you hold on to the sounds.) Now I'll say it smoothly. *Flip*. /fffllliiiip/. (Demonstrate with your finger again). *Flip*. Now I'll read my sentence. (Show the sentence strip.) Look at my underlined word. Let's say it slowly and then read it smoothly. /fffllliiiip/ *flip*. I'll read the sentence. Timothy can flip. Timothy, can you flip? Everyone, point and read with me. Timothy can flip." (Chorally read as you point to each word.)

Let's Get Some Practice

Continue with this practice. Have children continuously blend the target word—say the sounds slowly and read the word smoothly—and then read the sentence that includes the target word (for example, skip: Can Keyshawn skip?). If you notice children having difficulty blending, you can switch to sound-by-sound blending or adjust your word choice to CVC words. You may also find you need to echo read the sentences, meaning you point and read first and then the children chorally read as you point. My sentences use a variety of ending punctuation. You can keep it to periods or vary it. With my sentences here, I'll talk about the meaning of the punctuation.

Wrap It Up

"You are readers! You kept your eyes on the letters as you said sounds slowly and read words smoothly. Then you read sentences! Let's reread our question sentences. How do we know which ones are questions? That's right. . . our question mark! Can Keyshawn skip? Did Maria trip?" (Point and chorally read each sentence.)

Flex the Activity!

You can use your googly eye with this activity, too. You can also adjust this activity to encourage the children to read the blend as a unit and the ending rime—the vowel and what follows, like the *-ip* in *flip*. One way to encourage this is to have your blends on a card and your rimes on a card (for example, *fl-* on one card and *-ip* on another card). Say the sounds on the cards and then put the cards together to blend for the whole. In this case, rather than doing the continuous blending technique to "preread" the words before reading them in the sentences, you could blend the blend and rime on cards.

ACTIVITY Blending Lines

Get Things Ready

Create a series of blending lines—lines of three to six words that should be in children's blending grasp. This means you will choose decodable words with letter sounds you've previously taught. Blevins (2017) suggests seven lines with the first four highlighting a target feature, the next two with words reviewing previous features, and then a last line with challenge words. Blending lines end with two short, decodable sentences. For example, if your target feature was *SH* for /sh/ as in *ship*, you might have:

ship	shed	shot
cash	rush	wish
shed	shag	mesh
dish	shop	rash
hush	sat	shed
fish	his	sod

That ship is in the shed.

I wish I had that ship that is in the shed.

My example adjusts Blevins's suggestions a bit. I've taken my target /sh/ and made six lines with two sentences. My first line has /sh/ at the beginning of words, my second line has /sh/ at the end of words, and my next two lines has /sh/ at both the beginning and end. Then my fifth and sixth lines include words without /sh/. Adjusting for your purposes is fine as long as the words are decodable for children, meaning you are using letter sounds you've previously taught. The words you choose can be words from a book you plan to read—even the sentences. This would allow you to "frontload" words coming up in books they will be reading. You can write your blending lines on chart paper for a whole-group reference, but each child will need their own copy for individual practice.

Make an Introduction

"We'll practice our reading today by reading our blending lines. Let me show you what I mean. (Show the blending lines and point to the word lines.) We'll read these words line-by-line. Then we'll read the two sentences at the bottom of the page." (Point to the sentences).

Now for the Model

"Watch me. I'm going to read the first word in the first line and the first word in the second line. (Point to *ship* and use continuous blending.) I'll say each sound and then read the word smoothly. /shhhĭĭĭp/ (Move your finger under the letters as you say the sounds slowly.) *Ship.* Say the sounds with me. /shhhĭĭĭp/ (Move your finger under the letters as you chorally say the sounds slowly.) What's the word? *Ship.* Now my next word. (Point to *cash*.) /kăăăshhh/ (Move your finger under the letters as you say the sounds slowly.) *Cash.* Say the sounds with me. /kăăăshhh/ (Move your finger under the letters as you chorally say the sounds slowly.) What's the word? *Cash.* Now it's your turn."

Let's Get Some Practice

Continue using continuous blending to read each line as necessary. You can do this chorally as a group, but let your voice go to the background so children are doing the work. You can also have the children try out reading line-by-line individually. In kindergarten, I generally like to check in after each line. You will prompt by saying, "Say the sounds slowly," and "What's the word?" If the children have difficulty, put your finger under the erroneous sound and say the correct sound. Have the children repeat the sound as you point to the letter. Then direct them to start over and blend the sounds again.

> **Connect to a Book!**
>
> Blevins (2017) suggests you include words and even sentences from upcoming books in your blending lines. So, if you are reading a decodable text with children, think about words and sentences you might include in your blending lines. This would act as a nice scaffold to support children's reading of their decodable text.

Wrap It Up

"We read so many words! Let's read a few again." (Point to a few words randomly and have children chorally blend slowly and read smoothly.)

Manipulating to Build Flexibility

The following activities are designed to have children segment, isolate, and manipulate sounds. By working with individual sounds, or phonemes, children not only deepen their knowledge of *specific words*, but they further develop their ability to analyze sounds in words. Having a solid awareness of phonemes in words will not only help children to process words more fully, but it will also help them build their word recognition.

As you think about your choice of words in these activities, think about the learning goal. For example, if you are targeting initial blends in words, then you will want children to build and manipulate words with and without initial blends. Having children build words that *do* as well as words that *don't* will let them practice distinguishing between words with and without initial blends, such as *cap* and *clap*. An added bonus of these activities is the extra practice segmenting and blending individual sounds in words.

ACTIVITY Consonant Swap

Get Things Ready

With this game, you can add beginning or ending consonants. If you are playing for the first time, I'd suggest beginning consonants first. It is easier for children to manipulate beginning sounds rather than ending sounds. Make a set of cards or gather letter tiles or magnetic letters. If you are changing the beginning consonant, then you'll choose a short vowel word family for one of your cards and think about the words you can make. If you are changing the ending consonant, then you will have a consonant + vowel card and think about the words you can make. Here are some examples to illustrate.

CHANGING THE BEGINNING CONSONANT		CHANGING THE ENDING CONSONANT	
Possible Beginning Consonants	Short Vowel Family	Consonant + Vowel	Possible Ending Consonants
c, l, m, n, r, s, t, z	-ap	sa-	d, g, m, p, t, x
b, f, h, k, l, p, s	-it	bi-	b, d, g, n, t
b, d, h, j, l, m, r, t	-ug	le-	d, g, t

So, if I wanted to change up the beginning consonant, then I'd choose a short vowel family, making sure I've taught that short vowel and using consonant sounds I've already taught. I might make these cards:

You can do this activity as a group, or you can have individual sets for children. If each child will work with a set, then you'll want them to have a workspace. I usually use laminated construction paper since the letter tiles move more easily on a smooth surface.

Make an Introduction

"Today we'll make a bunch of words by changing only the beginning sound! Before we start, let's say the sounds we'll use at the beginning of our words." (Show your letter cards and have children chorally provide the sounds. Hold off on the -*ap* card.)

Now for the Model

"Watch me. I'm going to lay out my beginning sounds on this side. (Place your consonant cards on the left side of your workspace.) Now I have my card with the rest of the word. Let's say each sound and read it smoothly. /ă/ /p/. . . *ap*. (Point and say the sounds. Then run your finger under while you say *ap*). All of our words will end with *ap*. Here's my first word. I'm going to bring the /k/ over. (Bring the *C* over to the -*ap* card.) /k/ /ăp/. . . *cap*. Now I'm going to move the /k/ back and get my /m/. /m/ /ăp/. . . *map*. I've made *cap* and *map*. Your turn!"

Let's Get Some Practice

Continue with this process. I've chosen to make only real words, but you can use made-up words, too. You can keep a count of how many real words versus made-up words. Children like to see which group wins in the end! Either way, you'll tell them which card to pull over with each beginning sound change. Then you'll either say each sound and read the word smoothly as a group or you'll support children as they work individually. If a child is having difficulty, say the sounds smoothly and read the word smoothly. Have the child repeat.

Wrap It Up

"Look at all of the words you made today. Let's make one of our words again before we clean up. Everyone, bring over your /k/. (If a sound provided some challenge, I usually review it before wrapping up.) Let's say the sounds and read the word smoothly. /k/ /ăp/. . . *cap*."

Look For

With any of the activities in this section, you are looking for children to grow in their accuracy and ease of completing these phonemic shifts in words. All of these activities require close examination of words and will help children strengthen not only their letter sound knowledge but also their phonemic awareness.

Flex the Activity!

In chapter 3, you read about the game Spin a Letter to build letter name and/or sound knowledge. You can play that same game here. Instead of moving over the beginning consonant cards to build onto your short vowel word families, you spin for the beginning consonant.

ACTIVITY Change a Letter

☐ Get Things Ready

Decide on the words you'll use for this game. You'll want to choose words that include only the letters you've taught. Make a set of letter tiles for each child and for yourself. So, if you've taught *m, s, n, r, t, p, c, o,* and *a,* you have quite a few words you can make. I usually don't try to use all letters; instead, I'll intentionally choose based on newer letters or ones I've noticed are a bit troublesome for children alongside letters they are more confident with. Generally, I try to keep this to eight to ten letters or maybe fewer. For this example, I'm only including *a, o, m, p, s, t.* My plan is to make words such as *sap, map, mat, pat, pot.* You'll need a workspace for each child, too, such as a laminated piece of construction paper or card stock.

☐ Make an Introduction

"Today you'll read a word made with three letters. Then you'll change one of the letters to make a new word!"

☐ Now for the Model

"Watch me. First, I'm going to get my workspace ready. I'm going to put my letter tiles at the bottom of my workspace. Now I'm going to make my first word. (Bring *s, a,* and *p* to the top of your workspace.) Let's say the sounds slowly. /s/ /ă/ /p/. What's the word? *Sap.* Good! Now I'm going to change the *S* to *M.* What's the sound? (Point to *M* and encourage a choral response.) Let's say the sounds slowly. /m/ /ă/ /p/. What's the word? *Map.*"

☐ Let's Get Some Practice

Continue with the process as you tell children the letters to change, and they work to say each sound slowly and blend to read the word smoothly. If children have difficulty, you might want to move back to modeling. Children can repeat the process after your model. You might also need to encourage sound-by-sound blending if they have difficulty with continuous blending. If they continue to have difficulty, you might need to change only one part of the word.

☐ Wrap It Up

"You are readers! You thought about the letters you saw and said each sound slowly. Then you read the words! I'm going to make one last word for us. (Show *N-O-T.*) Let's say the sounds slowly. /n/ /ŏ/ /t/. What's the word? *Not.* Nice work, readers!"

> **Connect to a Book!**
>
> You don't have to limit your book connections to the short decodables that children are reading to practice their growing phonics knowledge. You can use just about any read-aloud as a springboard for this work. For example, *13 Ways to Eat a Fly* by Sue Heavenrich is a fun reverse counting book that has plenty of fun CVC connections, such as the words to describe various flies (for example, *big* or *thin*) or ways flies can be eaten (for example, frogs *zap* them and wasps *dig* them up).

ACTIVITY **Mix It Up!**

Get Things Ready

Make a set of letter tiles for each child as well as for you. Children will need a workspace. As with the other activities, I like using a laminated piece of construction paper or card stock as a workspace, and I make letter tiles out of card stock. You'll also need to choose a set of words you'll use; I like to use lists similar to Beck and Beck's (2013) word-building lists. These lists start with a word and then move to new words with only one phoneme change. This requires close examination of the words and will help children build their understanding of not only letter-to-sound matches but also their phonemic awareness. The following options illustrate an easier word list to a harder one.

	EASIER		**HARDER**
Focus	Short Vowel Introduction	Short Vowel Discrimination	Beginning Consonant Blends
Tiles Needed	r, a, t, p, n, s, m, c, b	h, i, d, t, a, s, b, p	c, l, a, p, n, s, i, o, t
Word List	rat	hid	clap
	rap	hit	lap
	nap	hat	nap
	sap	sat	snap
	sat	sit	lap
	mat	it	slap
	map	at	slip
	cap	bat	slop
	cat	bit	top
	bat	pit	stop

Make an Introduction

"We're going to play Mix It Up! today. We'll have to listen carefully to our words. We'll build a word and then mix it up by changing only one sound! First, I'll get my workspace ready." (Model laying out your letter tiles at the bottom of your workspace so that you can push up tiles to make words. Note: you can teach children to group vowels to the side, but that's definitely not required.)

Now for the Model

"Let's get ready with our sounds. (Hold up your letter tiles for the group to chorally say each sound.) We're ready. Watch me. I'll make the first word. My word is *clap*. (Say each sound as you hold up a finger.) /k/ /l/ /ă/ /p/. Four sounds. The first sound I hear is /k/. I'm going to push up my C. /k/ /lll/. . . that's L. I'll push up L. /k/ /l/ /ăăă/. . . A. I'll push up A. The last sound I hear is /k/ /l/ /ă/ /p/. . . *P*. I'll push up *P*. /k/ /l/ /ă/ /p/ (Put your finger under each letter as you say the sound.) *Clap*. (Run your finger under the word as you read it smoothly) Now we'll mix it up! Let's change *clap* into *lap*. What part of the word are we changing? The beginning, middle, or end? *Clap*. *Lap*. That's right. The beginning. /l/ /ă/ /p/. . . I need to take my *C* away. Let me check. /l/ /ă/ /p/ (Put your finger under each letter as you say the sound.) *Lap*. (Run your finger under the word as you read it smoothly.)

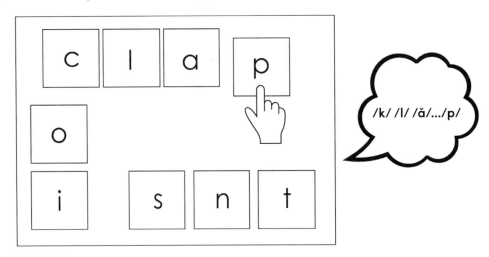

▢ Let's Get Some Practice

Support children laying out their letter tiles at the bottom of their workspace and continue this procedure of saying each sound smoothly, reading the words smoothly, and thinking about the one sound change from one word to the next. This work can be done as a group as children chorally say the sounds and read words and you guide the one sound change. Or you can have them say the sounds and build the words as you monitor their responses on their workspace. If children have difficulty, help them say each sound, and call attention to the number of sounds (for example, "Use your tiles to spell *nap*. Remember *nap* has three sounds.) They may have difficulty thinking about how the words are changing. If so, you might tell them what to do and then blend for the new word as you did in the Change a Letter activity. For example, you might say, "Let's change the beginning sound. Take /l/ away and replace it with /n/. Say the sounds and read the word smoothly. /n/ /ă/ /p/. . . *nap*."

▢ Wrap It Up

"Nice job, readers! You really had to think about words and their sounds. This will help you read and spell new words!"

ACTIVITY Double Duty Sorts

▢ Get Things Ready

Decide on your categories and choose a set of words you'll use for your sorting. Your words should include sounds you've previously taught. Collect a series of pictures that can fit your categories. You'll also want your keywords handy for the sound contrasts you are planning.

For example, let's say you have chosen initial sounds /sh/ and /ch/ as your categories. Your keywords might be *ship* for /sh/ and *chin* for /ch/. You might have *shop, shed, shut, chop, chip, chat* as your words and *shell, shark, sheep, chain, chicken, cheese* as your pictures. Notice the pictures can have more advanced patterns, such as the *ar* in *shark* and the *ee* in *cheese*, because we are only using pictures. *Ship* and *chop* are good choices for your words because you've previously taught consonant sounds and short vowels. I generally have six to twelve pictures and six to twelve words. In this activity, you'll sort first for sound contrasts with pictures and then for letter-sound contrasts with words. The "double duty" of this activity encourages children to analyze words closely for two key factors: the sounds they hear in words and the letters that represent those sounds.

Make an Introduction

"We're going to sort pictures into groups based on how the words begin. Then we'll read words that start with these same sounds. Today we'll think about words that begin with /sh/ and words that begin with /ch/."

Now for the Model

"Our first sound is the /ch/ at the beginning of /chhhhǐn/. (Place the *chin* keyword card in front of the group.) We are also going to listen to the /sh/ at the beginning of /shhhǐp/. (Place the *ship* keyword card in front of the group.) I'm going to sort this first picture: *cheese*. First, I need to think about how *cheese* starts. I hear /ch/ at the beginning of *cheese*. Let me see where it belongs. Does it begin like *ship*? Shhhhhhip. Ch-ch-cheese. No. Let me check *chin*. Ch-ch-chin—ch-ch-cheese. Yes. *Chin* and *cheese* both begin with /ch/. (Place your *cheese* pictures under the *chin* keyword.)

Here's our next picture: shhhhhhark. Ready? What's the first sound you hear in shhhhhhark? Now let's think about the category. Shhhhark—ch-ch-chin? Shhhhhhark—ship? Yes. *Shark* begins like *ship*. They both begin with /sh/." (Place your *shark* picture under the *ship* keyword.)

Let's Get Some Practice

Sort at least three pictures into each category, asking the children to name each picture aloud. After they say each picture, have them repeat the target sound. Once they've sorted all the pictures, say the pictures in each category and check your work—make sure the pictures all begin with /sh/ or /ch/. I like to tell children they are going to be sound sleuths! "Let's say all of the pictures in *chin*'s group. *Cheese, chain, chicken.* How do these words sound the same?"

Now for the Model

Note: since this is a two-step activity, we need a second round of modeling and practice as we bring in the letter-sound correspondence and words.

"Words beginning with the /sh/ like at the beginning of *shop, shark, shell,* and *sheep* begin with S-H. /sh/ is spelled S-H." Remove the picture cards as you bring out the *SH* pattern card. "Let's think about *ship.* Let's find the *SH* in *ship.*" Point out the word *ship* on the pattern card. You can underline or highlight it for extra emphasis. "Words beginning with the /ch/ like at the beginning of *chin, cheese, chain,* and *chicken* begin with C-H. /ch/ is spelled C-H." Remove the picture cards as you bring out the *CH* pattern card. "Let's think about *chin.* Let's find the *CH* in *chin.*" Point out the word *chin* on the pattern card. You can underline or highlight it for extra emphasis. "I'm going to sort this first word: *chop.* First, I need to think about how *chop* starts. I hear /ch/ at the beginning of *chop,* and I can see the *CH* pattern at the beginning. So, I know it sounds right: /ch/. And I know it looks right: *CH.*" Point to the *CH* in *chop* as you talk about how it looks.

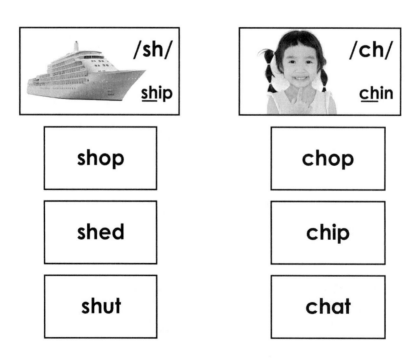

Let's Get Some Practice

Continue showing children the words, one at a time. Have children read each word aloud, supporting any decoding necessary. Then think about the word's category. Call their attention to the beginning sound of the word (**sounds** right) and the letter pattern (**looks** right). After sorting your words, review the words in each category. "Let's be word sleuths this time! Look at our /ch/ like the *chin* group. Read with me. *Chop, chip, chat.* What do all of these words have in common? That's right. They **sound** right: they begin with /ch/. Yes, they all begin with *C-H*, so they **look** right, too."

Wrap It Up

"We were sound sleuths *and* word sleuths today! What does *C-H* say? Let's say it together: /ch/. So, when you hear /ch/ in a word you are writing, write *C-H*. What does *S-H* say? Say it with me: /sh/. When you hear /sh/ in a word, you should write *S-H*. Let's write a word! How about *shed*? What is our first sound? /sh/. So, I'll write *S-H. Shed*. I hear /ĕ/, so I'll write *E. Shed*. Last, I hear /d/. That's *D. Shed. S-H-E-D*."

ACTIVITY Fast Reads

Get Things Ready

This is similar to an activity in chapter 4 where children practiced quickly naming letters or saying letter sounds. Create a page with approximately twelve to twenty words that exemplify sounds you are targeting. For example, I might make a page like this if I wanted the children to focus close attention on short vowels.

/ă/ cat	/ĕ/ jet	/ŏ/ pot	
let	chat	pet	hot
got	pat	bet	dot
get	bat	shot	met
set	not	hat	rot

You can treat these like the Blending Lines activity earlier in the chapter by having this on chart paper that is practiced in a group and perhaps used in a learning center. Or you can have individual copies for the children that they keep in a folder. I like to keep these so we can bring out previous "fast reads" and review.

Make an Introduction

"Today we're going to read words we've practiced already. Our goal is to practice these words until we can read them fast! Let's take a look at the sounds we've been practicing." (Show them your short vowels either on letter cards or on the letter wall. Have children chorally provide the letter sound and review your keywords for each.)

Now for the Model

"Watch me. I'm going to read the first line. (Read some words without hesitation and some through decoding.) Oh, I know the first word, so I'll say it smoothly. *Let*. I need to decode this next one. /chhăăăt/ *chat*. (Use the continuous blending technique.) I need to decode the next one, too. /pěěět/ *pet*. (Use continuous blending again.) And, I know this last one. *Hot*. I'm going to say my line again. *Let. Chat. Pet. Hot*. (Point and read each word.) Now you all read with me." (Point as you and children chorally read each word.)

Let's Get Some Practice

Move to the next line. Depending on the level of support children need, you can either have the children work on the line individually or you can support them as you work through each word together. You might even decide you need to model reading all lines as you did with the first line. If children have difficulty with a sound in a word, point to the letter and say the sound. Have children repeat the sound and then start over with the word as you guide them saying the sounds smoothly. If they have difficulty blending, you might need to use the sound-by-sound blending technique.

Wrap It Up

"Look at us. We read all of these words. We'll keep practicing so we can read them all fast. This will help you when you read books and even when you write!"

> **Flex the Activity!**
>
> Fast Reads do not have to be limited to decodable words and your target phonics features. You could also choose to practice high-frequency words. The children need to begin collecting a store of these words, too. So, providing them with this practice can be helpful. Note: this type of decontextualized practice should be accompanied by bringing their study and attention back to contextualized reading and writing.

Reading Words to Build Word Recognition

The ultimate goal of foundational fluency is not more phonics and decoding practice; the ultimate goal is to help the children become better readers, writers, and thinkers. This is why we need to explicitly support children's attempts to transfer what they know about words to contextual reading and writing. Here we'll focus on reading in text. Chapter 7 is devoted to early writing practice.

Building automaticity is critical to an early reader. Specifically, we want children to build a set of words they can read with ease and without the burden of decoding. This is a first step to building fluency. These words are decodable words, but they are also words with elements that are considered irregular. Sometimes our highly frequent words have irregular features. For example, the word *said* is highly frequent in texts, and the texts early readers use are no different. The irregular feature is the *ai* in *said.* It sounds like /ĕ/ rather than the /ā/ we expect from the *ai* long *a* letter combination.

While we don't expect our early readers to develop fluent reading immediately, we can support their development of a certain level of automaticity of these core high-frequency words, in addition to those decodable words with the features they are studying. To build automaticity, we can provide multiple opportunities for the children to decode and read words. One element of these multiple reads is repeated reads. Having a variety of materials the children can use to repeatedly practice reading words is common practice in early childhood classrooms. The following activities and games are meant to provide fun, engaging ways for our early readers to practice.

ACTIVITY Heart Words

Get Things Ready

Decide on a set of highly frequent words you want to teach children. I'm reminded of a kindergartner who piped up during a shared reading one day and said, "There's the word *the.* It's everywhere!" So, think like him and make a list of these "everywhere" words. You'll teach them intentionally over time and point them out when they come up in what you and children are reading. I've made a collection looking across sets such as Fry's *1000 Instant Words* (1996), Dolch words (1936), and word lists from *Word Matters* (Fountas and Pinnell, 1998). These are the top forty I put in my set of highly frequent words, presented in sets of ten by frequency. Once you have your set, think about the sounds you've taught and the words that are coming up frequently in books.

FIRST 10	SECOND 10	THIRD 10	FOURTH 10
the	for	that	all
of	on	was	from
and	as	are	so
a	I	with	me
to	at	they	can
in	be	no	said
is	or	one	this
you	had	up	have
it	not	but	do
he	an	if	she

For this activity, have your word written on a card and place Elkonin (1971) boxes underneath, making sure to match the number of boxes to the number of sounds in your target word (for example, *said* would have three boxes for the three sounds: /s/ /ĕ/ /d/). I like to make mine large enough to display in my classroom.

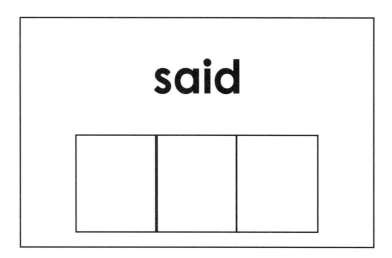

Make an Introduction

"We're going to practice words you'll see a lot in the books we read. Today we'll work with a word that you'll read in our book."

Now for the Model

"This is the word *said*. (Show the word card.) *Said* has three sounds: /s/ /ĕ/ /d/. (As you say each sound, either push a marker in a box or touch the box). The first sound I hear is /s/. (Touch the first box.) I know /s/ is the letter *s* and *said* starts with *s*. (Write *s* in the first box.) The next sound I hear is /ĕ/. Let's look at the letters in *said* that are spelling /ĕ/. It's not an *e*. It is *ai*. We need to know this part by heart. (Draw a heart at the top of the second box and write *ai* in the box.) Remember, *ai* is the part we must know by heart. I'm going to touch and say the sounds /s/ /ĕ/ /d/. My last sound is /d/. I know /d/ is the letter *d* and *said* ends with *d*. So, *said* is S-A-I-D. (Point as you say each letter name.) What's the word? *Said*. (Invite children to chorally say the word as you sweep your finger underneath the boxes.)

Note: this routine was informed by "Heart Word Magic" from Really Great Reading (https://www.reallygreatreading.com/). This website has many animated videos going through this process with highly frequent irregular words.

Let's Get Some Practice

Guide the children in reviewing the word by asking, "What is the first sound in *said*?" (Point to the first box as children chorally say /s/.) What letter? (Have children chorally say the letter name.) What is the last sound? (Point to the last box as children chorally say /d/.) What letter? (Have children chorally say the letter name.) What is the middle sound? (Point to the middle box as children chorally say /ĕ/.) What are the letters that spell /ĕ/? (Have children chorally say the letters *A-I*.) Then remind them the *ai* is the part they need to learn by heart. Your word card will now look like this.

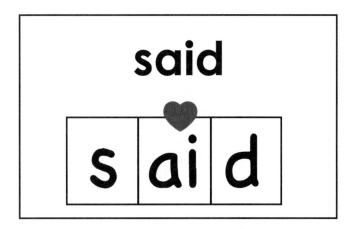

Wrap It Up

"Nice job reading our word today. What is our word? (Point to *said* and have children chorally read it.) There are three sounds in *said*. Say them with me. (Point to each box as you say the sounds.) What is the part we need to learn by heart? (Encourage children to respond, "*ai*.") *Said* will be in our book today. Look out for it!"

> **Connect to a Book!**
>
> Helping children notice these words in the texts they read as well as in the books you read aloud to them will help them "see them everywhere." For example, as you are reading *Sam and Dave Dig a Hole* by Mac Barnett, you can point out the word *said* as it comes up and reference your heart word. Or you can invite children to hunt for your heart word *said* on a page after you've read it.

ACTIVITY Around the World

Get Things Ready

Write previously learned high-frequency words on cards. Either have enough cards for each child or pair them so each pair gets one card. Sit in a circle and hand out cards.

Make an Introduction

"Today we'll play Around the World! We'll read our words around our circle. . . or around the world!

Now for the Model

"First, let's read our words together." As you hold up a word, chorally read each word. If children have difficulty, use your heart-word language to support their reading. You can refer to the word's heart-word card if it's on display. For this activity there isn't a model.

Let's Get Some Practice

Children will sit in a circle and read their cards aloud. Then you'll have them switch cards and go around the world. I usually go around the world by passing cards one to the right until everyone or every partnership has gotten the chance to read each word.

Wrap It Up

"Nice job reading our words. We know we'll see these words a lot when we read, so let's get one more round of practice. Read them with me." (Chorally read each word as you show the card.)

> **Flex the Activity!**
> You can play Around the World with decodable words for extra practice. You can also play around the world with letters. Children can name upper- and lowercase letters or they can provide letter sounds.

ACTIVITY Sentence Building

Get Things Ready

Collect decodable and irregular, highly frequent words that you've previously studied. The main goal of this activity is to have repeated practice with words in the context of a sentence. For example, you've previously taught *my, is, have, the, was.* You've also spent a lot of time practicing consonant sounds and short vowels. You might have words collected to make the following sentences:

- My mom is fun.
- You have my top.
- The top was fun.
- My mom was hot.

Make cards for each of these words; there are only ten. I try to reuse words in the sentences to keep the number of cards low.

You can do this as a whole-group activity where you are supporting them build and read each sentence as a group. Or you can make sets for each child. I usually have a workspace for each child if they are going to build and read their own sentences. I also keep a sticky note pad for quick adjustments like uppercase letters and ending punctuation.

Make an Introduction

"We are going to build sentences today! First, let's read the words we'll use in our sentences." (Show each card and chorally read. Support their reading as necessary.)

Now for the Model

"I'm going to put my word cards at the bottom of my workspace. Now I'm going to build my first sentence—My mom is fun. This is true. My mom *is* fun! I need to find *my.* I remember *my* from our heart words. M-Y. (Pull *my* to the top left of your workspace.) My mom. . . now I need to find *mom.* Here it is. . . M-O-M. (Place *mom* beside *my.*) My mom is. . . okay. *Is.* (Pull *is* up next.) My mom is fun. Here's *fun*. It's my only word that starts with /f/. (Pull *fun* up to complete your sentence.) Here is my sentence. Point and read with me. (Point to each word as you and children chorally read each word.) I know sentences start with an uppercase letter. (Write *my* with an uppercase *M* on a sticky note and put it over your *my*.) I also know my sentence needs to end with a period. (Write a period on a sticky note and put it at the end of your sentence.) Now let's point and read the sentence once more together." (Point to each word as the group chorally reads.)

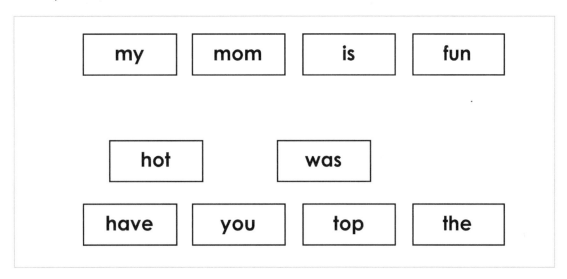

Let's Get Some Practice

"Okay. Let's pull all our words back to the bottom of the workspace. Let's make a new sentence. You have my top. Say it with me. You have my top. What's our first word?" Continue with this process as you build each sentence. Note: If I'm doing this as a group, I'll work through each sentence as in the model, inviting the children to be involved. If I'm having children build their own sentences, then I'll bring us back together and check each sentence as we go. If children have difficulty, read up to the word they are missing and guide them in thinking about the first sound. Or you can reduce their choice and pull up two words for them to consider. If they have difficulty reading the sentence when finished, point and read it to them and have them repeat.

Flex the Activity!

I've built this activity to focus on practice reading highly frequent words. You could switch it and focus on decodable words with sentences such as, *The frog can flip.* You can also have children hunt for words to clear your workspace. For example, if you are working as a group, you could invite children to come up one at a time to find specific words like "a word that rhymes with *stop*" or "a word that starts with /th/." Children must accurately read the word before they clear it.

Wrap It Up

"Wow. We built a lot of sentences today and got practice reading our words. I know you've seen some of these words many times in our books. Let's get one last read in! Read them with me." (Show the cards in random order as the children chorally read and you clear the workspace.)

ACTIVITY **Reading Decodable Texts**

Get Things Ready

Choose a small book or short text with words that are decodable for children. Sometimes these texts might be very focused on specific phonic features (for example, *Ted's Red Sled* published by Modern Curriculum Press has many short *e* words). But they can also cross many features that you've previously studied (for example, *Fran Can Flip* published by Flyleaf surveys across many consonant sounds as well as short *a* and *o*; Appleton-Smith, 2010). You can read this as a group and provide children with text copies. Or you could have a set of books for all children to have and read.

Make an Introduction

"We're going to read a book together. First, I'll read with you, and then you will get to read on your own!" Talk with children about the book's title, author, and illustrator. Then take children through a brief perusal of the book as you make note of some things happening in the illustrations. But the main purpose here is to introduce any words you think might be difficult. In which case, make note of them, write them on the board, and model either sound-by-sound blending or continuous blending.

Now for the Model

"Let's read. We'll read it one page at a time. First, you'll whisper-read to yourself, and then we'll read the same page together. Watch me whisper-read the first page." Whisper-read the first page as you move your finger under each word. Then invite the children to whisper-read the same page. After everyone has whisper-read the page, invite the children to go back to the beginning of the same page as you all point and read the page aloud.

Let's Get Some Practice

Read the rest of the book with children. First whisper-read the page and then chorally read the same page. After you've read the entire book in this way, you can invite children to whisper-read the whole book as you listen to them individually. If you feel the children need more support, you can chorally read the book for a second time rather than having them whisper-read individually. You can also pair them up to read to each other; in these cases, you will want to show them the procedure of taking turns as they read with a buddy.

Look For

During a reading, you are looking for a handful of things. First, you have the opportunity to observe children decoding as they use their letter sounds to blend for a word. Second, you can get an idea of how accurately they are blending words and any letter sounds they confuse in the context of book reading. Third, you can take a note of the irregular, highly frequent words you've taught and whether they are able to accurately read them in context. Lastly, you can get an understanding of their persistence and monitoring. Sometimes early readers try a word out and continue on even if their decoding attempt was unsuccessful. They may also move on even when the word does not make sense.

Wrap It Up

During the wrap-up, I usually revisit words we reviewed before reading the book. I always ask one or two questions about what happened in the book and encourage children to respond in complete sentences.

ACTIVITY Word Hunts in Books

Get Things Ready

Select a decodable text that has multiple examples of the target features. Make sure the book has already been read. Children can hunt in books, but you can also make text-only copies of books for children to have and circle or highlight their finds. Also, you can do this as a group and use highlighting tape in a book. If my book is large enough, I sometimes use Wikki Stix.

Make an Introduction

"Today we are going to hunt in books to find words we've been working on. This will give us some extra practice!"

Now for the Model

Early readers will need a great deal of support to have success with a word hunt. Model for them many times to ensure they understand the task. For example, let's say you are hunting for words with short e with *Ted's Red Sled*. You would read aloud page by page: "'So Ted went back to bed.' *So.* That doesn't have /ĕ/ like our keyword *bed. Ted.* That does. *Ted. Bed.* They both have /ĕ/. I'm going to highlight *Ted. So Ted went.* Hmmm. *Went* has an *e*, but it doesn't say /ĕ/. *So Ted went back. Back* has /ă/ and not /ĕ/. *To.* I know that doesn't work. *Bed. Bed* does have /ĕ/. Plus, it's our keyword! I'm going to highlight *bed.* On this page, we found *Ted* and *bed.*"

▢ Let's Get Some Practice

Continue with each page in this way and invite children to help you hunt for your words. Sometimes it's fun to set a goal to find ten words (or whatever number makes sense given your book). You can keep a tally and see how close you get!

▢ Wrap It Up

"We found so many words in our hunt today! Let's read our words." (Support children as you go through and chorally read the words you found and highlighted in your book.)

Classic Games

So many classic games lend themselves to practicing reading words, both in isolation and in context. In chapter 4, we looked at the classics Bingo and Matching. Both of these games work well here, too. You can play to practice decodable words; highly frequent, irregular words; or both! To play Bingo, you can create your bingo boards. I generally keep my board to sixteen cells at most. You want your games to be fast-paced, and too many cells can make the game too long.

You can have children draw word cards to match, or you can have them draw sentence cards to read and match the underlined word. Here is an example with a nine-cell board with short, simple sentences. I often have children partner up to support each other.

<<< B I N G O >>>		
was	that	from
are	or	can
all	have	do

__That__ cat is on a mat.

__Are__ you at the top?

I __can__ see the bed.

Matching can be played with words, but you can also find matches in different ways. You can match the same words or match words with a common feature (for example, matching by short vowel sound), or you can match a word to an underlined word in a sentence. Regardless, I usually have no more than ten pairs, or twenty cards. Card stock is useful for the cards because you cannot see the print when the cards are turned over. To make a match, matches always have to be read aloud. Children can also write each word from their matches. This extension of recording their matches allows for one quick, additional practice with the words.

TYPE OF MATCHING	EXAMPLES		HOW TO DO IT
Word to same word	cat	cat	Child matches word to same word and notes common spelling
Word to different word (decodable words only)	cat	hat	Child matches word to different word and notes common feature
Word to sentence	cat	The cat sat on the mat.	Child matches word with word used in a sentence

While not a game we think of as a classic, I love the Parking Lot game (Scanlon, Anderson, and Sweeney, 2017). It's such an easy, spur-of-the-moment game. Maybe it will become a classic for you as it has for me. To play this game, draw parking lots on pieces of paper with two rows of five or six spaces. Provide one parking lot for each child. I honestly draw them quickly on a dry-erase board, but you could have them laminated to pull out whenever you like. Write target words in each parking space, making sure words are right side up for children to read and each parking lot has the same words but in different spaces. Like the other games, these words can be decodable words, high-frequency words, or both. Children can have toy cars to park in their lot. For example, you might say, "Park your car on the word *where*." Or invite children to park and ask, "What space is your car in?" Once they have parked their cars, tell them they need to "back up" and get ready to park again. Here are two examples: the top with highly frequent words and the bottom with decodable words.

that	was	are	we	they	no
one	she	from	so	me	said

pat	hum	mop	sat	bed	lip
nut	top	big	met	rip	tag

To Sum It Up

Providing children with opportunities to build their foundational fluency skills and begin to build a bank of words they know without hesitation or the need to decode is essential for our early readers. The activities in this chapter can give the children the support and practice they need as they learn more about how print works, how to use letter sounds to blend and decode words, and how to practice reading words to build a collection of words they know. Including activities like the ones in this chapter as part of a comprehensive framework will help your learners become readers *and* writers.

CHAPTER SIX
Supporting Comprehension, Vocabulary, and World Knowledge

6

This chapter, while related to oral language, is focused on building early comprehension for both narrative and informational texts as well as building vocabulary and world knowledge through read-alouds. Activities will all include reading aloud for two purposes: helping children actively engage with text and building concept knowledge and vocabulary. To begin, let's take a look at the early literacy standards from the Head Start Early Learning Outcome Framework and the Common Core State Standards that address comprehension.

HEAD START EARLY LEARNING OUTCOME FRAMEWORK—36-60 MONTHS	COMMON CORE STATE STANDARDS— KINDERGARTEN
■ Retells familiar stories using props (36 months). ■ Asks to have several favorite books read over and over (36 months). ■ Uses pictures as a guide to talk about a story that has been read (36 months). ■ Asks or answers questions about what is happening in a book or story (36 months). ■ Identifies the feelings of characters in a book or story (36 months). ■ Retells or acts out a story that was read, putting events in the appropriate sequence, and demonstrating more sophisticated understanding of how events relate, such as cause and effect relationships (60 months). ■ Tells fictional or personal stories using a sequence of at least 2-3 connected events (60 months). ■ Identifies characters and main events in books and stories (60 months).	■ With prompting and support, ask and answer questions about key details in a text narrative and informational texts. ■ With prompting and support, retell familiar stories, including key details, in narrative text. ■ With prompting and support, identify the main topic and retell key details in informational text. ■ With prompting and support, identify characters, settings, and major events in a story in narrative text. ■ With prompting and support, describe the connection between two individuals, events, ideas, or pieces of information in informational text. ■ Ask and answer questions about unknown words in a text in narrative and informational texts.

HEAD START EARLY LEARNING OUTCOME FRAMEWORK—36-60 MONTHS	COMMON CORE STATE STANDARDS— KINDERGARTEN
■ Answers questions about details of a story with increasingly specific information, such as when asked, "Who was Mary?" responds, "She was the girl who was riding the horse and then got hurt" (60 months).	■ Name the author and illustrator of a text and define the role of each in presenting the ideas or information in a text.
■ Answers increasingly complex inferential questions that require making predictions based on multiple pieces of information from the story; inferring characters' feelings or intentions; or providing evaluations of judgments that are grounded in the text (60 months).	■ With prompting and support, describe the relationship between illustrations and the story in which they appear.
	■ With prompting and support, compare and contrast adventures and experiences of characters in familiar narrative texts.
■ Provides a summary of a story, highlighting a number of the key ideas in the story and how they relate (60 months).	■ With prompting and support, identify basic similarities in and differences between two informational texts on the same topic.
	■ With prompting and support, identify the reasons an author gives to support points in an informational text.
	■ Actively engage in group reading activities with purpose and understanding.

First off, reading aloud to children can be simply that—reading aloud. There are times in the day when you will be reading aloud for fun. These books may be fun choices you just want to share, or perhaps children are having an "off" day and need something to redirect their energy. Or maybe you've covered a difficult topic in math or reading/phonics, and they need a mental break. In these moments, take a few minutes and simply read aloud to enjoy a book and each other.

Books also help us create our classroom community. We share an experience through a book, especially books that elicit a laugh or a cry. Take Mo Willems's Elephant and Piggie series—a series that guarantees a good belly laugh or two while also teaching about being a good friend. Or the heaviness we feel when we follow alongside the invisible boy in Trudy Ludwig's The Invisible Boy or see Vanessa's experience in Kerascoët's I Walk with Vanessa.

Let's think about the books we choose. First, books read aloud in early childhood classrooms can be grouped into narrative (fiction), expository (nonfiction), and mixed genres with narrative as the most commonly read aloud in early childhood classrooms (Pentimonti, Zucker, and Justice, 2011). So, a first consideration is looking to include more books across these three groups. Second, we are more likely to infuse higher-level thinking into our interactive read-alouds when we read books that have more sophisticated language and vocabulary. Consider the language sophistication of the book and the potential vocabulary words. Lastly, books can be windows to help us learn about other worlds or think about perspectives other than our own. They can also be mirrors, acknowledging children's worth. "The world is best if we all learn to respect, appreciate, and honor our mutual humanity—and strive to understand the different ways in which people and societies think and live (Yokota and Teale, 2017). With this in mind, consider how a book might open our eyes to other things or encourage empathy.

Now, let's think about the read-aloud itself. Reading aloud is a performance—it's storytelling. It takes time and intentional practice to get better at it. Think about these qualities to make the experience even richer for children.

TONE	PITCH	PACE, PAUSE, VOLUME
Match your tone to the mood of the text as you consider the author's purpose	Change it up by character	Create suspense with a slowed pace, dramatic pauses, and increased volume as excitement builds
▪ *Outside In* by Deborah Underwood is described as "quietly profound" and should be read as such. ▪ Ryan T. Higgins's Mother Bruce series is as silly as it comes, inviting a silly, fun-loving tone.	▪ *Grumpy Monkey* by Suzanne Lang includes one grumpy monkey who encounters many friends who try to cheer him up. ▪ Each color monster in *The Color Monster: A Story About Emotions* by Anna Llenas lends itself to a changing pitch relative to its mood.	▪ Follow the eggs in *The Great Eggscape* by Jory John to see if they are ever reunited as you build suspense. ▪ See if Tiny can figure out how to hug his friend with his tiny arms in *Tiny T. Rex and the Impossible Hug* by Jonathan Stutzman as you read with dramatic effect.

Reading aloud isn't just about performance, though. There is another equally important ingredient—active participation. Studies have shown that the way we read aloud to children is just as important to how frequently we read aloud to them (Whitehurst and Lonigan, 2001). It makes sense. When children are active participants during the read-aloud, they show greater language and literacy gains than if we simply read the book to them.

All of this said, the focus of this chapter is about intentional vocabulary, world knowledge, and comprehension development through reading aloud. No doubt, your classroom is already flooded with read-alouds. Read-aloud practice that includes a style of interactive reading to encourage discussion about the book is a key ingredient (National Early Literacy Panel, 2008). In early childhood classrooms, reading aloud to children supports later reading comprehension through building vocabulary and world knowledge as well as providing a space to practice higher-level thinking skills like inferential thinking skills (Storch and Whitehurst, 2002).

Vocabulary

A read-aloud sparks conversation. Through the content of the book and these conversations, children's vocabularies grow. This type of vocabulary growth is incidental, but you can also be intentional about the words you are highlighting and helping children learn. In fact, children learn more vocabulary when they hear stories more than once and when teachers provide word explanations (Beck and McKeown, 2007). Creating a language-learning classroom is a good first step.

For now, let's consider our word choice. Beck, McKeown, and Kucan (2013) suggest a few considerations. First, you want to target "tier two" words. These are words that you are likely to encounter in a wide variety of texts and are a part of the oral language of a "mature language user." Second, choose words that can be explained in familiar words they already know. Lastly, think about whether they are important to our understanding of key events or concepts in the book and if the children are likely to use the words in their everyday conversations in the classroom and beyond. The bottom line is you want to evaluate a word's instructional potential and thematic or topical relatedness.

Murray (2010) estimates that 40 percent of English words are *polysemous*, meaning they have multiple meanings. Think about the word *run*. It's estimated to have 645 distinct meanings. National Public Radio ran a story in 2011 asking, "Has *run* run amok?" (Winchester, 2011). I might go for a *run* with a nose that is *running* and get a *run* in my tights when I *run* into a branch while I'm *running* against the clock! Consider whether a word has more than one meaning. You can explicitly explain the differences between these words' meanings. For example, when reading *Tall, Tall Tree* by Anthony D. Fredericks and learning about redwood trees, a child might ask about a dog because of the word *bark*. But, of course, in this case, the author is talking about bark on the trees. So, you may choose a word that is more a part of our everyday word register, or Beck, McKeown, and Kucan's "tier one" words, but has a new meaning.

After considering word choice, think about the remaining principles. I'll unpack them with the book *Poe Won't Go* by Kelly DiPucchio and demonstrate with one word from the book— *concentrate*. My child-friendly explanation is that to *concentrate* is to think very carefully about what you are doing. In *Poe Won't Go*, Marigold concentrates when she listens to Poe. Marigold says you can speak elephant if you listen hard enough or if you concentrate hard enough. I'd have the children say the word with me—*concentrate*. I concentrate when I'm planning what we do in class. This is a time I think very carefully about what I'm doing. Or I concentrate when I'm learning something new such as how to swing a golf club. I'd have the children share when they concentrate by saying, "I concentrate when I ___." We'd play a quick thumbs-up, thumbs-down game with scenarios to interact with the word: eating lunch (thumbs-down) or sliding at recess (thumbs-down) or trying to spell a new word (thumbs-up). With multiple readings across the week and at various times in the day, I'd offer additional practice and observe their use.

World Knowledge

Our world knowledge plays a major role in our comprehension of language, both oral and written. Successful reading comprehension depends heavily on how much we know about a topic. Your read-alouds can help build world knowledge in a multitude of ways, but here I'll mention two. First, children need to understand how different texts are structured. Young children need to learn about the structure of narrative books with characters and the problems they experience that lead to some sort of resolution. They also need to learn about the ways expository books are structured and how we use features like graphs and diagrams or bolded words. Second, children learn a great deal about the world through read-alouds. Reading a book like *The Honeybee* by Kirsten Hall can introduce children to honeybees and their important work, or a book like *Jabari Jumps* by Gaia Cornwall details a young boy's fear of jumping off the high dive and how he solves that problem, or a book like *Giraffes* by Laura Marsh gives children the opportunity to explore features of expository books such as captions and diagrams while also learning more about giraffes and where they live. The activities in this chapter provide opportunities for you to explore the structures of these books you read aloud in your classrooms.

Comprehension

Successful comprehension is dependent on language abilities that the children have been developing since birth. However, successful comprehension when listening to (or reading) books depends on more than our language abilities. Children also need to draw upon higher-level skills such as inferencing, monitoring comprehension, and using text structure. Think about this little story: *I was walking with a bowl of popcorn. I tripped. I had to grab a broom.* To understand what's happened here, you have to infer that I spilled the popcorn when I tripped to explain why I grabbed a broom. If you don't make that inference, you will wonder what a broom has to do with the story as you monitor your comprehension. Consider this little story: *My dog loves to be outside. I take him for a walk every day, but today he slipped out of his collar. Then he ran down the street away from me!* Now, you are using your knowledge about the problem/solution structure of narrative texts and predicting that either he comes back or I catch up to him.

Children learn more from our read-alouds when they are active participants in activities that we've intentionally planned. When it comes to comprehension, we want to encourage them to be strategic about their thinking. They'll be more engaged with our read-alouds when we challenge them to think about the books on a deeper level. We encourage them to think deeper through the questions we ask and the interactions we provide for them to have with us and with each other. We encourage them to make connections and predictions, to ask questions and visualize, to infer and determine importance.

This isn't to say there isn't a home for literal comprehension; for example, this establishes the foundation upon which we build our higher-level thinking. Think about it this way: you needed to know I had that bowl of popcorn when I tripped in order to infer that I spilled it. Our young children need prompting to move their language in this direction. Zucker and Landry (2010) suggested a 70 percent to 30 percent split of literal to inferential thinking/questioning during our read-alouds. While I acknowledge this split, the activities in this chapter primarily focus on how we can encourage this higher-level, strategic thinking while listening to a read-aloud.

Read-Aloud Routines

We get the best results from interactive and engaging read-aloud routines that are thoughtfully *and* intentionally planned with an eye to vocabulary, world knowledge, and comprehension development. To this end, we'll follow a framework of how we support children before reading, during reading, and after reading. We'll also consider how we support their deeper thinking through repeated reading routines.

REPEATED READINGS

Not every book should be a part of our repeated reading routine; some are meant for a solo reading for a needed break, a needed laugh, or an interesting sidebar. It is our target books for intentional practice that follow a repeated reading routine. Repeated reading helps to build vocabulary because having several exposures to words in a book give children more opportunities to associate and store new words. Repeated readings also help children move their attention to learn about other things. For example, perhaps they were focused on print concepts in the first reading but the content of the story in the second and third readings. Many suggest 45 minutes per day of reading aloud, which could include three 15-minute sessions

(Shanahan and Lonigan, 2013). Specifically, current guidance recommends you read a book at least three times over a short period of time such as a week or two (Paulson and Moats, 2018). You might think about your repeated interactive read-alouds in this way:

PURPOSE	WHAT TO DO
First Read: gain a basic, overarching understanding of the book	■ Introduce target vocabulary with child-friendly explanations contextualized in the book. ■ Ask mostly literal questions to create a baseline of understanding. ■ Think aloud to model how you make inferences about a character's feelings or establish problems and predict possible solutions and so on. ■ Wrap up with questions to encourage higher-level thinking.
Second Read: deepen understanding by pointing out new information and vocabulary	■ Focus on your target vocabulary with child-friendly explanations within the context of the book and beyond. ■ Engage children with opportunities for higher-level thinking, including activities to engage with target vocabulary.
Third Read: ensure overall comprehension	■ Encourage connections to prior knowledge (for example, similar context, synonym for vocabulary word). ■ Narrative: Review story structure with problem, events, and solution. Talk about character feelings and motivation. ■ Expository: Review key concepts and vocabulary. Connect to previously learned information.

BEFORE, DURING, AND AFTER

These individual readings follow a before, during, and after reading framework. Before reading, you might preteach key vocabulary, introduce a concept such as visualizing to help children understand what the author is telling them, or activate prior knowledge. Ultimately, you are setting a purpose for the reading. During reading, you will have your intentional stopping points where you make connections, monitor children's understanding, and generate questions. Basically, during reading you are actively engaging with the book and staying focused. After reading, you can help children think about the book and what they just learned. You are building up to a deeper understanding. For example, you might lead children in a discussion about a conflict that was resolved or how a character changed in the book.

The upcoming read-alouds in the activities will follow this before, during, after framework. While we know you'll be reading many of these books multiple times, these readings will be outlined for one read-aloud session. This said, if you are reading a lengthy book or a book with a hefty concept, break it up over a couple of reading sittings or take a brain break. You might invite children to turn and talk or even take a walk around the room. You could have them act out something in the book or stop and ask them to skywrite an important word as you say the letter names. While the upcoming activities can be used with a variety of books, each one will be tied to a specific book for illustration. We'll begin with activities to teach vocabulary and move to activities to support narrative structure, building world knowledge through expository books, and introducing higher-level thinking through comprehension strategies.

Teach Vocabulary

What are best practices for facilitating vocabulary learning? Beck, McKeown, and Kucan (2013) map out the following principles in mind to keep in mind.

- Choose words intentionally and build upon them over time.

- Provide child-friendly explanations for new words.

- Contextualize words within *and* beyond the read-aloud.

- Have children say words aloud.

- Offer frequent activities to get them to interact with the words.

- Include periodic reviews.

- Observe children's use of the words.

In the following activities, let's see how these principles are implemented during an interactive read-aloud.

ACTIVITY Introducing Vocabulary

Get Things Ready

Choose your book; narrative or expository is completely fine. You'll need to prepare a few things. For each word, you will need a child-friendly explanation, a sentence to give it context with a question or two about that context, and a quick way to help them connect with the word. For this activity, I'm going to quickly use an activity called "have you ever. . . " to help them connect with the words (Beck, McKeown, and Kucan, 2013). Here are six words from *Hoot Owl* by Sean Taylor as an example: *midnight, disguise, gobble, wise, helpless, disappear.* Here's the word *midnight* laid out as an example.

MIDNIGHT		
Child-friendly explanation	**Context sentence + questions**	**Quick connection**
this is the middle of the night when we are asleep	I woke up at midnight last night, and it was so dark I couldn't see the end of my bed! ■ When did I wake up? ■ Was it day or night? How do you know?	Have you ever. . . woken up in the middle of the night. . . past midnight? What was it like in your house?

I usually keep the words to two or three per reading, meaning I'll get to all six after three repeated readings.

Make an Introduction

"We are going to learn some new words today. We'll hear these words in the book we're reading—*Hoot Owl* by Sean Taylor and illustrated by Jean Jullian. (Show the book.) A hoot owl is a type of owl." (It's actually called a barred owl, but you don't need to tell children that.) "It's a good name for an owl since the sound an owl makes is called a *hoot*. Let me hear a soft hoot. . . at the count of three. 1, 2, 3. . . hoot."

Now for the Model

"Our first word is *midnight*. Say it with me. *Midnight*. Some of you may have heard this word before. Let me tell you about it. Midnight is the middle of the night when we are asleep. I woke up at midnight last night, and it was so dark I couldn't see the end of my bed! When did I wake up? (Encourage responses, making sure they are saying *midnight*.) Was it day or night? How do you know? (Encourage responses, making sure to reiterate midnight is the middle of the night when we are asleep.) Have you ever. . . woken up in the middle of the night, after midnight? Thumbs-up if you have ever woken up past midnight. It looks like almost all of us have been awake after midnight. Let's turn and talk with our talking partners. Here's our question: What is it like in your house after midnight?" (Come back together and talk about descriptors of a house at night: dark, quiet, everyone asleep, etc.)

"Our second word is *disguise*. Say it with me. *Disguise*. A disguise is something you put on so no one knows who you are. The wolf in 'Little Red Riding Hood' wore a disguise when he acted like Granny. Little Red thought he *was* Granny! What did the wolf wear?" (Encourage responses, making sure they are saying *disguise*.) "Why did he wear a disguise?" (Encourage responses, making sure to note Little Red wouldn't know who he was.) "Have you ever worn a disguise or know someone else who has? Thumbs-up if you have ever worn a disguise. Thumbs-up if you know someone else who wore a disguise. Let's get back with our talking partners. Describe the disguise." (Come back together and note how the disguise made it hard for people to know who they were.) "In this book, the hoot owl is looking for something good to eat. Let's read and find out what he finds to eat. And remember, thumbs-up when you hear *midnight* and *disguise*!"

Let's Get Some Practice

"When I'm reading today, listen for our two words: *midnight* and *disguise*. When you hear one of them, put your thumbs up!" Put your thumb up when you come to the words and stop briefly to narrate how the author is using the words in the context of the book. It might sound something like this: "Thumbs-up! I have my thumb up and so do you. The author starts out saying 'the darkness of midnight is all around me.' We talked about how midnight is the middle of the night when it is dark. And look how dark the illustrator made it! The midnight sky is black. What's our word? *Midnight*. Yes, the darkness of midnight!" You'll also have at least one other stopping point when you revisit the question of what he finds to eat and how a disguise factors in.

Wrap It Up

"We had fun reading about Hoot Owl and how he finally found a tasty pizza to eat! We also read our words *midnight* and *disguise*. Everybody, when was owl out? During the day? Or at midnight? (Encourage a choral response: midnight!) And, everybody, Hoot Owl is a master of. . . ? (Encourage a choral response: disguise!) Today during writing, we are going to draw disguises for ourselves and write about how no one knows who we are!"

Look For

As you provide more opportunities for children to practice vocabulary words, you will look for times they use the words appropriately. You can keep a chart of this to have a record. You could also make a chart where you have these words posted with a visual from your book and put stickers by the words every time you notice someone using them, including yourself as you model using the words. Your chart might look like this. (Note: stars indicate times we used the words.)

Thumbs-Up/Thumbs-Down

Get Things Ready

This is an activity to review previously learned vocabulary words. Collect six to ten words. Then create a brief context for the children to give a thumbs-up or a thumbs-down. I'll use our six words from *Hoot Owl* by Sean Taylor as an example. Notice I have thumbs-up and thumbs-down examples to use in random order.

WORD	BRIEF CONTEXT
midnight	■ It is midnight in the morning when I wake up. ■ It is midnight when I'm asleep at night.
disguise	■ I wear a disguise every day to school. ■ I wear a disguise on Halloween.
wise	■ I am wise when I eat so much ice cream, I get a belly ache. ■ I am wise when I take turns going down the slide.
gobble	■ I gobble up food I don't like. ■ I gobble up my favorite vegetable.
helpless	■ I am helpless showing a visitor where our pencil sharpener is. ■ I am helpless tying shoes because I don't know how to tie shoes yet.
disappear	■ Look at our door. Keyshawn walked in and disappeared. ■ Look at our door. Abigail walked out and disappeared.

Make an Introduction

"We're going to practice our words from *Hoot Owl*. We'll play thumbs-up/thumbs-down. I'm going to use the word in a sentence. If I use it correctly, we'll put our thumbs up. If I use it wrong, we'll put our thumbs down."

Now for the Model

"I'll go first. My word is *gobble*. Here's my sentence: I gobble up food I don't like. Nooooo! Thumbs-down. I used gobble wrong. I remember *gobble* means eating really fast, especially with foods we like. Hoot owl wanted to gobble up the rabbit."

Let's Get Some Practice

Present the children with a new word and say your sentence. Support them as they put their thumbs up or down by reminding them of the word's meaning and how it was used in the book as necessary. With each word, engage them in a discussion of why they put their thumbs up or down as they connect the sentence context with the word's meaning.

Wrap It Up

"Nice job thinking about our words from *Hoot Owl*! Let's see how many times we hear someone use one of our words or how many times we can use them ourselves! I don't know about you, but I brought one of my favorite snacks today for lunch. I'm going to gobble it down!"

> **Flex the Activity!**
>
> You could play thumbs-up/thumbs-down in a slightly different way. Instead of creating sentence contexts, you would think of examples and nonexamples of your vocabulary words. You could have the children put their thumbs up if you give an example of a disguise and thumbs down if it's not an example of a disguise: a police officer wearing a uniform, me wearing a wig and sunglasses, hoot owl wearing a carrot costume, a doctor wearing a long, white coat, you wearing a mask and a hat.

ACTIVITY Act Out Vocabulary

Get Things Ready

While you can do this activity when you first introduce a vocabulary word, it's also a fun way to review previously taught words. You might think only verbs will work, but any type of word can work. For example, for the noun *disguise*, you would tell the children you are acting out a time when you wore a disguise as you describe what you did, using the word *disguise* frequently. Adjectives can work, too. Take the word *helpless*. You could act out a time you were helpless because you had hurt your hand and couldn't open a jar. So, to prepare for this activity, you'll want to have some scenarios children can act out. You can always act out the word as it appears in the book.

Make an Introduction

"We're going to act out our vocabulary words today! I'll say a word and remind us what it means. Then we'll think about ways we can act out that word."

Now for the Model

"Watch me. My word is *disguise*. What's my word? (Children chorally respond.) I remember a disguise is something you put on so that no one knows who you are. I'm going to act out how Hoot Owl was a master of disguise. (Act out, narrating as you go, how he made the carrot costume and put it on to trick the rabbit.) I'm going to be Hoot Owl. I'm going to make my disguise. I'm making a carrot costume so I can disguise myself from the rabbit. I'm going to put on my carrot costume and act like a carrot. This way the rabbit won't know who I am. I'm a master of disguise! What's my word?" Notice I used the word five times.

Let's Get Some Practice

You could follow this up by asking the children about a time they wore a disguise and no one knew who they were. Then invite one child to act out for the rest as you narrate what they are doing and use the word multiple times. Or you could move to the next word. Remember to provide the meaning again before acting it out. You could act out a scenario yourself, act out a scenario from the book, remind them of the scenario from the book and invite a child to act it out, etc. If needed, you could show a picture from the book to remind them about the context of the story. The bottom line is you are acting out or supporting children acting out while you narrate and use the word multiple times.

▮ Wrap It Up

"Acting out our words is a fun way for us to learn them. It will help us remember our new words. Let's pay attention to when we can use these words today! I already saw someone being wise today! Amelia was wise when she walked carefully around the circle to line up, because we had our book tubs out and she knew she needed to be careful so she wouldn't trip. Amelia was wise to walk around!"

Support Narrative Structure

In some ways, supporting narrative structure is building world knowledge. Events in our lives often mirror the elements of a story. For example, events sometimes have a beginning, middle, and end; they happen in a particular time and place; there are people who are involved; sometimes we experience conflict or a problem that hopefully gets resolved; and we sometimes learn a life lesson. So, children are already primed for this type of thinking, and they can think about what's most relevant to a story when they know about narrative story structure. The following activities will provide children with practice in understanding how stories work.

ACTIVITY Story Map

▮ Get Things Ready

Choose a book that has enough detail that you can discuss how the story begins, what happens in the middle, and how the story ends. I'm going to use Lisa Mantchev's *Strictly No Elephants* as an example. You'll need chart paper set up like this:

Beginning	Middle	End

▮ Make an Introduction

"We're going to make a story map today. A story map will help us think about the different parts of the story, such as what happens in the beginning, the middle, and the end." (Point to each part on your chart paper as you say it.) "It'll help us retell our story."

▮ Now for the Model

"Today we'll reread *Strictly No Elephants*. The author is Lisa Mantchev, and the illustrator is Taeeun Yoo. When we finish, we'll make a story map to help us think about the important things that happened in the story." As you read, stop at predetermined spots to discuss different story events as you emphasize things that happen in the beginning (setting the scene and establishing the problem), the middle (establishing the problem and attempting to solve it), and the end (resolving the problem). Notice, I said *reread*. The first read was focused on learning new words (for example, *strict/strictly, allow*) and talking about the lessons the author wanted to teach us about friendship.

Let's Get Some Practice

After reading, prompt children for events that happened at the beginning, middle, and end of the story. You will draw a quick picture and write a brief description. Then encourage the children to retell the story in their own words. You could do this by choosing children using your equity sticks to give you the beginning, then the middle, and then the end. Or you could have children turn and talk with a partner to talk about each part, one part at a time. You might find you need to model the retelling first and then invite them to retell.

Wrap It Up

"We made a story map to help us remember the important events in *Strictly No Elephants*. Our story map helped us retell our story and reminded us about the author's lessons about friendship. You can use the story map to help you retell the story to a friend today. I'll put our book in our library center!"

Connect to a Book!

As noted earlier, you will want to choose books with enough detail within the beginning, middle, and end to lend themselves to rich conversation. Moreover, you want stories with problems children can connect with. The following are some additional options:

- *Mother Bruce* by Ryan T. Higgins—the story of a grumpy bear who reluctantly finds himself the stand-in mother to gaggle of baby geese.

- *Alan's Big, Scary Teeth* by Jarvis—a tale about an alligator who likes to scare animals in the jungle with his scary teeth. But they are false teeth, and one day he finds they've gone missing.

- *Creepy Pair of Underwear* by Aaron Reynolds—the story of a rabbit who is all grown up and not afraid of the dark. . . that is, until he gets a creepy pair of underwear.

- *Out!* by Arree Chung—a book of very few words that tells a funny story about a baby who is not quite ready for bed and the dog who is trying to keep baby safe.

- *The Smallest Girl in the Smallest Grade* by Justin Roberts—a story of a small girl who hardly gets noticed but finds her voice to make a difference when she stands up to a bully.

- *Rulers of the Playground* by Joseph Kuefler—a story about two children who want to rule the playground but make playing there not much fun.

Let's Get to the Problem. . . and the Solution!

Get Things Ready

Select a book that has a clear problem with multiple attempts to solve it. You'll want to read the book and map out your predetermined stopping places where you can stop to fill out your before, during, and after chart. This time, though, your chart will highlight problem, attempts to fix it, and solution. I'll use *Charlotte the Scientist Is Squished* by Camille Andros as an example here. We'll do this work as a rereading of the book. Our first reading was devoted to connecting to Charlotte's problem and establishing an understanding of scientific experiments and why she needs more space. Set up your chart like this:

Problem (beginning)	Attempts to fix it (middle)	Solution (end)

Make an Introduction

"Let's reread *Charlotte the Scientist is Squished*. Remember what it means to be *squished*? It means you don't have any space. Let's squish in for a minute. (Encourage the children to move so that they have no space between each other.) Let's remember this when we read and think about Charlotte's problem. You may already have ideas, but let's get started reading first. And, as we read, let's think about what we do when we have a problem. We try to fix it and then find a solution."

Now for the Model

In this reading, you will fill out the chart that lists the problem, attempts to fix it, and the solution as you go. However, if you find children need more time with you modeling this type of thinking, engage them in a discussion as you read and fill in your chart after the reading.

Let's Get Some Practice

As you read, stop along the way to establish the problem. In this story, the problem isn't just that Charlotte is squished. It's because Charlotte does not have the space she needs to conduct her science experiments. Once established, draw a quick picture of her problem and label it with writing (Charlotte is squished and can't do her experiments). Then stop again along the way to record her attempts (she tries to make her siblings disappear, make herself invisible, etc.). Finally, after finishing the story, record how her problem gets solved (she finds the space she needs in her spaceship that she parks beside her family's house).

▢ Wrap It Up

"Nice work thinking about Charlotte's problem and all of the ways she tried to fix her problem. (Refer to your chart to encourage the children to list some of her attempts.) How did she end up solving her problem? (Encourage responses using your chart.) You can use our chart to help you retell the story to a friend today. I'll put *Charlotte the Scientist is Squished* in our library center!"

> **Flex the Activity!**
>
> A story map can help children practice retelling. Retelling is an important first step to summarization, which is an important part of reading comprehension in later grades. Give children a purpose for retelling such as it helps you remember what you've read and check your understanding. Or it is a great way to share a story or something you learned with a friend or a family member. For narrative, I will look to incorporate key characters, the setting, the problem and solution, and any other key events. You can also retell the expository books you are reading. For expository, I consider the topic, the author's purpose, the main idea, and at least two (and up to four or five) supporting details. A KWL chart or Venn diagram can be used to help support retellings.

ACTIVITY I Know How You Feel!

▢ Get Things Ready

Characters' feelings play a big role in narrative structure and help drive the plot. Choose a series of books where characters have feelings children can connect to such as *Green Pants* by Kenneth Kraelgel, *Horrible Bear!* by Ame Dyckman, *A Bike Like Sergio's* by Maribeth Boelts. For illustration here, I'll use *Jabari Jumps* by Gaia Cornwall. Make an anchor chart that outlines for children how we can learn about character feelings: their thoughts, or what they say, and their actions. You might have a chart like this:

You can also put gestures to this with your finger pointing to your head for "thoughts" and "sayings," move your arms like you are running in place for "actions," and then put your hands to your heart for "feelings." Identify your stopping points where your character has thoughts or actions that reveal their feelings. You can chart this by recording thoughts and actions. You can also pair your chart with hand gestures (for example, hand to heart for *feelings*).

Make an Introduction

"Today we are going to read *Jabari Jumps*. Gaia Cornwall is the author, and the illustrator is. . . guess who? Gaia Cornwall. She wrote the story *and* drew the pictures. While I read, I'm going to stop along the way when I've learned something about Jabari that will help me understand how he feels. Before we get started, let's look at the cover. Can you tell by the way he is standing on the diving board how he might feel? Have you ever felt that way? Turn and talk with your partner."

Now for the Model

As you come to your stopping points, explicitly point out your character's thoughts/sayings or actions and how you think they feel. For example, Jabari starts to let other children go ahead of him when he is in the line for the high dive. I'd stop here and say, "I'm noticing Jabari's actions here. He is letting the other children go ahead of him. This makes me think about this time I was nervous about trying a handstand. I kept trying to do it, but then I'd stop. I think he may be nervous, and that's why he keeps letting other children in front of him. So, his actions help me think about his feelings—that he's nervous. Maybe he's scared, too. I'm going to write this down under actions: He let children go first in line. Then I'm going to write nervous and scared under feelings. Let's keep reading to see what else we find out about how he feels."

Let's Get Some Practice

Keep reading and stopping as you go along. Before or after sharing your thinking, have children turn and talk to share their thoughts with their talking partners. You might need to have a sentence stem for them: "I think Jabari feels ___ because ___." If children are having difficulty, you can support their thinking by using the illustrations and talking about the expressions on Jabari's face. Or you can reduce the choices by asking if Jabari feels excited or scared. Then ask why. Or you can keep sharing your thinking and then ask them to share about a time they felt like Jabari.

Wrap It Up

"We thought about Jabari's thoughts, what he said, and his actions to help us understand his feelings. This helped us understand the problem in the story. He was scared about jumping off the high dive. How did we know he felt scared?" Encourage responses using his thoughts, sayings, and actions from the story as well as how their experiences helped them think about how Jabari must have felt.

> ### Connect to a Book!
> Books where the character's feelings change with the arc of the story are also good options. For example, *Hannah and Sugar* by Kate Berube follows a little girl named Hannah who is afraid of dogs at the beginning of the story and finds a special friend in Sugar, a dog in her neighborhood, by the end. Another option is *A Dog Wearing Shoes* by Sangmi Ko where Mini goes from wanting to keep a lost dog to wanting to help find the dog's owner in the end.

ACTIVITY Let's Compare!

Get Things Ready

You'll want a book where you can compare two characters like Cyril and Pat in Emily Gravett's *Cyril and Pat* or Jonah and Lennox in Joseph Kuefler's *Rulers on the Playground*. You can also compare characters across two books, such as *The Invisible Boy* by Trudy Ludwig and *The Smallest Girl in the Smallest Grade* by Justin Roberts. Read your book(s) and make note of where you will stop to highlight how these characters are alike and how they differ. You'll need chart paper to make a Venn diagram to compare and contrast the two characters. So, my Venn diagram of two characters who are a lot alike, Cyril and Pat, would look like this:

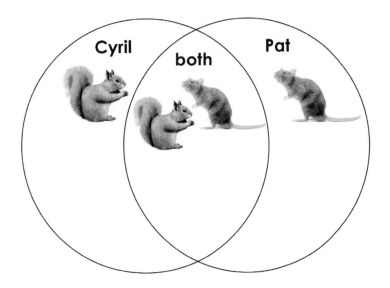

Make an Introduction

"We're going to read *Cyril and Pat* today. When we are reading, we are going to pay close attention to two characters in the story—Cyril and Pat. We're going to talk about them as we are reading. We're going to compare them. Get ready for Let's Compare!"

Now for the Model

Read the book as you normally would with your predetermined stopping points. The driving plot of the story is that Cyril has found a kindred spirit in Pat, but Cyril is a squirrel and Pat is a rat. Cyril's friends say squirrels can't be friends with rats. Stop as you go to highlight their similarities and this one big difference. I like to repeat 'Let's Compare!' when I get to one of these spots.

Let's Get Some Practice

"Let's take a look at my chart here. See my circles? This is called a Venn diagram. Let's say it together. Venn diagram. Our Venn diagram will help us organize our thinking about our characters, Cyril and Pat. See over here. (Point to the "both" circle.) This says both. We're going to put the ways Cyril and Pat are alike here. For things that are different, we'll put in the circle just for Cyril (Point to Cyril) and or here for Pat (Point to Pat)." As you guide children in a discussion about these characters, you'll be noticing many ways they are alike and one big way they are different—Cyril is a squirrel and Pat is a rat. Record on the Venn diagram as you go. You can use your oral language routines of expansions and questions to encourage more discussion and detail (see chapter 2). You can use the turn and talk strategy to get children talking to each other and thinking how Cyril and Pat are alike and different. You might need to support their conversations with sentence stems (for example, "One way Cyril and Pat are alike is. . .").

Wrap It Up

"We thought of many ways Cyril and Pat are alike and wrote it on our Venn diagram. We also thought about one big way they are different! How are they different? (Encourage the children to talk about squirrels and rats.) We compared our characters. Our Venn diagram helps us organize our ideas. I'm going to put our Venn diagram in our writing center. Today in the writing center, write about how Cyril and Pat are alike. You can pick any way you want!"

Flex the Activity!

Think about how you can intentionally incorporate both vocabulary and character study in your reading. For example, in *Cyril and Pat*, you might choose these three vocabulary words to target: *clever*, *brilliant*, and *outrun*. See the chart below that maps out how you might incorporate learning *clever* in your before, during, after routine.

Before Reading	Introduce one of your vocabulary words with a child-friendly explanation and context sentence + question:
	• *Clever* describes someone who can quickly solve a problem:
	Keyshawn was <u>clever</u> the other day at the word work center. He needed a letter *e* but couldn't find it in his letter tiles, so he made one out of paper. What was Keyshawn's problem? How did he quickly solve it?
	• Introduce using a Venn diagram to compare characters
	• Set your purpose for reading: pay close attention how Cyril and Pat are alike and how they are different.
During Reading	Read aloud and maintain the story thread and stop at your predetermined stopping points:
	• Key points where Cyril and Pat are alike
	• Key points where Cyril and Pat are different
	• Think aloud the context of the story where Pat is described as *clever* and connect to your child-friendly explanation.

| After Reading | ■ Turn to the illustration in the book where Pat was clever and ask what made Pat clever (encouraging the explanation of Pat quickly solving a problem). |
| | ■ Fill out the Venn diagram as you highlight character similarities and differences. |

Build World Knowledge

We learn new things by being taught by someone or by reading, or listening to, expository texts. It's easier for children to learn new concepts from our read-alouds if they also learn the process of connecting these new concepts to each other as well as previously learned knowledge. In other words, we are helping them structure and organize their world knowledge—something that develops over time and is modified and refined based on our experiences. These activities are offered to help children learn this process of connecting to build their world knowledge as they organize information based on common structures found in expository texts (for example, descriptive, compare/contrast, cause/effect). But first, we'll start with an approach to "reading to learn" from a book—thinking about what you know before you start, asking questions either before or as you go, and reflecting on what you learned. To do this, we'll use a KWL chart (Ogle, 1986).

ACTIVITY KWL Chart

Get Things Ready

This activity sets the stage for reading expository texts. Readers usually think about what they already know about a topic before reading. So, you'll want to choose a topic most children know about. I'm going to choose birds, specifically birds' nests. My book to illustrate a KWL is *Bird Builds a Nest* by Martin Jenkins. My main goal here is to demonstrate three things:

■ We read books to learn new things.

■ We connect to what we already know and see how this new knowledge fits.

■ We interact with books as we read to help us remember things we are learning.

The *K* stands for "what do I know" about a topic. I always say the *W* stands for "what I will learn about" (a slight variation of the "what I want to learn" from the original KWL), and the *L* stands for "what I learned." Set your chart up like this:

K what do I know	W what will I learn	L what did I learn

Make an Introduction

"We're going to use this chart today to help us organize what we know about bird nests. It will also help us remember the things we already know about bird's nests and the things we learn today from our book."

Now for the Model

"This chart is called a KWL chart. (Point to the letters as you say them.) When I get ready to read a book about something I am learning about, I always first think about what I already know. So, today we are reading about a bird's nest. I'm going to think about what I already know. That's my K. I know that a bird's nest is the bird's home. I'm going to write that in my K column. Home. I also want to ask myself some questions. Things I think I will learn about from my book. That's the W. I think I will learn about the things a bird uses to make the nest. I'm going to ask that question. What is a nest made of?"

Let's Get Some Practice

Let the children contribute to the K and W parts of the chart by facilitating a conversation about what they already know. You could have them turn and talk with their talking partners with the sentence stem, "I know birds ____." You can support asking questions by looking at some of the illustrations/pictures in the book. Sometimes you will find yourself posing questions that you know won't be answered. That's okay. Books don't answer every question. You could use your oral language routine of questioning to extend their thinking (see chapter 2). Then move to the reading. Stop periodically to answer questions or think aloud about things you are learning. That's the L part of the chart. For example, throughout *Bird Builds a Nest*, we find out birds use twigs small enough for them to carry and softer things like dried grass and feathers. As you read

Connect to a Book!

There are so many excellent expository books with topics of interest for our early learners. Each of these helps to build their world knowledge. Here are just a few suggestions:

- *Bat Loves the Night* by Nicola Davies— through a storytelling voice, this book captures a bat's life over the course of one night giving the reader (and listener) loads of information about bats.

- *Wolf Pups Join the Pack* by the American Museum of Natural History—a book that details a year in a wolf pup's life with engaging nature photography.

- *Trapped: A Whale's Rescue* by Robert Burleigh—a book inspired by true events that highlights the importance of our role in supporting and protecting all living creatures.

- *Tree of Wonder: The Many Marvelous Lives of a Rainforest Tree* by Kate Mesmer—a book that includes both accessible text for children and companion information for you to share as well as a fun hook inviting readers to hunt for and count the animals in the illustrations.

- *Hippos Are Huge!* by Jonathan London— another book that includes both accessible text for children and companion information for you to share.

- *Giant Squid* by Candice Fleming—a Robert F. Sibert Information Honor Book that includes a great deal of information about giant squid and more appropriate for our kindergartners.

these pages, stop and note you have learned something to put in your *L* column and write it in. I also add questions to my *W* as we go, too. We might even be reminded of something else we already knew for the *K* column. Remember, one of my goals is to demonstrate how we interact with books as we read; it's an active process rather than passive.

▢ Wrap It Up

"We did a great job thinking about bird's nests today. We thought about what we already knew. We wrote down some questions about what we thought we would learn. And we learned a lot! Let's review what we learned." Take a minute to talk through the *L* column.

ACTIVITY Learning Map

▢ Get Things Ready

Choose a book that will provide details about your topic. I'm going to use *Gray Squirrels* by G.G. Lake from the Woodland Wildlife series. These books have a table of contents that can speak to your categories for the map. You can build your map as you read or have it already set up. For *Gray Squirrels*, I've decided to build my map before reading to set up our purpose. My main goal is the same one as for the KWL activity–demonstrate the active process of learning from the books we read.

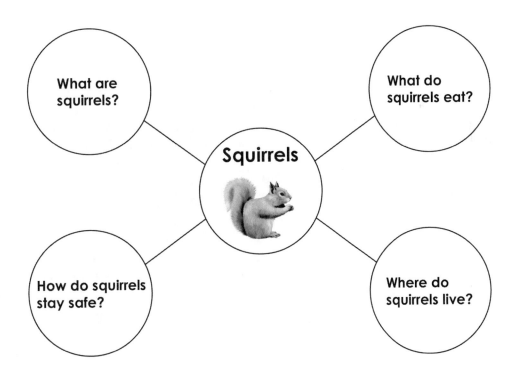

Make an Introduction

"We're going to map out our thinking today to help us organize what we are learning about squirrels. It will also help us remember the things we learn today from our book—*Gray Squirrels* by G.G. Lake. I'm going to call this a *learning map*."

Now for the Model

"G.G. Lake wrote this book to describe gray squirrels and tell us about their lives. When we read books where an author is telling us more about one thing, we can map out what we are learning and even things we already know. Watch me. I'm going to start our map. I have a circle in the middle with the word *squirrels* and a picture of a squirrel. I'm going to start thinking about squirrels and ask myself: What are squirrels? I'm going to draw a line from my squirrels circle and write my question. I might also put some things here that I already know. Turn and talk to your partner to think about what you know about squirrels." (Give children a brief moment to talk to their partners. Bring them back to share back and record appropriate responses such as small animal, bushy tail. Use questions and elaborations as discussed in chapter 2.) "Now I'm going to look at my book's table of contents. This tells me what G.G. Lake is going to tell us about. So, I know I'll read about their homes, the food they eat, how they stay safe, and baby squirrels. (Point to the table of contents.) I'm going to go ahead and draw lines from my circle to ask more questions. I'm going to read about their homes, so I'm going to ask: Where do squirrels live? (Quickly add your other questions.) Okay. Let's start reading. We'll stop when we read something that answers our questions." Note: I usually don't draw the circles until after, so we have plenty of space.

Let's Get Some Practice

As you read, stop to discuss your questions and record answers. You can engage the children by having them turn and talk or by inviting different children to respond using your equity sticks. You can also use oral language practices like questions and elaborations to extend their thinking. If needed, you can reread a sentence or section and invite them to listen for something specific.

Wrap It Up

"Wow. Look at our learning map! We learned a lot about squirrels. Let's review what we learned. (Take a minute to talk through your learning map.) I'm going to post our learning map about squirrels in our science center. You can practice telling your friends about squirrels or you can draw and write about squirrels."

Connect to a Book!

Learning maps (often called semantic maps) don't have to always be matched with expository books. You could have a discussion about squirrels before reading *Cyril and Pat*. Your map might begin with a map like the one here about gray squirrels to unpack with children about squirrels before reading the narrative book about the friendship between a squirrel (Cyril) and a rat (Pat). You can also pair your expository texts with narrative companions. For example, our book *Gray Squirrels* could be paired with *Cyril and Pat* (from the Comparing Characters activity). See the chart on the next page for suggestions for studying wolves and bats.

NARRATIVE OPTIONS	TOPIC	EXPOSITORY OPTIONS
■ *Bear and Wolf* by Daniel Salmieri ■ *Little Wolf's First Howling* by Laura McGee Kvasnosky ■ *The Little Wolf* by Hilary Yelvington	wolves	■ *I Wish I Was a Wolf* by Jennifer Bové ■ *Wolves* by Laura Marsh ■ *Safari Readers: Wolves* by Tristan Walters
■ *I Am Bat* by Morag Hood ■ *Bat Book* series by Brian Lies ■ *Superbat* by Matt Carr	bats	■ *All About Bats* by Caryn Jenner ■ *Bats* by Elizabeth Carney ■ *Zipping, Zapping, Zooming Bats* by Ann Earle

ACTIVITY Alike and Different

Get Things Ready

Two graphic organizers you can use to compare and contrast are Venn diagrams and comparison charts. I'm going to use a comparison chart with this activity. I like to set it up ahead of time on chart paper, and I usually do this activity after I've read books about the things I want to compare (for example, moths vs. butterflies, squares vs. circles). Here, though, we're going to create our chart as we go. There are also compare/contrast books you can read that set it up for you, such as *Sharks and Dolphins* by Kevin Kurtz. In fact, this book comes from a series called A Compare and Contrast Book.

Make an Introduction

"Sometimes the books we read compare things. When we compare things, we think about how they are alike and how they are different. Today we are going to compare sharks and dolphins."

Now for the Model

"We're going to put all of our thoughts in this chart. It will help us remember how sharks and dolphins are alike plus how they are different. Here's our book, *Sharks and Dolphins*, and our author is Kevin Kurtz. He wrote this book to help us learn about sharks and dolphins. He wanted us to learn how they are alike and how they are different. We're going to read about where they live, how they look, the kind of animal they are, and how they eat. (Point to your chart categories as you go.) I might know some things already. I think sharks and dolphins both live in the ocean. I'm going to read to make sure about that, so let's get started. (Start reading and stop to think aloud how you use the chart.) Our author starts out telling us something about where they live. They both live in the ocean. They are alike in that way—they both live in the ocean. So, I'm going to write that here to remind us one way they are alike. They both live in the ocean."

Sharks		Dolphins
	where they live ocean	
	how they look	
	kind of animal	
	how they eat	

Let's Get Some Practice

As you read, stop at your predetermined spots to talk about what you learned about their similarities and differences and note them on your chart. You can use language practices like elaborations and questions to encourage responses. You can also have children turn and talk or use your equity sticks to manage contributions. Doing this may take some time, so even with shorter books, you might need to break this up into more than one reading.

Flex the Activity!

You can also do this activity with your narrative texts. Like the Venn diagram with Cyril and Pat, you can compare characters with a comparison chart. You can also compare books like fractured fairy tales. With fractured fairy tales, I compare them across story elements (for example, setting, characters, events). You could read a version of the original Goldilocks fairy tale. Then read some fractured tales such as *Goldi Rocks* by Corey Rosen Schwartz and Beth Coulton, *Goldy Luck and the Three Pandas* by Natasha Kim, and *Goldilocks and the Three Dinosaurs* by Mo Willems.

Wrap It Up

"Let's look at our chart. We learned so much about how sharks and dolphins are alike and how they're different. Tell me one way they are alike. Start by saying 'They both. . .' (Use equity sticks to call on a child.) Now let's say one way they are different. Start by saying 'They are different because. . .' I'm going to put our chart in the science center. You can choose a way they are alike or a way they are different to draw and write about!"

ACTIVITY Cause and Effect

Get Things Ready

Make a cause-and-effect chart on chart paper. Choose a book that has a clear cause and effect structure. I'm going to use *Weather* by Kristin Baird Rattini; this book will help us think about what causes different types of weather.

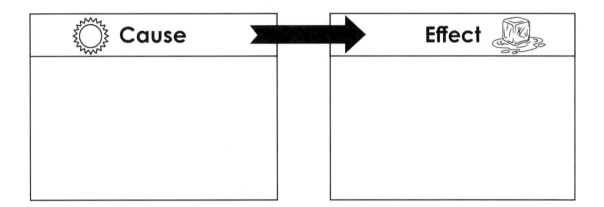

You can discuss and write the cause and effect in the chart. When I'm first teaching cause and effect, I write the cause and effect on sentence strips before the reading. Then I can show the children a pairing (for example, cause strip with its corresponding effect strip).

Make an Introduction

"Sometimes I read books because I want to understand the world around me. Everything happens for a reason. There is a cause for every effect. Let's think about these words: *cause* and *effect*. A *cause* explains why something happens. The *effect* is the thing that happens."

Now for the Model

"What would happen if you left a piece of ice outside in the sun? Turn and talk with your partner. Start by saying, 'If I left ice outside in the sun.' (Have the children turn and talk. Then bring them back to talk about the effect.) Okay. What would happen if you left a piece of ice in the sun? Yes. It would melt. That's the effect. . . melting. Let's think about the cause. Why would it melt? Turn and talk. Start by saying, 'It would melt because. . .' (Turn and talk again to identify the cause.) Now why would the ice melt? You got it. It melts because the sun is hot. That's the cause. Watch me. I'm going to draw a sun here with the word *cause* to remind us. A cause explains why something happens. Now I'm going to draw melting ice by *effect* to remind us that the effect is the thing that happens."

Let's Get Some Practice

Read your book with your predetermined stopping points. These points should be placed where the cause and effect are clear. If you've prewritten sentence strips, you might have:

Water droplets in clouds freeze.	Snow falls.

You would read the sentence strips and talk with the children about which one is the cause and which one is the effect. Then place them accordingly as you use the terms *cause* and *effect* many times to reinforce.

Wrap It Up

"Let's look at our chart. We learned a lot about the causes for different kinds of weather. Remember, our causes have effects. I'm going to read a cause and you tell me the effect. Ready? Water droplets in clouds freeze. What's the effect? Think. (Have children think and then encourage responses.) Now I'm going to say an effect. You tell me the cause. Ready? Snow falls. What's the cause? Think. (Have children think again and then encourage responses.) Our chart will stay right here. Let's get ready to do some writing. You will draw a cause and effect. Then we'll write about it."

> **Flex the Activity!**
>
> You can also use a cause-and-effect chart with narrative. Some options are *A Funny Thing Happened on the Way to School* by Davide Cali and Benjamin Chaud, *Pig the Pug* by Aaron Blabey, or *The Lumberjack's Beard* by Duncan Beedie. As you discuss cause and effect with narratives, make sure to identify story elements like characters, problem, and solutions.

Introduce Comprehension Strategies

Earlier, I noted comprehension is an active process not a passive one. But what is the reader (or listener) doing? Years of research have shown that readers employ a number of comprehension strategies (NRP, 2000). "Comprehension strategies are conscious plans that readers apply and adapt to make sense of text and get the most out of what they read" (Honig, Diamond, and Gutlohn, 2018). These strategies are often taught in elementary school. The activities here are designed for those of us in early childhood classrooms to encourage active listening and encourage higher-level thinking. We'll concentrate on visualizing, making connections, making predictions, asking questions, and making inferences.

ACTIVITY Visualize—Let's Make a Movie!

▢ Get Things Ready

Choose a book that evokes mental images; books use descriptive language that paints a picture. For this activity, I'm going to offer up a short text you can use to demonstrate and practice making a movie.

> *It is a warm and breezy day.*
> *The trees are swaying, and my hair is blowing.*
> *We all sit down on a blanket.*
> *It's so soft.*
> *I put my hand over the grass and let it tickle me.*
> *I lie back to watch the clouds float by in the blue sky.*
> *I see a cloud that looks like a giraffe. Oh look! There's a cat!*
> *I can hear the ice jingle in my cup of lemonade.*
> *I take a drink. It tastes sweet and tangy!*

I like to use visuals and hand gestures for these active comprehension strategies. The visual I use for making a movie is a movie camera, and my hand gesture is the movie gesture for charades. If you already use hand gestures for different things in your classroom (for example, agreement, questions, answers), then you might want to stick to visuals to avoid confusion. Whichever you choose, point it out and use it frequently during the read-aloud.

▢ Make an Introduction

"When we read a book, we use our imagination. Our imagination will help us 'see' what the author is telling us. The author's words can help us imagine things in the book. We might know what something looks like, what it feels like, or what it smells like. We might know what something sounds like or maybe even how something tastes. I'm going to read a short story today. While I'm reading, you will all close your eyes and make a movie in your mind as I read. I'm going to use this sign to let you know I'm making a movie in my head." Demonstrate your movie gesture and encourage children to practice. Make sure to use it frequently during the read-aloud.

▢ Now for the Model

"Let me show you how we'll do this. When I start reading, you'll close your eyes when I start reading. I'm going to read my story two times. First, I want you to make our movie sign if you start seeing a movie in your mind of what I'm describing to you. (Close your eyes and demonstrate the movie gesture.) If your movie goes away, put your hands down. (Keeping your eyes closed, put your hands down, and look disappointed.) I'll read that part again to help the movie come back. And, then you can make our movie sign again! The movie in your mind helps you understand the story. It also helps you remember it. Plus, it makes reading fun! Now close your eyes. Make our movie sign as soon as the movie starts!" Read as you normally would but put special emphasis on sensory words. Once you are finished, invite children to share briefly about their movies.

⬜ Let's Get Some Practice

Read the story again, having them to make the movie sign as the movies in their heads start. Ask questions this time to have them reflect on their movies. You might call on certain children to ask them what they see, feel, hear, taste, and smell. Use questioning and elaborations to get more detail. If needed, reread a sentence to help.

⬜ Wrap It Up

"If you make a movie in your mind when you hear a story, you'll see what's happening. (Make the movie sign.) This will help you understand the story! If your movie stops, you can ask me to read a part again to help. Great job listening and using your imagination to make your movie!"

> **Connect to a Book!**
>
> I've often seen teachers use books such as *Owl Moon* by Jane Yolen and *The Seashore Book* by Charlotte Zolotow. These books definitely help us make mental images or movies in our heads. There are many new titles that are also good choices, such as *A Small Blue Whale* by Beth Ferry or *Snow* by Cynthia Rylant.

ACTIVITY Make Connections

⬜ Get Things Ready

Choose a book with which children will be able to easily connect, meaning they have some background knowledge or similar experiences. You can do this activity with an expository topic, and you can take children on a virtual field trip to establish background knowledge to support making connections. These field trips include pictures, stories, and video of whatever your content is to establish shared knowledge. You can also do this activity with narrative texts, which is what I'll do here with the book *Lubna and Pebble* by Wendy Meddour. Read the book and make note of connections to your own life and potential connections children might have so that you have a few intentional stopping points.

As I noted with visualization, I like to introduce a visual and a hand signal with these active reading strategies. For making connections, I use a speech bubble as a visual, and I use a hand gesture by moving my hand back and forth (see image below). Whichever you choose, point it out/use it frequently during the read-aloud.

Make an Introduction

"When we read today, we're going to make connections. A connection is what you do when something in the story reminds you of your own life. They help us understand what we're reading, and they help us remember. When we make a connection, we'll use this sign." Demonstrate your hand gesture and invite the children to practice. Make sure to use it frequently during the read-aloud.

Now for the Model

"I'm going to show you how I make connections and then you'll make your own. (Read aloud pages 1–6.) Okay. I'm making a connection here to when I was a child. I had a pet rock like Lubna. My rock was also smooth and shiny. On this page, it says, 'Somehow she knew they'd keep her safe.' The author is talking about her dad and her pet rock. I felt that way about my parents and my pet rock, too. I carried it with me every day. It made me feel safe. My connection helps me think about how Lubna feels. (Read the next two pages.) I'm going to make another connection! Lubna draws a smiley face on her rock and names it Pebble. I did the same thing. I wanted my pet rock to smile back at me, and I named my rock. I called my rock Pet Rock. My connection helps me understand how much she cares for Pebble, because I remember how much I cared for my pet rock."

Let's Get Some Practice

Continue to read the book and ask "have you ever" questions to help children make connections. Have children turn and talk with a partner, giving them a sentence stem to get their conversation started, and support them in using complete sentences in their responses. After children talk with their partners, come back as a group and use equity sticks to hear one or two children's connections. Make sure to note how their connections help them understand. I usually keep my stopping points to three to five per book.

Wrap It Up

"We made connections between our story and our own lives. (Make your hand gesture.) Making connections helps us understand what we're reading. We'll practice making connections with other books! Today in your writing center, you can draw and write about one of your connections with *Lubna and Pebble*."

Look For

With all of these strategies to encourage active listening that promotes comprehension and higher-level thinking, you will be observing children's responses to your activities. You are looking for children to make logical observations. You will also look for them to spontaneously use these strategies. I often make a chart of the strategies I plan to address over the year (for example, visualization, questioning, prediction) so I can have a record of dates when I observe them doing these things during our read-alouds without my prompting. My hand gestures help with this. For example, in a later read-aloud, I may observe children using my "make connections" hand gesture. I can encourage their responses to hear and evaluate their connections. See the example observation chart on the next page.

Name	Visualization	Connections	Predictions	Questions	Inference	Notes
Keyshawn	2/12 2/29	2/29				visualize with prompting 2/12, spontaneous visualization and connected with my prompting, 2/29
Abigail						
Maria						

ACTIVITY Making Predictions

Get Things Ready

For this introduction to predicting, choose a book with a title and cover with enough detail for making predictions. I'm going to use *Watch Out for Wolf!* by Anica Mrose Rissi. It's a good option because it has well-known fairy tale characters, lots of detail, and a title that gives us some clues as to what the book is about. Make a chart so you can record predictions and check to confirm or note if your thinking changed. A possible visual for prediction is a book + face, and a gesture might be making a book with your hands. Whichever you choose, point it out and use it frequently during the read-aloud.

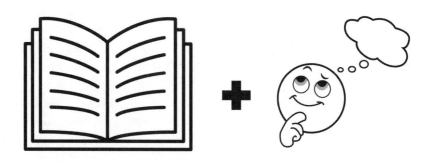

Make an Introduction

"Today we are going to read a new book. But before we read, we're going to look at the cover and think about the title to help us make a prediction. A *prediction* is a guess about what might happen later. Making predictions help us understand what's happening in our book. So, we're going to make a prediction before we read and then check it as we're reading to see if we were right. When I'm thinking about my prediction, I'm going to make a book sign." Demonstrate the book sign and invite children to practice. Make sure to use it during your read-aloud.

Now for the Model

"The title of the book is *Watch Out for Wolf!* Now let's look at the cover. (Give the children a minute to explore the cover illustration.) Okay. Let's share what we notice on the cover." Using your equity sticks, encourage responses. For this book, the main points are about the fairy-tale characters, the things they are carrying such as the present, and the looming wolf in the background. Guide the children toward a likely prediction, and explain why the prediction is likely (for example, they are going to a birthday party). Make the prediction gesture as you restate it. Write the prediction on the chart and make a quick drawing. Then make a second prediction that you know isn't going to happen (for example, the wolf tries to gobble up the animals), making the prediction gesture. This is a critical step because it allows you to demonstrate how our predictions, even though they could happen, sometimes do not come to fruition. You can also demonstrate how you adjust predictions as you are reading based on the story.

Let's Get Some Practice

Start reading and remind children of their purpose: to find out if the predictions are right. "When I read today, I am going to think about my predictions and see if they are right. If my predictions are not right, that's okay! I can think about what's happening in the story and make a new prediction." Read and briefly make note of evidence to support your first prediction (for example, they are making a cake and blowing up balloons). Then read to the point where you can evaluate your first prediction, the right one. Evaluate the prediction by saying, "Our prediction was right. They are having a birthday party. I know because they decorated and handed out invitations. This picture looks like a birthday party with the cake, balloons, and streamers. I'm going to put a check by our prediction here—they are going to a birthday party. We used the clues from the title and the cover to help us make a prediction. Let's read on to find out what's happening with the wolf. We predicted the wolf would gobble them up."

Read on to rethink your second, wrong prediction, and stop when the wolf opens the door. Say, "Okay. I'm going to stop here. I'm looking at this picture and thinking about wolf's face. It looks like a sweet smile. I think maybe she wants to come to the party. We predicted the wolf would want to gobble them up. But now that I see this picture, I'm not sure. I'm going to put a question mark on my chart by that prediction. Let's keep going!" Turn the page, see and read the big reveal, and say, "The party is a surprise party for wolf! She didn't want to gobble them up. That didn't happen in this story. Sometimes our predictions aren't quite right. When we read and find out what's happening, we can make new predictions just like I did when I saw the wolf's sweet smile."

🔲 Wrap It Up

"We made predictions using the title and cover of our book. One of our predictions was right and one was not. That's okay! We make predictions and read to see what happens. Sometimes we see our predictions work out. Sometimes our predictions don't work out, and we make new predictions. Nice job listening and thinking about what happens in our story!"

ACTIVITY Inferences

🔲 Get Things Ready

Choose a book that lends itself to making inferences. To make an inference, children will need to bring in their prior knowledge and draw on their experiences. So, make sure the books you choose are ones children can relate to. Also, remember inferential questions will often begin with *why* or *how*. Once you make a choice, read your book and determine your stopping points. I usually write on sticky notes and put them right on the page as reminders. For inferences, my visual is a lightbulb shining and my hand gesture is putting my index finger to my temple. Whichever you choose, point it out and use it frequently during the read-aloud.

🔲 Make an Introduction

"We are going to make inferences when we read today. When I make an inference, I use what I know from my experiences and what the author has told me in the book to figure something out. An inference is when you figure something out that someone has not told you. Like this. (Pretend you are tired and yawn.) How am I feeling? (Encourage responses.) Yes, I'm sleepy. Did I tell you that? No, I didn't. You made an inference! You thought about your own experience. You yawn when you're sleepy. You saw me looking tired and then I yawned. You put those things together to make the inference that I was sleepy!" Demonstrate the inference sign and invite children to practice. Make sure to use it during your read-aloud.

🔲 Now for the Model

"Let's make inferences in our story today. Sometimes authors don't tell us things, but we can figure it out by using these clues to make an inference. Today we'll read *Truman* by Jean Reidy. (Read the first six pages.) I'm going to stop here. The author doesn't tell me where Sarah is going, but I can use clues to help me. (Put your index finger to your temple.) The author says Sarah is up for breakfast, is wearing a new sweater, and has a backpack. I see the backpack in the picture, too. I'm thinking about when I'm up in the morning and take a backpack with me. That's when I'm going to school. So, my inference is (put your index finger to your temple again): I think Sarah is going to school. But I also think she's going to school without Truman, because the author says zero tortoises rode along in the backpack."

Read the next four pages and stop again to make another inference. "I'm going to stop again. The author doesn't tell me what Sarah is thinking, but I want to make an inference here because I have some clues. (Put your finger to your temple.) She gave Truman extra green beans. She also gives him a kiss and tells him to be brave. When I do special things like that for a friend, it's because I care about them or I'm worried about them. Here's my inference. I think Sarah is worried Truman will miss her, so she gives him something special and tells him to be brave."

Let's Get Some Practice

Continue reading to your next stopping points and support children as they infer. For example, my next stopping point is about how Truman feels. So, stop and ask children how Truman feels and how they know. Let them turn and talk and then share back their thoughts. If children have difficulty, you can either model as you infer and explain your inference, or you can reread key parts of the book and then restate your question.

Wrap It Up

"We made inferences today! Remember, an inference is when you figure something out that the author hasn't told you. You use your own experiences and the clues the author gives you to make an inference. Like today—the author told us Sarah had a backpack but didn't say where she was going. We made an inference that she was going to school because of that clue, and we thought about when we wear a backpack."

Flex the Activity!

We can use graphic organizers like the KWL chart or the comparison chart with our comprehension strategies, too. For example, with an inference, we can have a column for our experience, the book clues, and our inference. I usually set mine up like this to reinforce our experience plus book clues equals the inference.

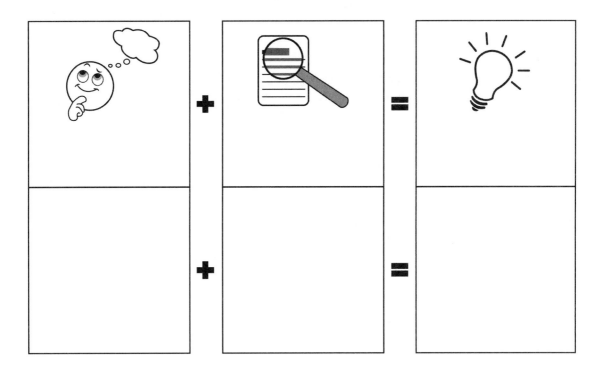

ACTIVITY Ask a Question—Set a Purpose

Get Things Ready

Make your book choice and read to think about questions you can ask *before* reading. With this activity, you'll read a book three times over a short period, usually within a week's time. For each reading, set a guiding question to have a purpose for the reading. As you choose guiding questions, consider a few things: Do the questions have a few possible answers? Do the questions consider the whole book? Do they require higher-level thinking? For the first question, I usually choose a question that is more literal. I might ask children to describe or recall. Then, for subsequent questions, I'll ask higher-level questions that encourage connections, comparisons, inferences, etc. In the book *Tiny T. Rex and the Very Dark Dark* by Jonathan Stutzman, I might ask:

- First Reading—What did Rex and Pointy do to get ready for their campout?

  - This question is literal and asks them to recall things from the whole story.

- Second Reading—Have you ever been scared about doing something? How does it connect to our story?

  - These questions require higher-level thinking as children make connections and offer different possible answers.

- Third Reading—Why did Rex and Pointy feel happy in the end?

  - This question calls upon the higher-level thinking of inference.

Make an Introduction

"Today when we read, we are going to think about one big question. We'll stop along the way to see if we've learned anything to help us answer our big question. Today we'll read *Tiny T. Rex and the Very Dark Dark* by Jonathan Stutzman. Our big question is: What did Rex and Pointy do to get ready for their campout?"

Now for the Model

Read the first few pages of the book, allowing for Rex and Pointy to start their planning. "I'm going to stop here. I see an answer to our big question. Let's remember our big question. What did Rex and Pointy do to get ready for their campout? The author tells us here what they did first. I'll reread it. First, we will build a hiding fort. I'm going to draw a hiding fort to remind us."

Let's Get Some Practice

Continue reading with your predetermined stopping points to check in on the question. At each stopping point, restate the question and have children either turn and talk or respond using equity sticks. Make quick drawings as you go for a reference after reading.

▢ Wrap It Up

"We thought about all of the things Rex and Pointy did to get ready for their campout. Turn and talk with your partner to think about everything they did. Start your conversation with, 'One thing Rex and Pointy did was. . .' and 'Another thing they did was. . .' "

To Sum It Up

The work you do supporting children's vocabulary and world knowledge development, their understanding about story structure, and their engagement with higher-level thinking through comprehension strategies builds a necessary foundation for their later literacy development. As discussed in chapter 1, our early literacy instruction must address the skills found within the word recognition component as well as those within the oral language component of the simple view. Successful reading depends upon being able to decode and read words as well as making meaning of what is read. Incorporating the activities from this chapter alongside the other activities in this book will move children toward a smooth transition to early reading and writing.

Flex the Activity!

You can engage children in asking their own questions while listening by using visualizing, connecting, and predicting. After practicing these strategies and observing children correctly using them, you can introduce questions they can ask as they are listening to books. For example, with visualization, ask questions such as, "What do I see?" With connection, ask questions such as, "What connection can I make?" With prediction, ask yourself, "What do I think might happen next?" You can stop at predetermined points during your read-aloud and ask what they are wondering about to encourage them to self-question.

7

CHAPTER SEVEN
Scaffolding Early Writers

As children are building the foundational skills of writing, they will explore through both less structured and very structured writing activities to help them learn more about the form and function of print. This chapter outlines writing from letter formation to spelling to writing composition and provides activities that will help you support development across these areas concurrently in your classroom. To begin, let's take a look at the early literacy standards from the Head Start Early Learning Outcome Framework and the Common Core State Standards that address writing. As you can see, these standards span development from scribbling and learning to make straight or curved lines to writing a sentence with capitalization to ending punctuation.

HEAD START EARLY LEARNING OUTCOME FRAMEWORK—36-60 MONTHS	COMMON CORE STATE STANDARDS— KINDERGARTEN

▪ Draws pictures using scribbles and talks with others about what they have made (36 months).
 	
 ▪ Draws straight lines or curved lines (36 months).
 	
 ▪ Makes letter-like marks or scribbles on paper (36 months).
 	
 ▪ Creates a variety of written products that may or may not phonetically relate to intended messages (60 months).
 	
 ▪ Shows an interest in copying simple words posted in the classroom (60 months).
 	
 ▪ Attempts to independently write some words using invented spelling, such as K for kite (60 months).
	▪ Demonstrates command of the conventions of standard English capitalization, punctuation, and spelling when writing.
	
	   • Capitalizes the first word in a sentence.
	
	   • Recognizes and names end punctuation.
	
	   • Writes a letter or letters for most consonant and short-vowel sounds (phonemes).
	
	   • Spells simple words phonetically, drawing on knowledge of sound-letter relationships.
	
	 ▪ Prints many upper- and lowercase letters.
	
	 ▪ Uses a combination of drawing, dictating, and writing to compose opinion pieces in which they tell a reader the topic or the name of the book they are writing about and state an opinion or preference about the topic or book (for example, "My favorite book is. . . ").

HEAD START EARLY LEARNING OUTCOME FRAMEWORK—36–60 MONTHS	COMMON CORE STATE STANDARDS— KINDERGARTEN
■ Writes first name correctly or close to correctly (60 months). ■ Writes (draws, illustrates) for a variety of purposes and demonstrates evidence of many aspects of print conventions, such as creating a book that moves left to right (60 months).	■ Uses a combination of drawing, dictating, and writing to compose informative/explanatory texts in which they name what they are writing about and supply some information about the topic. ■ Uses a combination of drawing, dictating, and writing to narrate a single event or several loosely linked events, tells about the events in the order in which they occurred, and provides a reaction to what happened. ■ With guidance and support from adults, responds to questions and suggestions from peers and adds details to strengthen writing as needed. ■ With guidance and support from adults, explores a variety of digital tools to produce and publish writing, including in collaboration with peers. ■ Participates in shared research and writing projects (for example, explores a number of books by a favorite author and expresses opinions about them). ■ With guidance and support from adults, recalls information from experiences or gathers information from provided sources to answer a question.

Children learn how print works in their writing as well. They watch people write all around them, and they want in on the game. Much of this is pretend play, but it leads to an important exploration of the forms and functions of print that lead to representing words on a page. I'm reminded of my own daughter who came to me one day with scribbles on a page and proudly stated, "Look what I wrote." She followed up with a question, "What does it say?" I encouraged *her* to tell me what it said. Her response, "I can't read." This is an illustration of the motivation to participate in the act of writing despite limited knowledge about the forms and functions of print. She knew one important thing: we write to communicate and share.

For our young children, writing serves as a window into their language and literacy development. We want them to feel comfortable and confident in expressing themselves through writing, so we provide a forum for them to take risks and explore written language. In this chapter, we'll consider three dimensions of children's early writing: handwriting and letter formation, spelling, and writing composition.

Handwriting and Letter Formation

While letters are arbitrary abstract symbols that represent our sounds in English, they are critical to early literacy success. We don't just have twenty-six letters; we have upper- and lowercase versions. Children tend to learn uppercase letters first and more easily. There is good reason for this. Let's compare upper- and lowercase letters to think about why.

UPPERCASE LETTERS	ASPECTS	LOWERCASE LETTERS
Start at the top examples: *A, N, Q*	Starting place	Start at different places examples: *a, b, e*
The same height examples: *A, C, R, Z*	Height	Aren't the same height examples: *c, f, g*
More distinct examples: *A, C, E, P W*	Distinctness	Some have only subtle differences examples: *a, b, d, p, q*
More prevalent in ABC books and environmental print (for example, signs)	Prevalence	

Out of these fifty-two letters, there are only twelve whose upper- and lowercase shapes are identical (for example, *Ss, Xx,* and *Oo*) or almost so (for example, *Pp, Jj, Kk*). This leaves children with forty distinctive letters to learn. Some letters share common visual features, such as *b/d, m/n,* and *v/w*. Letters work differently than anything young children have previously experienced. In other words, I could take a cup and turn it around, upside down, or right side up, and it's always a cup. But consider *b*. If I flip it, it becomes *d*. If I turn it upside down, it becomes a *p*. If I flip it and turn it upside down, it could be a *q*.

Letter formation instruction is not only a critical piece of early writing instruction, but it is also important for building alphabet knowledge. When we teach formation, we require children to look more closely and think about the distinguishing features of each letter. More than that, young children are hands-on, and providing them with opportunities to form letters takes advantage of that. Their growing knowledge of letter forms and increasingly developed fine motor skills allows them to write letters.

Spelling

A big part of writing for our early learners is making connections between letters and sounds as they learn to represent, or spell, words in print. Children appear to move through levels of spelling development. While they may move back and forth across these levels, you will notice a pattern to their spelling/writing attempts over time. For example, Bud, a kindergartner, wrote five consonant-vowel-consonant words with medial short *a* with good accuracy and with great consideration. He segmented each sound, thought about letters that corresponded with the sounds, and looked for letter-formation support when needed. The process took time and was labor intensive. He then went to write about superheroes in his journal. He drew a picture and proceeded to write his story using a combination of mock-linear forms and random letters. At this point, he wanted to have the ease of getting his ideas down on the paper. Even though Bud showed evidence of two levels of spelling/writing development, children will generally follow an expected progression, starting with drawings and scribbles.

DRAWING AND SCRIBBLING

Like my own daughter, young children begin to experiment with writing using drawings and scribbles as a result of a budding interest in print. Encourage children to talk about their writing, and you'll begin to see how they understand the connection between writing and language. They may also include mock-linear scribbles like we see in this sample of five words from the Phonological Awareness Literacy Screener—Kindergarten (Invernizzi, Juel, Swank, and Meier, 2003-2017). This kindergartner was asked to write *jam*, *rob*, *fun*, *sip*, and *let*. Notice his "scribbles" are linear, and in fact, he wrote left to right, demonstrating his understanding not only of the linearity of writing but also its directionality.

LETTER-LIKE FORMS

As children begin to notice letters and make note of their global shapes, they'll try writing letter-like forms. They realize now that there is a difference between drawings and letters. They just don't know yet how to form letters and may or may not know letter names. You may even notice some letters in their writing, especially the letters in their name. This sample is the same five words written by another kindergartner. Notice the letter-like forms in this sample, such as the word *rob* in number two, begin with a letter similar to an uppercase E or F and the circles/dots in *jam*, *fun*, and *let*.

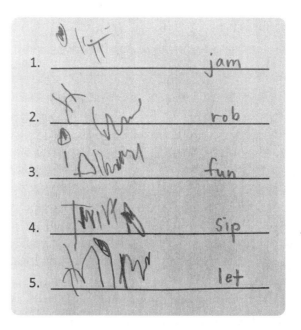

RANDOM LETTERS

As children begin to learn about letter formation, they start to include random letters in their writing. In fact, learning how to make the letters in their names helps to propel them to start using letters in their writing. The more letters they learn, the more letters you'll see in their random strings. They also start to remember what certain words look like, especially words in their everyday environment or those that are special to them. So, you might even see noticeable words pop up in their random letter strings. These may or may not have any meaning or connection to what they are writing about. Take a look at these two samples. In the one on the left, a kindergartner has learned his name: Willie. He exclusively uses the letters in his name to represent his thoughts in print. To the right, you can see a prekindergartner who is straddling two levels of development. This child , one we looked at in chapter 1, is using mock-linear writing as a way to efficiently get her story on paper about visiting with her cousins. Interspersed in her writing are the words *MOM, DAD,* and *LOVE*—all words that are special to her with some shared meaning to her story.

SALIENT AND INITIAL SOUNDS

When children's experiences highlight the sounds that make up our words—phonemes—as well as letter-sound correspondences, they begin representing salient sounds and initial sounds in words. A *salient sound* is a sound in a word that stands out for a variety of possible reasons. Your lips might pop together when you make it (for example, the /p/ in *lip*) or the sound may be similar the sound that starts a child's name (for example, the /k/ in *Kamara*) or it's a sound with a letter connection they know (for example, the child writes *rob* as *B* because they know /b/ is *B* but not the letter-sound connections for other sounds in *rob*). As children become more aware of phonemes, they will begin to segment the onset from words (for example, the /j/ in *jam*). Because of this, we also will start to see children representing whole words with single letters: the initial sound. They know a lot of letters but just don't have the phonemic awareness needed to represent more sounds.

Let's look at the following two samples. The one on the left is a five-word spelling sample, and the one on the right is from the same kindergartner's journal where she wrote about cooking with her mom. Notice her attention to salient and initial sounds. In the spelling sample, she writes *J* for *jam*, *B* for *rob*, *N* for *fun*, *P* for *sip*, and *L* for *let*. These are sometimes initial sounds and sometimes the more salient sounds in the word. Her writing sample clearly demonstrates her attention to initial sounds with *K* for cook, *W* for *with*, *M* for *my*, and *MOO* for *mom*.

LETTER-SOUND CORRESPONDENCES

Finally, as children become more experienced at segmenting sounds in words and their letter-sound knowledge increases, their writing clearly represents words, even if they are misspelled. They haven't yet mastered conventional spelling (for example, long *a* can be spelled in a few ways, such as the *ai* in *train* or the *ay* in *tray*), but their writing begins to become more readable, especially within a context. Look at the sample on the left. In this prekindergartner's spelling of five consonant-vowel-consonant words (*sad, hug, lip, net, job*), we see more attention to the sounds in words. While the words are not spelled correctly, the child's spelling attempts make sense.

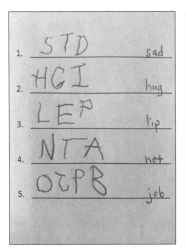 

For example, *lep* for *lip* makes sense because *e* for short *i* is a common misrepresentation of that medial short vowel with young children. On the right, the kindergartner writes about his dog who likes to eat people food and drink cold water. You likely don't need me to tell you that, though, because his spellings of these words, while most not correct, are close approximations making it readable.

Writing Composition

It might seem odd to think about composition for our young children, but composing is a way for them to practice their formation, try out letters for the sounds they might hear in a word, and express their ideas in another form. With this in mind, children are building composition skills whether they are scribbling, drawing, or even writing random letters to communicate.

This prekindergartner's story is scribbles and drawings; yet, it is an elaborate story about a ghost, a dragon, and a monster. They poked his sister, and he saved her with the help of his parents. While he didn't connect letters to sounds and write words strung together into sentences, he did demonstrate the concept of organizing an idea (a ghost, dragon, and monster poking his sister and him saving the day) and an attempt to reflect that idea on paper. Children's understanding of and perception about writing is a reflection of their experiences with literacy in their everyday lives. We can see how this child's experiences with books have provided him with a story to tell. So, although no words were written and no sentences were provided to express his story in print, his story is still what I'd call a composition!

Writing in Your Classroom

With all this information in mind, writing in your classroom takes on a multipronged approach. You attend to children's early attempts at writing by helping them learn how to form letters. You support their burgeoning spelling skills as they shift from scribbling and drawing to representing sounds they hear with letters. You also provide opportunities for them to observe you as a writer and explore writing their own messages. Each of the following activities are offered to support you with this multipronged approach.

Letter Formation

The number of balls a child is juggling while writing can seem overwhelming. Helping them get a handle on letter formation can lessen the number. In fact, handwriting instruction has been shown to positively impact future writing quality, length, and fluency (Santangelo and Graham, 2015). This work starts with learning the contours of these abstract symbols of our written language, such as straight and curved lines. Supporting children putting these forms together to make letters is a next step (for example, an uppercase G includes a curved line around and a straight line in the middle and back). Then we work to help them discriminate between, and form, letters with subtle differences, such as lowercase b and d.

Name writing is a good place to start with not only the purpose of writing but also to encourage letter formation. At first, children may be matching letters in their names with letter tiles, like Build Your Name and Disappearing Names from chapter 4. Children will be especially interested in practicing the letters of their names. In fact, it is one of the first words a child learns to write (Both-de Vries and Bus, 2008). Provide multiple opportunities to practice name writing, such as a morning sign-ins, surveys of the class, signing up for centers, and signing their names on artwork. Model writing your name often, and encourage any attempt at writing their names from a scribble to a first letter. Children can have name plates for models, and peer helpers can support their friends in name writing. The following three activities will help lay the foundation for children to learn to write their names.

ACTIVITY Skywriting—Lines

Get Things Ready

Create cards or a chart with the following:

- One big vertical line

- One little vertical line (half-length of tall vertical)

- One horizontal line

- One line the length of big vertical slanting right to left

- One line the length of big vertical slanting left to right

- Two little slanting lines

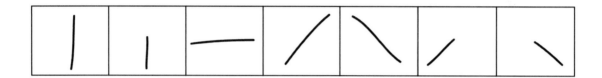

When making these lines in the air, the first step is always where to begin with the starting point (for example, "top," "middle," or "bottom"). I usually put the "top" just above my head, the "middle" at my eye level, and "bottom" at my shoulders. Consistent positions are helpful.

Make an Introduction

"Everyone, get your magic pencils out! We're going to skywrite. Here's my magic pencil. (Hold your pointer finger on your dominant hand in the air.) Show me your magic pencils. We're going to practice straight lines in the air that we'll use when we write letters." (You might need to demonstrate the difference between straight lines and curved lines. Children can walk in a straight line or curvy lines to help them connect to the concepts.)

Now for the Model

Note: Make sure children are facing forward and your back is to the group to ensure they see the correct view of your arm as you form letters. This means you need to have your arm to the side rather than directly in front of you. I usually make my lines based on the majority of dominance (meaning, most children are "righties," so I demonstrate with my right). You might need to provide some adjustments for any children who are "lefties."

You can give them a brief explanation about why you have your back turned. "We are going to skywrite some lines that we'll use all year when we write letters. The first is a big line down. (Point to the line on your card or chart.) I start my magic pencil at the top and then draw a big, straight line down to the bottom. (Trace the line on the card or chart.) Follow me. Magic pencils up. Start at the top and write a big line down."

Let's Get Some Practice

Repeat this process as you provide practice with all lines. I use the similar language to what I will use with letter formation. For example, in Handwriting Without Tears, you use the term *big* line rather than *long* line. Here are some ideas of language you might use.

|	start at the top, big line down
|	start at the middle, little line down
—	start at the top, straight line across
/	start at the bottom, big slant line up to the top
\	start at the top, big slant line down to the bottom
/	start at the bottom, little slant line up to the middle
\	start at the middle, little slant line down to the bottom

If children have difficulty, consider practicing fewer lines at a time. You may also need to provide hand-over-hand support. You can also practice on the carpet, on sandpaper, in sand, and so on. Children can form these lines with playdough and lay them atop a card with the target line. Plus, you'll  want to have opportunities for them to practice on paper with crayons or little golf pencils (the kind you get at a mini-golf course). The main thing is to use consistent language regardless of the practice.

Wrap It Up

"We did some skywriting to practice the lines we'll use to write letters. You can also use your magic pencil on your leg or on the carpet if you need to practice a line before writing."

ACTIVITY Skywriting—Curves and Circles

Get Things Ready

Create cards or a chart with the following:

- Big curves
- Little curves
- Big circle
- Little circle

When making curved lines and circles in the air, the first step is always where to begin with the starting point (for example, "top," "middle," or "bottom"). As with straight lines, I usually put the "top" just above my head, the "middle" at my eye level, and "bottom" at my shoulders. Consistent positions are helpful.

Make an Introduction

"Let's get out our magic pencils! We're going to skywrite. (Hold your pointer finger on your dominant hand in the air.) Show me your magic pencils. We're going to practice curved lines and circles in the air that we'll use when we write letters."

Now for the Model

Note: Make sure children are facing forward and your back is to the group to ensure they see the correct view of your arm as you form letters. This means you need to have your arm to the side rather than directly in front of you. I usually make my lines based on the majority of dominance (meaning, most children are "righties," so I demonstrate with my right). You might need to provide some adjustments for any children who are "lefties." You can give them a brief explanation about why you have your back turned.

"We are going to skywrite curves and circles that we'll use all year when we write letters. The first is a big curve. (Point to the big curve on your card or chart.) I start my magic pencil at the top and then draw a big curve that goes all the way down to the bottom. (Trace the line on the card or chart.) Follow me. Magic pencils up. Start at the top and big curve."

Let's Get Some Practice

Repeat this process as you provide practice with all lines. I use the similar language to what I will use with letter formation. For example, in Handwriting Without Tears, some curves start with the "magic c" (for example, lowercase *a, c, d, g, o, q,* and even *s*—begin with a little "magic c"). Here are some ideas of language you might use.

( )	Start at the middle, little curve down to the bottom
c ɔ ∩ ∪	Start at the middle, little curve down to the bottom (these can face up, down, right, and left—adjust starting point accordingly)
◯	Start at the top, big circle all the way down to the bottom and back up to the top
◯	Start at the middle, little circle down to the bottom and back up to the middle

If children have difficulty, consider practicing fewer at a time (focus only on circles, big and little). You may also need to provide hand-over-hand support. You can also practice on the carpet, on sandpaper, in sand, and so on. I've used "goopy bags," too. A goopy bag is a good, sealable plastic bag with some hair gel colored with food coloring (and some glitter if you want!). Tips for success: Choose a high-quality bag, choose a darker color of gel, don't use too much gel, and use the goopy bag on a light-colored background such as a dry-erase board for high contrast so children can easily see the letter they make. You'll want to provide opportunities for them to practice on paper with crayons or little golf pencils. As with writing straight lines, the main thing is to use consistent language regardless of the practice.

Wrap It Up

"Nice work! We practiced curves and circles that we'll use to write letters. Remember, you can write on your legs or the carpet if you need to practice before writing."

Flex the Activity!

In chapter 4, we explored an activity called Letter Shape Sort in which children sort letters by straight or curved lines. These activities are complementary of each other: Letter Shape Sort, Skywriting Lines, and Skywriting Curves and Circles.

ACTIVITY Forming Letters

Get Things Ready

Once children are starting to get comfortable with the global contours of written letters (straight lines, curves, and circles), begin to put these together to form letters. If you have a handwriting curriculum already in place, you can use that. If not, and you are looking for some guidance, here are some ideas. First, make a collection of "moves" you make forming letters, beginning in uppercase. For example, with A, you might say, "Big line. Big line. Little line across." Or with I, you might say, "Big line. Little line top. Little line bottom." My main thinking around this is that the language needs to be consistent and used often and that you don't want it to be too wordy— simple is best.

Make an Introduction

"Today we'll practice making uppercase A. Everyone take a look at uppercase A. (Point out uppercase A on your letter wall, on a card, or written on the board). Raise your hand if A is your name letter!"

Now for the Model

"I'm going to trace my uppercase A first. Start at the top. Big line. Back to the top. Big line. Little line across the middle. (Trace your letter as you narrate your moves.) Now I'm going to skywrite uppercase A with my magic pencil. Watch me." (Put your finger up just above your head with your back turned to make sure children have the correct view when you are forming the letter.) "Start at the top. Big line. Back to the top. Big line. Little line across the middle. I'm going to write it this time. Start at the top. Big line. Back to the top. Big line. Little line across the middle." (Write on the board as you narrate your moves.)

Let's Get Some Practice

Have children skywrite uppercase A as you narrate (and skywrite if you need to provide a model). Follow up with

Connect to a Book!

A Squiggly Story by Andrew Larsen tells the story of a boy who wants to write stories like his big sister. His problem is he knows letters but doesn't know how to write the words he wants to use. He ends up writing a story about the beach and sharks, oh my! And, he uses the letters he knows and slants and squiggles. It's a perfect story to encourage children to start writing using what they know. As the big sis says in the story, they're the boss of their stories.

practice on paper or dry-erase board. If we are just learning, I usually have children do this as a group as we write together. If we are getting extra practice, then I might have children at tables writing as I move around the room, supporting as needed.

Wrap It Up

"We worked on Amelia and Ali's name letter today! Let's skywrite uppercase *A*. Start at the top. Big line. Back to the top. Big line. Little line across the middle. You can practice uppercase *A* and use it in your writing!"

Spelling

Spelling is another dimension of young children's writing. Their spelling reflects their understanding of the alphabetic principle. Letter-sound knowledge and phonemic awareness (sensitivity to the individual sounds in spoken words) are critical understandings to develop the alphabetic principle. Spelling pulls together these understandings and the ability to put them together on paper. The more opportunities children have to attempt to write words, the more they'll learn about bringing these skills together to spell words.

ACTIVITY Say It, Write It

Get Things Ready

Identify a sequence of words based on the features you are studying. For example, if you are studying short *o* word families, then you could include *pot, hop, log, chop, fog, hot, shot, mop, hog, dot*. Ten to twelve words are usually enough for this activity. I usually do this activity using Elkonin boxes, which help make the "separation" of sounds more concrete for children. Consider the word *chop*. You can clearly illustrate for the children that *CH* makes one sound (it's in one box) but is two letters. Follow the same process above as you write each letter (or letter combination like *CH*) rather than move a letter tile. Usually, I put my Elkonin box page in a sheet protector to use with dry-erase markers. Children are accustomed to using boxes to push and say sounds (see chapter 3), so this is a familiar task.

Make an Introduction

"We are going to spell words today and play Say It, Write It. We've been thinking about words with /ŏ/ like in the middle of *hot*. So, let's write words that have /ŏ/ in the middle."

Now for the Model

"Watch me first. My first word is *dot*. First, I'll say each sound. /d/ /ŏ/ /t/. . . dot. /d/. . . D. So, I'll write *D* in my first box. /ŏ/. . . O. I'll write *O* in my next box. /t/. . . T. Now I'll write *T* in the last box. /d/ /ŏ/ /t/. . . dot." (Point to each letter as you say the sound. Sweep your finger under the boxes as you say the whole word.)

Let's Get Some Practice

Continue with this process as you direct the children to a new word. If children have difficulty, model first and then chorally say each sound and write each letter.

Wrap It Up

"Nice job writing our words today! When you are spelling a new word for you, say it and then write it."

Flex the Activity!

In chapter 5, you read about the activity Mix It Up! Rather than say a sound and write the letter, you push and say letter tiles. These two activities can complement each other. For example, you might have children push and say markers first (Push It, Say It from chapter 3), make the word with letter tiles (Mix It Up! from chapter 5), and then write the word (Say It, Write It here in chapter 7). I usually have a page made for this that I keep in sheet protectors to use over and over with a dry-erase marker.

ACTIVITY Listen for the Vowel

Get Things Ready

Collect a list of consonant-vowel-consonant words that include the vowel you want children to get extra practice with.

Make an Introduction

"Today we are going to play a game called Listen for the Vowel! First, I'll write a vowel on the board. (Write a large lowercase *o* on the board.) Then I'll say a word, and you'll show me a thumbs-up if the word has this vowel spelling or a thumbs-down if it doesn't."

Now for the Model

"Today we're going to listen for /ŏ/. This vowel is the letter *o*. It makes /ŏ/. What's the name of this vowel letter? What sound does it make?" (Repeat this review with any additional vowels you'll use for the activity. You can absolutely keep this to only one vowel.) "I'm going to say some words. Then I'll put a thumbs-up if it has /ŏ/ in the middle or a thumbs-down if it doesn't. The word is *hot*. /hŏŏŏt/. I hear /ŏ/ in the middle of *hot*. /hŏŏŏt/. Thumbs-up. (Point to *O* written on the board.) Everyone, thumbs-up!"

Let's Get Some Practice

Continue with this process as you say new consonant-vowel-consonant words. For example, you might say *big* and ask if the word has /ŏ/. With *big*, you'd do a thumbs-down and then ask what letter makes that sound. If children have difficulty, demonstrate saying the word as you elongate the medial vowel. You can also use words with the target sound at the beginning (for example, *otter, octopus*) since it is easier for children to hear initial sounds. You could also give children their own dry-erase boards and have them write the vowel letter for each word as you have them say the sound as they write.

Wrap It Up

"Good job listening for the vowel sounds in the middle of words. Listening to the sounds in words will help you become better spellers!"

> **Connect to a Book!**
>
> You can listen for the medial vowel in *spot* after reading *A Little Spot of Courage* by Diane Alber. This book is part of a series helping children think about emotions such as courage and confidence. Or pull out words such as *cat* and *Meg* from *The Good Egg* by Jory John. Not only are you using your books as a springboard, but you are also demonstrating for the children that these activities apply to real words in the books they read.

What's the Middle Letter?

Get Things Ready

Create a set of vowel letter cards for each child and one for yourself. Or you can fold paper in half to make little "tents" for each vowel; make a set for each child and for yourself. These sit and children can pick them up easily. You can also put your vowels on different-colored cards/tents. This will help you get a quick look at their choices. Make a list of consonant-vowel-consonant words. Here's a collection across short vowels you can pull from.

/ă/	/ĕ/	/ĭ/	/ŏ/	/ŭ/
cat	met	pig	lot	nut
gab	fed	sit	mop	tub
tag	pep	rib	pod	mud
hat	bet	lip	rob	bus
wax	wed	hid	box	cup

■ **Make an Introduction**

"Today we'll listen for the vowels in the middle of words. When I say a word, we'll listen for the vowel we hear in the middle. First, let's review our sounds." (Show each vowel and review each short vowel sound.)

■ **Now for the Model**

"I'll go first. My word is *tag*. /tăăăg/. . . I hear /ă/. So, I'll hold up my *A* card."

■ **Let's Get Some Practice**

Continue saying words, elongating the medial vowel, and inviting children to hold up the appropriate vowel card. If children have difficulty, reduce the choice from all five vowels to only two or three. Or model and have children repeat after you. "/lŏŏŏt/. . . I hear /ŏ/ in the middle. *O* says /ŏ/. (Hold up your *O* card.) Say *lot*. *Lot*. What's the vowel? /ŏ/. . . now hold up your *O* card and say it with me. . . *O* says /ŏ/."

■ **Wrap It Up**

"Good job listening for the vowel sounds in the middle of words. Listening to the sounds in words will help you become better spellers!"

ACTIVITY **Word Ladders**

■ **Get Things Ready**

Decide on a sequence of words similar to the Mix It Up! activity from chapter 5. With these lists, you will have one sound change to encourage a close analysis of the words. For example, if you are focusing on words with short *o*, you might have a list like *dot, hot, hop, chop, bop, bog, log, lot, shot, shop*. I like to do this activity on paper.

Make an Introduction

"Today we'll make word ladders! You have to listen carefully. I'll tell you a word to write. Then I'll tell you a new word that is different by only one sound like *hop* and *hot*. They both have /h/ at the beginning and /ŏ/ in the middle. But *hop* ends with /p/ and *hot* ends with /t/."

Now for the Model

"Let's write our word ladders! Watch me get started. I'll make the first word. My word is *dot*. /d/ /ŏ/ /t/ (Say each sound as you hold up a finger.) Three sounds. /d/. . . D. (Write a D.) /ŏ/. . . O. (Write O.) /t/. . . T. (Write T.) *Dot*. (Sweep your finger under the words as you read it.) Now my next word is *hot*. What part of the word are we changing? The beginning, middle, or end? *Dot. Hot*. That's right. The beginning. /h/ /ŏ/ /t/. . . /h/. . . H. (Write H. You are writing *hot* under *dot*.) /ŏ/. . . O. (Write O.) /t/. . . T. (Write T.) *Hot*. (Sweep your finger under the words as you read it.) *Dot. Hot*. (Point to each word as you read it.)

Let's Get Some Practice

Continue with this process as you write your word ladder, moving to *chop, bop, bog, log, lot, shot, shop*. If children have difficulty, model writing the word and then chorally segment and write each letter.

Wrap It Up

"We wrote ten words today. All of them have /ŏ/ in the middle! Let's read them all. Point and read with me."

Look For

You not only want children to develop their accuracy in identifying the corresponding letter for the sounds in these consonant-vowel-consonant words, but you also want to monitor their ease in writing the letters and their increased automaticity in making the sound-to-letter match.

ACTIVITY Quick Write

Get Things Ready

Choose a set of words you will ask the children to spell. These words should mirror the features you are studying. If you were studying digraphs (a combination of two letters that make one sound, like *ch* for /ch/), you could choose the following words: *hop, shop, cop, chop, hat, that, hut, shut, hip, chip*. I usually play Quick Write by writing on individual dry-erase boards because they are easy to flip and show.

This activity can be adjusted. Rather than write words, you can write for letter sounds. For example, you could say, "Write /d/." The children will write a *D*, upper- or lowercase, on their dry-erase boards to flip and show.

Make an Introduction

"Today we'll play Quick Write! I'm going to say a word, and you'll write it. Then I'll say, 'Show me,' and you'll flip your board."

Now for the Model

"I'll go first. My word is *hop.* First, I'll say the sounds /hŏŏŏp/ (Put your fingers up as you say each sound.) Now I'll write for each sound I hear. /h/ (Write *h.*) /ŏ/ (Write *o.*) /t/ (Write *t*). *Hot.* (Sweep your finger under the word as you say it.) Watch this. Show me!" (Demonstrate how to flip your board.)

Let's Get Some Practice

Continue with this process as you provide new words. If children have difficulty, model saying each sound and writing it. Then have them repeat on their own boards as you chorally say each sound.

Wrap It Up

"We listened to our sounds as we spelled words today! We'll keep practicing so you can get faster writing your words."

Flex the Activity!

You can play a version of Quick Write that I call Show Me! This activity includes building words with letter tiles. I make Show Me! pockets by folding a piece of card stock not quite in half, leaving about two inches extra on one side. Fold that two-inch lip up to make a pocket. Staple the ends of the pocket. I've found that stapling on the pocket to make slots for your letter tiles is helpful so that your tiles won't slip around. I make my tiles as rectangles with the letters positioned at the top to leave blank space where the tile will be stuck in the Show Me! pocket. As with the Mix It Up! from chapter 5, only give the children the letter cards they will need to make the words you have chosen to work with for the activity.

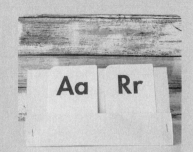

ACTIVITY **My Very Own Words**

Get Things Ready

Once you have introduced words as heart words (see chapter 5), you can provide practice writing these words. You might build a small collection over time (in kindergarten) of words on cards that children keep on a ring or stapled in a little book for them to practice. To practice writing these words, I set up a page with the heart word on the top and then space to write underneath.

Make an Introduction

"Today we are going to practice writing our heart word *the,* like in this sentence: I put *the* pencil on *the* table." (Point to the word on your heart-word card.)

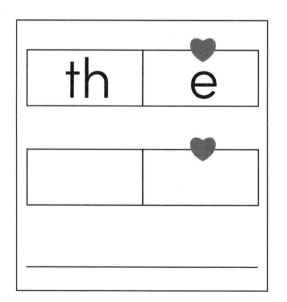

Now for the Model

"Watch me. Remember, *the* has two sounds. /th/ /ŭ/. The first sound is /th/. We know that is spelled with *TH*. (Point to your heart word and the *TH* in the first box.) The second sound is /ŭ/. The /ŭ/ is spelled with *E*. This is the part we must remember by heart. (Point to your heart word and the *E* in the second box.)

Let's Get Some Practice

Give each child a heart-word page, and have them orally segment the sounds in *the*. Now direct their attention to the heart-word page. Have them point to the *TH* and *E* as they say the two sounds. Ask them which part they need to know by heart. Then say each sound again as they write in the middle boxes on the page. Have them say each sound once more as they write *the* on the line at the bottom. To end the activity, say "What's our word? *The*. Yes! I'm going to write it in a sentence: 'I put the pencil on the table.'" Invite children to come up and circle or underline *the* in the sentence.

> **Connect to a Book!**
>
> While reading (or after), call attention to heart words. For example, in *Drum Dream Girl* by Margarita Engle, you could invite the children to find the word *the* in the line "On an island of music in a city of drumbeats the drum dream girl dreamed".

Wrap It Up

"Writing our heart words helps us remember them. Plus, knowing which part we have to remember by heart helps us remember them, too! How do we spell *the*? Let's say it together *T-H-E*."

Writing Composition

Reading aloud is commonplace in early childhood classrooms. Traditionally, writing has gotten less attention (Puranik, Al Otaiba, Sidler, and Greulick, 2014). We can make a difference by intentionally guiding the children in thinking about what to write, how to get it down on paper, the sounds in words, connecting those sounds to letters, and writing those letters on the page with attention to letter formation and pencil grip. That's a lot of balls for a young child to juggle. Providing them with multiple, scaffolded opportunities to write makes a difference in early literacy development (Dickinson and Tabors, 2001; National Early Literacy Panel, 2008; Whitehurst and Lonigan, 1998) as does providing opportunities for them to observe us as readers and writers and showing a genuine interest in their writing—be it a drawing, a scribble, or a string of random letters (Morrow, 2005). Often this practice comes in the form of modeled writing, shared writing, interactive writing, and independent writing. You'll see aspects of all of these in the following activities.

WRITING OPPORTUNITIES	WHAT'S THE PURPOSE?	WHAT IS IT?
Modeled	Introduce new forms of writing	Teacher thinks aloud while writing in an effort to explicitly demonstrate for young writers
Shared	Reinforce ideas children already know	Joint activity in which teacher involves children in thinking about aspects of writing, such as letter-sound connections, while you are thinking aloud spelling a word
Interactive	Reinforce ideas children already know	Joint activity where teachers involve children in the actual writing as appropriate based on individual children's skill sets
Independent	Reinforce ideas children already know	Children have the opportunity to practice all aspects of writing from formation to the alphabetic principle to their self-concept as writers

The way you scaffold these experiences will depend not only on the aspect of writing you want to support (for example, formation, spelling, composition) but also the level of writing a child displays (Cabell, Tortorelli, and Gerde, 2013). For example, during journaling, you might ask a child who is scribbling or drawing when writing to tell you about their drawing as you write their words.

Now let's think about a child who is attending to salient and initial sounds. You would ask the child to tell you what they want to write, and you enunciate words to help them hear more than the initial sound. Ultimately, you play a crucial role in helping children develop early writing skills (Hall, Simpson, Guo, and Wang, 2015). Each of these activities allow for modeled, shared, or interactive writing that will support children's independent writing.

ACTIVITY Letter and Word Hunt

Get Things Ready

Gather a clipboard, paper, and a writing utensil. For little hands, broken crayons (not the fat ones) and golf pencils are a good size. Their small size supports a better pencil grip because you can't use a fist grip with these short, thin writing utensils. Pencil grips can also help when needed as well as Y-shaped ergonomic pencils.

You can play this any way you want, but I like to put it to music and keep hunting, reading, and writing until I stop the music. Here we'll learn how to hunt (this activity is also called Read and Write the Room) so only one child at a time is usually involved. This can, however, be a whole-group activity or a center activity once children know how to productively hunt for letters and words. If you are studying a theme, you can hang cards with key vocabulary and pictures for children to hunt for and find. Or if you are focused on a particular set of letters, hang many upper- and lowercase letters around the room for extra practice reading and writing.

Make an Introduction

"You have practiced your letters, and we've learned that you can put letters together to make words. Today we'll go around our classroom and hunt for letters and words. Then we'll read and write letters and words on our papers!"

Now for the Model

"Watch me get started. I have my clipboard with my paper and my pencil. I'm going to start walking around the room to hunt for letters and words. I've already found one on our letter wall! I see my name letter. I'm going to read it and write it. It's the letter *T*. I'll write an uppercase *T* and a lowercase *t*. Okay, I'll keep hunting. Look! Here's a word. I'll read it. It's my keyword for the letter *T*. *Top*. I'll write *top*. T-O-P. . . *top*."

Let's Get Some Practice

"It's your turn. I'm going to pick a friend to hunt for letters or words to read and write." Choose a child using equity sticks or whatever system you use. Pass off your clipboard. As they hunt, encourage them to think aloud. Once a letter or word is found, have the other children repeat what the child has found. Continue having children hunt one by one until your time runs out. If a child has difficulty, model how to ask a friend to help read the letter or word.

Wrap It Up

"Great work, readers and writers. We found letters and words. Remember, our letters go together to make words. We'll hunt for letters and words in our classroom a few more times like this. Then we'll start playing as a big group all together!"

> **Connect to a Book!**
>
> *A Way with Wild Things* by Larissa Theule is about a shy girl who blends into the background when people come around. The illustrations by Sara Palacios are fun for finding the girl as she blends into the picture. This book not only helps you talk about shyness, but it can also set the stage for hunting for letters and words. Or if you are learning about life cycles, you might read *Cactus and Flower: A Book About Life Cycles* by Sarah Williamson. You can hunt in the book for letters and words and then display key words (with pictures) around the room for your next classroom hunt.

ACTIVITY Sentence Frames

Get Things Ready

You can do this activity with any sentence frame. For example, you just took children on a walk around the school or a nature walk outside. When you come back to the classroom, you use the sentence frame: "___ saw a ___ on our walk." Repetitive books provide a perfect springboard to sentence frames. You can use old favorites such as *Brown Bear, Brown Bear, What Do You See?* by Eric Carle, *I Went Walking* by Sue Williams, and *Silly Sally* by Audrey Wood. With *I Went Walking*, you might have this frame: "I saw a ___ ___ looking at me." Here are some newer titles you could check out:

- *Fussy Flamingo* by Shelly Vaughan James

- *A Hippy Hoppy Toad* by Peggy Archer

- *Go Sleep in Your Own Bed!* by Candace Fleming

- *Hooray for Today* by Brian Won

- *Tiptoe Joe* by Ginger Foglesong Gibson

- *Two Little Monkeys* by Mem Fox

- *Where Bear?* by Sophy Henn

- *I Need a Hug* by Aaron Blabey

- *Toad on a Road* by Stephen Shaskan

- *Bug Soup: What's in Your Lunchbox?* by Vince Cleghorne

I'm going to use *A Bear Sat on My Porch Today* by Jane Yolen and the sentence frame "A ___ sat on my porch today." I'll provide enough papers with my sentence frame for each child.

Make an Introduction

"We just finished *A Bear Sat on My Porch Today*. Let's write sentences about who sat on the porch! First, we'll draw a picture and then we'll write our sentences."

Now for the Model

"I'll go first. Here's my sentence frame. It says 'A ___ sat on my porch today.' (Point and read the sentence frame.) I'm going to fill in the blank to make a complete sentence. My animal is a cat! First, I'll draw my cat. (Draw a quick sketch of a cat.) Now I'll write *cat* in the blank. I have to say each sound. /k/ /ă/ /t/ (Put a finger up for each sound.) /k/. . . C or K. I'm going to use C. /ă/. . . A. /t/. . . T. (As you sound out and name the letter, write the letter in the blank.) Let's read my sentence together. 'A cat sat on my porch today.' (Point and read the sentence.)"

Name _____

A __cat__ sat on my porch today.

Name _____

A _____ sat on my porch today.

Let's Get Some Practice

Support each child as they choose their animal, draw it, and then sound out to write it. As children finish, have them point and read their sentences. You may want to write the words using "adult writing" by their "kid writing" attempts.

Wrap It Up

"Let's read our sentences. I'll go first. I'll hold my paper up so you can see my drawing. Then I'll point and read my sentence. 'A cat sat on my porch.'"

> **Flex the Activity!**
> You can collect these sentence frames and make a class book. These sentences can be used for activities such as Be the Word from chapter 5 as you emphasize words in sentences.

ACTIVITY Start with a Picture

Get Things Ready

Collect pictures from magazines, or print some pictures. You can choose for children or provide a collection from which they can choose. The only consideration of your picture choices is to make sure each lends itself to writing a sentence: a who or a what and what is happening. I like to set up a page that is blank on top with lines for writing on the bottom.

Make an Introduction

"Remember, letters go together to make words. And words go together to make sentences. We are going to write sentences today. We'll use pictures to help us think of ideas for our sentences."

Now for the Model

"A sentence tells who or what we are talking about. It also tells us what they are doing or what is happening. I'm going to write about this picture. It shows kids on a slide. I need a who or what—the kids. Now I need to say what they are doing—sliding. My sentence is: *The kids slide*. Now I need to count my words. I'm going to hold up a finger for each word I say. *The. Kids. Slide*. Three words. I'll start with the first one. *The*. Oh. This is one of our heart words. Let me find it. (Point out the heart-word card for *the* on your wall. (See chapter 5 for an explanation of heart words) *T-H-E. The*. (Write the word.) I need to remember that my sentences start with uppercase letters. So, my first letter needs to be uppercase. The kids slide. My next word is *kids*. I need to listen for my sounds to write *kids*. (Demonstrate saying each sound and writing a letter for each sound.) *The kids*. Now I'll write my last word, *slide*. (Demonstrate saying each sound and writing a letter for each sound. For this word, I'll spell it correctly but not make a big deal about the silent *e*.) Now I end my sentence with a period. *The kids slide*." (Point and read your sentence.)

Let's Get Some Practice

Provide opportunities for children to practice writing sentences as you provide feedback. Your level of support will depend on children. For example, you might need to model more and/or write additional sentences using the interactive writing technique. Or, you can partner children to write a sentence together. Or, children write their own sentences as you provide support. You may find you want to provide "adult writing" to coincide with their "kid writing." I usually do this for children who are still pretend writing to demonstrate making letter-sound connections.

▢ Wrap It Up

"We wrote sentences! We thought about the who or the what in the picture. We also thought about what they did or what was happening. And, we wrote sentences! Remember, sentences start with uppercase letters and end with punctuation. My sentence, *The kids slide*, has an uppercase *T* at the beginning and a period at the end. Look at Mia's sentence. (Point and read as you point out her uppercase start and ending punctuation.) She wrote, *The kids run!* She has an uppercase *T* at the beginning and an exclamation point at the end. Why did she choose an exclamation point?"

> **Flex the Activity!**
> This activity can be further scaffolded by providing a sentence frame. You will just need to make sure your frame and pictures complement each other. For example, you can provide pictures of children doing things (for example, swinging, swimming, eating ice cream) with the sentence frame "___ likes to ___."

ACTIVITY Make a List

▢ Get Things Ready

All you'll need for this activity is chart paper (or your whiteboard) and a marker.

▢ Make an Introduction

"People write for different reasons. Sometimes they make lists to remember things. I do this when I go to the grocery story to remind myself of the things I need to buy. We'll make a list of things we'll need to make ice cream sundaes!"

▢ Now for the Model

"At the top of my page, I'll write the title: *Shopping List*. I'm going to start my list here at the top under my title. The first thing we need is ice cream. I'll write that first. This is two words. . . *ice* and *cream*. (Hold up a finger for each word.) I'll write *ice* first. What's the first sound in *ice*? /ī/. . . so I'll write the letter *I* first. My next sound is /s/. What letter says /s/? I know *C* sometimes says /s/. I'll finish writing my word using *C* for /s/. (Finish writing *ice* and make little mention of the silent *e*.) Now let's write *cream*. *Ice cream*. Let's say our sounds. /krrrēēēmmm/. (Hold up a finger for each sound you say.) What's my first sound? /k/. . . that can be *C* or *K*. I'm going to write *C*. /krrrēēēmmm/. /krrrr/. . . /r/. What letter says /r/? *R*. /krrrēēēmmm/. /ēēē/. *E*. . . okay. I'll write *E*. What's my last sound? /krrrēēēmmm/. /mmm/. What letter should I write? *M*. Yes." Note: You can write using invented spelling to demonstrate for children, or you can write using conventional spellings. If the latter, make little note about the advanced patterns (for example, the vowel-consonant-*e* in *ice* and the vowel team in *cream*).

Let's Get Some Practice

Invite children to come up and help write the remainder of your list. Differentiate their contributions based on their understandings. For example, invite a child to write a letter if they are working on letter formation, and invite another child to identify a beginning sound and write the letter that represents it if they are using letters to represent some sounds in words.

Wrap It Up

"We made our list for our ice cream sundaes. Let's read down our list." (Point as you chorally read the list.)

Connect to a Book!

Plan your list after reading *Gorilla Loves Vanilla* by Chae Strathie or *Make Your Own Ice Cream Sundae* by Fran Newman-D'Amico. Or create a different list inspired by another book. For example, you might make a list of supplies for planting a garden after reading *Lola Plants a Garden* by Anna McQuinn, read *Everything You Need for a Treehouse* by Carter Higgins and create a list for a magical treehouse, or create a list of party supplies after reading *The Piñata That the Farm Maiden Hung* by Samantha R. Vamos.

ACTIVITY Make a Web

Get Things Ready

All you'll need for this activity is chart paper, a marker, and a nonfiction book on your topic. I'm going to use *Gray Squirrels* by G.G. Lake from the Woodland Wildlife series. I like to print out a color picture of whatever we're learning about, so I'll print a picture of a gray squirrel to put in the middle of our web.

Make an Introduction

"We've been learning about animals, and this week we've read about animals that live in forests. Today we're going to make a web about gray squirrels. See my gray squirrel. (Write *gray squirrel* by your picture.) Let's think together about the things we've learned about gray squirrels."

Now for the Model

"Our gray squirrel is in the middle. I'm going to draw a line away from the picture and add a fact we've learned about gray squirrels. Hmmm. . . I learned gray squirrels are tree jumpers. I'm going to write that on our web." (Write *tree jumpers* and emphasize letter sounds children know as you write. Draw a circle around your fact.)

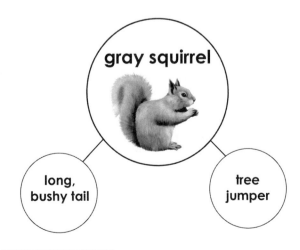

Let's Get Some Practice

"What else did we learn about gray squirrels? Think. (Give children a minute to think of a fact.) Now let's turn and talk to our partners. (For this to be productive, you will need to teach them about "turn and talk"—see chapter 2.) Okay. Let's come back together in 3, 2, 1." Use your equity sticks or whatever method you use to call on a child. Draw your line, reinforce letter-sound correspondences as appropriate, and circle the fact. Continue until you've completed your web and reread facts to review as you go. If children have difficulty thinking about facts, pull out your book to reread a page or ask questions such as, "Do gray squirrels have short, stubby tails?" You can also draw pictures when reasonable to go with your fact (for example, a bushy tail).

Wrap It Up

"We've learned so much about animals that live in the forest! And today we thought about gray squirrels. Let's read through our facts. (Point and read facts.) I'll post this web in our science center for you to read or use to make your own."

ACTIVITY Write About a Shared Activity

Get Things Ready

All you need for this activity is a shared experience plus chart paper and markers. I usually like to have sentence starters to support our story already written to generate ideas and support the cognitive load of the activity. These shared experiences don't have to be special events; they can be everyday events such as recess.

Make an Introduction

"Today we're going to write a story about the fun we have at recess. I've written the title on my paper already. I'll point and read it for you. Fun at Recess." (Point and read the title.)

Now for the Model

"I've gotten our story started by writing the beginning of each sentence. You'll help me think about how we can end each sentence. I'll show you how with our first sentence. Here I have it started. It says, 'Today we went to recess and. . .' I need to write something to finish this sentence. I'm thinking we should say how much fun we had. I'll read the sentence again and add what I want to say to make sure it makes sense. 'Today we went to recess and had so much fun.' That makes sense. I'm going to write those words at the end of the sentence: *had so much fun*. (Hold up a finger for each word you say.) That's four words." Encourage children to help you remember what word comes next in the sentence, and as you write each word, emphasize letter sounds children know. Reinforce writing conventions such as starting sentences with uppercase letters, ending with punctuation, and spacing between words.

Let's Get Some Practice

"Now you'll help me finish the next two sentences in our story. Here's our next sentence. 'When we were at recess, we. . .' What is one thing you did?" Allow time for children to think and then respond. You could have them turn and talk to encourage contributions from all children. Go through the same process of orally completing the sentence to check that it makes sense, counting words, and emphasizing sounds as you write words (or use your heart words as appropriate). Make sure to reinforce writing conventions such as uppercase letters, punctuation, and spacing. Then move to your last sentence: "We also had fun. . ."

Wrap It Up

"Now that we've finished our story, let's read it. (Point as you chorally read the story.) I want to draw a picture about the story we just wrote. What should we draw? Turn and talk with your partner. Think about what we should draw." After children have time to talk, bring them back together to get ideas of what to draw. As you draw, think aloud what you are drawing, and invite children to suggest things to add to your drawing.

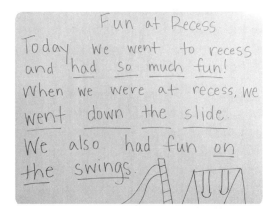

Look For

Ultimately, you are looking for children to begin to apply letter-sound connections to their writing (for example, *K* for *kitten*) and to demonstrate an understanding of the functions of print in prekindergarten. As kindergartners, you will be looking for the children to write a complete sentence following basic writing conventions and applying letter-sound connections with increasing independence.

ACTIVITY Class Books

Get Things Ready

Class books are well loved and get a lot of attention, so I usually like to write them on paper and then laminate them before putting them together. Many schools have binding machines, and plastic bindings are inexpensive. But you can always use rings, tie with yarn, put in a three-ring binder, bind with embroidery thread, and so on. Or you can make an accordion book. The main takeaway here is there are many, many ways to make a book!

You can make class books about so many different things. For example, you could have a collection of forest-animal webs (for example, gray squirrel) that you collect in a book or use as inspiration to write a sentence about each animal. For this example, we'll write a class book inspired by *The Panda Problem* by Deborah

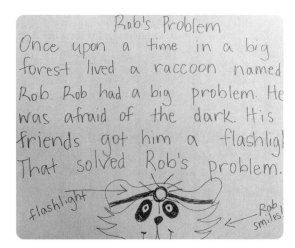

Underwood. In this book, Panda is the main character who needs to have a problem so that the problem can be solved because, as Panda learns, that's how stories work.

Make an Introduction

"Remember our book *The Panda Problem?* Panda was our main character, and Panda had a problem. What was Panda's problem? That's right! He needed a problem! We learned that stories have characters who have problems that get solved. Today we'll write a story and decide on a main character, the problem, and the solution. We'll write our own story!"

Now for the Model

"Let's get our story started. The first thing we'll do is introduce our main character. I want my story to take place in the forest, so I'm going to write about a raccoon. Our main character is a raccoon. I know stories sometimes start out with 'once upon a time,' so I'm going to use that. Once upon a time in a big forest lived a raccoon named Rob." Demonstrate writing while you think aloud key points such as uppercase letters, spacing, letter-sound connections to write words like *big* and *Rob*, heart words, and ending punctuation.

Let's Get Some Practice

Continue writing your story as you encourage children to think about the problem. As with Panda in *The Panda Problem*, the problem can be silly (for example, raining jellybeans). Using the shared writing technique, you can invite children to help form sentences to tell your story, think about writing conventions (for example, uppercase letters, spacing), and write words as you emphasize letter-sound correspondences. You can write class books with prereaders, too. You would just emphasize concepts about print such as moving left to right and perhaps initial sounds or letter formation.

Wrap It Up

"We wrote a book! We thought about how our character needs a problem and that problem needs to get solved. We'll read our book together a few times, and I'll make it available to you in our class library!"

Flex the Activity!

You can connect to the Name Song activity in chapter 4. You could invite children to draw a picture about themselves and fill in a sentence frame like "___ likes ___." Or you could invite them to bring in something special from home or a picture of them doing some of their favorite things to make a page for each child to go in the book. Perhaps each page could have the following sentence frames/starters: "My name is ___. I love to ___." You could highlight different children each day to create your book. This will for sure be a loved book that gets many readers over the year!

Connect to a Book!

Another fun book is *One Day, The End: Short, Very Short, Shorter-Than-Ever Stories* by Rebecca Kai Dotlich. This is a book about stories that get started but don't have problems or solutions. It's a good contrast to demonstrate how problems and their solutions make stories more entertaining.

ACTIVITY Speech Bubbles

Get Things Ready

Find a book that clearly illustrates speech bubbles and how a character's words can help tell a story. One I like to use is *You Will Be My Friend!* by Peter Brown. In this book, the dialogue is in quotation bubbles, which are prominently placed on the page. I usually pose a question for check-in that I can use with this activity, such as, "What's your favorite ice cream flavor?" or "Are bugs cool or creepy?" You'll need chart paper for your story using speech bubbles.

Make an Introduction

"In *You Will Be My Friend!*, Lucy is so excited to find a friend. She talks to many animals to find one. (Open to a page with speech bubbles.) See these? They are called speech bubbles. That's how we know what Lucy is saying. Here she says, "I'm going to make a new friend today! Mom! Isn't that exciting!" (Point and read each speech bubble.)

Now for the Model

"You can use speech bubbles in your drawings. Today when you checked in, I asked if you thought bugs were cool or creepy. In our morning meeting, ten of us said they are creepy and five said they are cool. I'm going to pick one of you who thinks they're creepy and one of you who said cool. (Randomly choose two children's names.) I pick Mia and Javier. I'm going to draw Mia and Javier, and then I'm going to have them talk to each other using speech bubbles like in our book. Mia thinks bugs are cool, so she says, 'Bugs are cool.' I'm going to make a speech bubble by Mia and write, 'Bugs are cool.' (Emphasize the letter sounds in the words to highlight taught sounds as you use the shared writing technique.) Now Javier is going to say something to Mia. He thinks bugs are creepy. So, he'll say, 'Bugs are creepy.' Watch me make a speech bubble by Javier and write what he says. (Again, emphasize letter sounds in the words as you write and invite children to take part in shared writing.)

Let's Get Some Practice

"Now you'll draw yourself and a friend. You'll make a speech bubble for each of you and write, 'Bugs are cool,' or 'Bugs are creepy.' Use our question of the day to find out what your friend thinks about bugs!" Support children drawing a picture quickly and using speech bubbles to write dialogue. You can support children by having the sentences already set like I did here, or you can have sentence frames they'll use in their speech bubbles. As children write, support their letter-sound connections and use of writing conventions (for example, uppercase letters, punctuation).

Wrap It Up

"Nice work using speech bubbles in your drawings today. Your speech bubbles told a message about what we think about bugs! Think about other times you can use speech bubbles. Let's all try to use speech bubbles in our journals today!"

ACTIVITY Journals

Get Things Ready

Make journals for all children. I usually make journals with paper set up for drawing at the top and lined at the bottom for writing. Then I hole-punch and collect pages in pocket folders with brads. You'll also want to collect writing utensils (for example, little golf pencils) and a binder clip to mark your place. Many teachers like date stamps for journal entries; I use a self-ink stamp. This lesson introduces the concept of journaling for writing practice.

Make an Introduction

"Today we're going to get journals for our writing! Let me show you my journal. I use it whenever I want to write about something that happened or something new I learned. You'll get your journals today, so you'll have a special place to write things in, too!"

Now for the Model

"I know this is my journal because it has my name and my picture on its cover. Let me show you my journal. You see this binder clip? This lets me know which page to write on when I'm ready. It's like a bookmark. (Open your journal using the binder clip.) Now that I know which page I'll write on, I'm ready to get started. I'll use my date stamp. Watch me use it. All you do is put it down flat at the top right of your page and push straight down quickly. (Make your date stamp and show the children.) Now I need to decide what I want to write. I'm going to write about a walk I went on this weekend with my daughter in my neighborhood. It started to rain when we were halfway back to our house, so we started to run. We got so wet that it looked like we had taken a shower! (Draw a picture to represent your story as you are telling it.) Now I'm going to write a sentence to tell about my drawing. I'm going to write, 'My daughter and I ran home in the rain!'" (Think aloud while you write your sentence. Count the words. Talk about using an uppercase letter to start, punctuation at the end, and spacing between words. Emphasize using letter-sound correspondences as well as when you can use a heart word.)

Let's Get Some Practice

Give each child a journal with their picture and name on the cover. Help them find the page with the binder clip. Then help each child put their date in the upper right-hand corner. Now they are ready to write. Remind them of the first step: Think about what you want to write about. Then draw a picture. After you have your picture, write your sentence. Support each child as necessary. For example, you might have a child dictate to you and you record what they say about their picture. Or you might have a child tell you about their picture and write a sentence frame for them. Or you might count the number of words in the child's sentence, draw a line for each word, and support them writing words. Or you might provide "adult writing" with the child's "kid writing."

▢ Wrap It Up

"We can write our thoughts and stories in our journals. Think about what you want to tell with your writing. Then draw a picture and write your message! We'll keep working in our journals." I like having a particular time of the day for journaling when I can move around the room and support children's writing and provide feedback as I reinforce letter-sound correspondences and other writing conventions we've learned.

> **Connect to a Book!**
>
> You can write in journals about a theme or topic of study. You can also write in response to a book you are getting ready to read, are reading, or have just finished reading. For example, after reading *Ruby Finds a Worry* by Tom Percival, you can talk about times we've been worried like Ruby, and children can write in their journals.

ACTIVITY Heart Ideas

▢ Get Things Ready

Set up your chart paper and make a heart paper for each child. You'll also need writing utensils. To set up your heart papers, write "Heart Ideas" at the top (or put a red heart where the word *heart* would be) and then create a list underneath. Children can put their heart ideas in the front pocket of their journals.

▢ Make an Introduction

"Authors love to write! When authors write stories, they think about people or things they care a lot about. Today we're going to make a list of ideas we'd love to write about. We'll call them our 'heart ideas.' Whenever you aren't sure what to write about, you can take a look at your heart ideas.

▢ Now for the Model

"See what I've written at the top of my page? It says 'Heart Ideas.' I'm going to list at least four things I care about that I'd like to write about. I can write more, but I'm going to start with four. Okay, I'm going to close my eyes and think about something or somebody I love. (Close your eyes and indicate you are thinking.) The first thing I'm thinking about is my family. I'm going to draw my family. (Draw and label the picture.) Something else I love is my dog, Desmond. So, I'm going to draw him next. (Draw and label the picture.) Continue with this process until you have four things drawn and labeled.

▢ Let's Get Some Practice

Partner children so they can "turn and talk" about what they would like to draw for their heart ideas. Distribute heart-ideas papers and support the children as they begin to draw their ideas. Move around the room and label their drawings and support them as they think about their ideas. It's usually good to have a list already in your head for suggestions. I usually think about themes or topics we've been studying as well as some tried-and-true topics such as bugs, toys, friends, birthdays, holidays, and seasons.

Wrap It Up

"Each of you came up with some great heart ideas. Remember, when you are writing in your journal and can't think of something to write, you can look at your heart ideas!"

> **Flex the Activity!**
>
> Pictures are worth a thousand words. Sometimes children can't think of ideas for writing, and a picture can help. I keep a collection of pictures, too, that I also call heart ideas. You can talk to children about using the heart-ideas box as you do with the Start with a Picture activity from this chapter.

ACTIVITY Write a Letter to a Character

Get Things Ready

Choose a book with an engaging character. *Gustavo, the Shy Ghost* by Flavia Z. Drago or *Carmela Full of Wishes* by Matt de la Peña are a couple of choices. Read the book to the children. You can write a letter after reading the story or before you are finished. For example, in *Gustavo, the Shy Ghost*, Gustavo is so shy he has trouble making friends. After you have established his problem in the story, stop reading and write a letter to Gustavo to give him advice. Or in *Carmela Full of Wishes*, she finds a dandelion ready to blow and make a wish. Write a letter to Carmela to ask about her wish and offer ideas. For this activity, you will be using the interactive writing technique and inviting children to help you write.

Make an Introduction

"We've been reading *Mother Bruce* by Ryan T. Higgins this week. Today we're going to write a letter to Bruce from the gosling's mother. If someone takes care of your babies, what kind of letter might you write them? I agree! A thank-you letter."

Now for the Model

"Let's pretend we are the mother goose. Since this is a letter to Bruce, we'll write *Dear Bruce* to start. So, I'm going to write the word *Dear*. (Write *Dear* on your chart paper. Invite children to help make letter-sound connections with /d/ at the beginning and /r/ at the end.) Now I'll write *Bruce*. Let's listen for the first sound in *Bruce*. . . /b/ /b/ *Bruce*. What letter makes /b/? *B*. Yes. Since this is his name, we will use an uppercase *B*. (Invite a child to come up and write *B* on the chart paper. Then write the rest of *Bruce*.) Let's read what we have so far: 'Dear Bruce.'" (Point as you read.)

Let's Get Some Practice

"Let's think about what we want to tell Bruce. Think about all of the things Bruce does for the goslings in the story. Turn and talk with your partner to think about what we should tell him." Bring the children back to the group and talk about how you would start with a statement of thank you. Then give two reasons why you are thankful. For example, you might say, "Thank you for taking care of my goslings. You kept them safe. You gave them food." Write one sentence at a time, count the number of words in a sentence, and talk about conventions of writing (for example, start at the left, begin with an uppercase letter). Invite children to come up to write letters after making letter-sound connections to the words. Invite children to punctuate your sentences. You might even have a child come up to write a word, such as a heart word like *you*. As you finish a sentence, point and echo read it.

Wrap It Up

"Let's read our thank-you letter together. (Point as you chorally read the letter.) I'm going to hang our letter so you can read it again. See if you can find letters and words you know!"

Flex the Activity!

Alternatively, you can write a letter to a favorite author. After reading two or three books from an author, you can talk about writing a letter to the author to talk about your favorite books. You could have children vote on their favorite as they check in one morning and sign their names. Then you can count the names and provide a total before you begin your letter. For example, *Mother Bruce* is a series by Ryan T. Higgins. Children can vote on their favorite Mother Bruce book and write a letter to Ryan Higgins about their favorite parts.

ACTIVITY Message Board

Get Things Ready

Create an area in your classroom for the message board. Post a message (I usually use an oversized sticky note) with *To* at the top and *From* at the bottom as a model for children when they write their own messages. I always keep the message simple and highlight *To* and *From* so they can copy these key words for their messages. Have a collection of sticky notes and writing utensils at the message board for easy use. Note: I've found I need to buy super sticky notes so they stay posted.

Make an Introduction

"Sometimes I have something to tell someone, but they're busy or not here. When that happens, I can write them a note and leave it here on our message board. Today we'll write a note. Our notes will always have the name of who we are writing to, our message or what we want to say, and our name so they know who the note is from. You can write notes to me or a friend." (Be sure to include other adults in the room such as the classroom assistant).

Now for the Model

"There are three things you need on a note. (Show your oversized sticky note.) First, I'll write the word *To* and the name of the person I'm writing my note to. Second, I'll write my message. This is what I want to say. Third, I'll write *From* and my name so the person knows who wrote the message. Watch me write a note to Ms. Preston. I need our pencils sharpened, and I want to ask her to do that while I'm thinking about it. The first thing I need to do is write the word *To* and her name, *Ms. Preston*. Then I need to write my message. "Please sharpen our pencils." The last thing I need to do is write the word *From* and put my name, *Ms. Hayes*." (Model writing on your oversized sticky note as you emphasize letter-sound connections, writing conventions, and the three parts of the message.) "I can also draw some pencils because it's okay to write a message with pictures or words. My note is finished, so I'll post it here on my message board."

Let's Get Some Practice

Practice writing another note together. I usually write to someone to tell them about the message board. Make sure to use another oversized sticky note so all children can see it. Use the shared writing technique to create the message, and make sure to highlight the three parts of the message. Come back to the message board for as many days as you think you should so that children feel confident and comfortable using it. You might find prewritten messages can be helpful. For example, you might have To: ___ and From: ___ at the top and the bottom with a space between for the message, which can be pictures or words.

Wrap It Up

"Now we know how to write notes and leave them on our message board. You can write notes to someone, and we'll check our message board every day. Make sure you check, too, because you might get a message!" Note: Your message board can become stagnant quickly if you don't regularly use it yourself and encourage children to use it. I usually have a set time of the day when I check it with the class. I also monitor the board to make sure all children get at least one message every week; I keep a checklist to make note of when I leave a message so I can easily keep up with it.

ACTIVITY Nonfiction Writing

Get Things Ready

This activity works well after you've read a nonfiction book or after you've completed a thematic study. I often pair it with a graphic organizer like the web in this chapter. You'll need chart paper, a marker, and any graphic organizer or book you are using as a reference. In this example, I'm using the book *Can an Aardvark Bark?* by Melissa Stewart. Each child will need paper for practice, or you can have them write in their journals.

Make an Introduction

"We learned a lot about how animals communicate in our book *Can an Aardvark Bark?* We write for different reasons. Sometimes we want to tell a story, and sometimes we want to share information to learn about something new. Nonfiction writing helps us learn new information and facts about something."

Now for the Model

"Let's write about the ways animals communicate. In our book, we learned that some animals bark like a seal and a tree frog. We learned that a woodchuck can whistle. Hedgehogs and dolphins squeal. Porcupines, bears, and beavers whine. (As you are talking, write down ways animals communicate: *bark, whistle, squeal, whine*.) What are other ways animals communicate? (Encourage answers such as gorillas laughing and salamanders growling. Add these to your list.) I'm going to write about seals. First, I'll draw a picture of a seal. Now, I'll write my sentence about my picture. Remember, a sentence has words. *Seals can bark. Seals. Can. Bark.* (Hold up fingers as you say each word.) Three words. I'll start with my first word, *seals.*"

(Continue with each word as you write your sentence and emphasize letter-sound connections and writing conventions.)

▢ Let's Get Some Practice

Give each child their journal. Invite children to draw their pictures first. Support each child as necessary. For example, some children may need to dictate to you about their pictures while you write their words. For others, you might write a sentence frame such as "Beavers and bears ___" and help them make letter-sound connections to complete the sentence frame or refer them to your list from the model. Other children might need less support; you might ask them about their picture, help them narrow in on a simple descriptive sentence, write a line for each word, and support them as they write each word.

▢ Wrap It Up

"It was fun to learn about all of the ways animals communicate! We have lots of facts about this. We could even turn these facts into a nonfiction book about the ways they communicate. Let's plan to do that!"

To Sum It Up

In the end, writing is an essential practice for our early learners, even before they can form letters and make letter-sound connections. The activities in this chapter span from handwriting and letter formation to spelling to writing composition. Ultimately, we want to instill in children the functions of print through their own writing. They write to communicate. We also want to provide an authentic purpose for applying their letter-sound knowledge and practicing writing conventions like spacing and punctuation. The more practice they get, the more feedback you can provide. This will help increase their accuracy and overall fluency of writing words and sentences. While early writing is only one part of the bigger early literacy picture, it is an important one.

8

CHAPTER EIGHT
Putting It All Together

The aim of this book is to arm you with early literacy activities that you can use in your classroom. To use these activities with intentionality, it is important to consider four things: 1) developmental trends in literacy, 2) developmentally appropriate practices, 3) assessment procedures to identify what the children have learned and whether they are meeting age expectations, and 4) the standards to use as a guidepost. This is all in an effort to help children reach their full potential.

Research over the past four decades has demonstrated over and over that early reading difficulties more often than not lead to later reading difficulties (for example, Fletcher and Lyon, 1998; Heckman, Moon, Pinto, Savelyev, and Yavitz, 2010; Juel, 1988). In other words, reading difficulties early on in a child's schooling do not tend to resolve on their own. As Solari, McGinty, and Hall (2021) put it, "We now understand that we should not believe there is such a thing as a 'late bloomer' when it comes to reading development." Teachers who develop a deep understanding of instruction (including the activities in this book) and pay attention to their children's literacy needs will positively affect the early literacy growth of the children in their classrooms.

Developmental Trends in Literacy

Let's bring it back to something we thought about in chapter 1—the Simple View of Reading (Gough and Tumner, 1986). Here are a few quick reminders about this framework. First, the key concept Gough and Tumner relay to educators is that a reader relies on both word decoding

and language comprehension to understand the written texts they read. Second, the framework seems simple, but in fact, it is complex and multifaceted. Third, thinking about this framework can help us understand literacy developmental trends of the children in our classrooms, which, in turn, help us think more intentionally about our early literacy instruction and assessment.

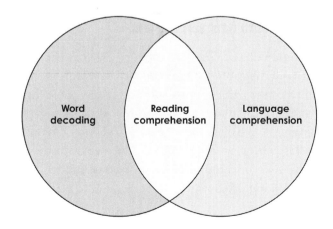

Literacy instruction in our early education classrooms must include attention across all areas mapped out in the chapters of this book. Let's take each chapter's focus and see how it relates to the Simple View of Reading.

- Instruction targeting phonological awareness (chapter 3), the alphabetic code (chapter 4), word recognition and foundational fluency (chapter 5), and early writing (chapter 7) helps children begin to develop the word-decoding component of the framework.

- Instruction targeting oral language (chapter 2) and vocabulary, comprehension, and world knowledge (chapter 6) helps children build upon their existing language comprehension.

Providing the children with the opportunity to practice early literacy skills across the Simple View of Reading builds the foundation for skilled, fluent reading and writing in the elementary school grades. A curriculum focused on these components of language and early literacy provides significant benefits for children (Shanahan and Lonigan, 2013). You may already have an early literacy curriculum in place. A strong curriculum combined with a knowledgeable teacher can make a difference for a child that lasts a lifetime. After reading this book, you might find yourself wanting to reflect upon your curriculum. A helpful resource that is readily available online is the *Language and Literacy Preschool Curriculum Consumer Report* published by the National Center on Quality Teaching and Learning (2015). It not only provides guidance on evaluating the strengths and weaknesses curricula, but it also offers a thorough evaluation of seven commonly used prekindergarten curricula (for example, *Read It Again-PreK!*).

Early Literacy Instruction and Developmentally Appropriate Practices

As an early childhood educator, you are attuned to developmentally appropriate practices—instruction that is designed to be engaging and appropriate for children in early childhood programs. This core concept guiding your instruction is the basis of a rich learning environment where the children can explore and learn. It is important for them to have intentional instruction that is explicit, systematic, and sequential. This means your teaching is intentional and deliberate, including both teacher-directed and child-directed activities. The activities throughout this book exemplify this idea of intentionality through teacher- and child-directed activities.

Assessment to Gauge Progress

Developmentally appropriate practice involves intentional and deliberate instruction, and assessments support our intentionality. Assessments provide us with valuable information about what the children have learned and what to teach, as well as offer a framework for communicating with families about what their children are learning in our classrooms. Comprehensive assessment includes a range of tools like one-to-one child assessments, portfolios, and observations. Armed with valuable assessment information, you can determine what the children already know, support what they still need to learn, and identify children who need additional supports.

We have many informal assessments at our fingertips to help us better understand children's early literacy knowledge. Common assessments of early literacy address both the word decoding and language comprehension components of the Simple View of Reading. Let's take a look at common assessment options, what they measure, example questions or prompts, and when they are typically assessed.

	COMMON OPTIONS	WHAT THEY MEASURE	EXAMPLE QUESTIONS/ PROMPTS	WHEN
Word Decoding	Alphabet Knowledge	Recognize letter names and sounds	▪ What is this letter's name? ▪ What sound does this letter make?	Prekindergarten Kindergarten
	Phonological Awareness	▪ Recognize and produce rhyme ▪ Segment words in a spoken sentence ▪ Blend and segment syllables ▪ Blend onset-rime ▪ Segment initial sounds ▪ Segment phonemes in a spoken word	▪ Do these words rhyme: *pig* and *wig*? ▪ How many words are in this sentence? *I ride the bus to school.* ▪ How many word parts are in *cookie*? ▪ Listen: /f/ / ŏx/ What word did I say? ▪ What is the first sound in *mop*? ▪ How many sounds do you hear in *sat*?	Prekindergarten* Kindergarten *Note: rhyme production and phoneme segmentation are not typically assessed until kindergarten.
	Phonics/ Decoding	Phonic elements Word decoding	▪ What sound do these letters make? (Show child letters and letter combinations such as *SH* to provide sounds.) ▪ What is this word? (Show child CVC words such as *sat, hop* to decode.)	Kindergarten

	COMMON OPTIONS	WHAT THEY MEASURE	EXAMPLE QUESTIONS/ PROMPTS	WHEN
Word Decoding	Word Recognition	■ Read highly frequent words (for example, *the, is*) in isolation ■ Recognize words in the context of a short passage	■ Read each of these words to me. (Show child a set of words organized by frequency or grade-level expectation.) ■ Read this story to me. (Show child a short passage that is usually chosen using grade-level guidance.)	Kindergarten
	Early Writing	■ Name writing ■ Spelling ■ Informal writing	■ Write your name. ■ Spell the word *sat*. ■ Write a sentence about what you did at recess.	Kindergarten (Note: name writing is typically a prekindergarten task.)
Language Comprehension	Concepts About Print	Understand: ■ Purpose of print ■ Parts of a book (for example, front/ back) ■ Directionality (for example, move left to right and top to bottom) ■ Difference between letters and words ■ Words are separated by spaces	■ Show me the front of the book. ■ Show me the picture. Show me the words. ■ Where should I start reading? ■ If I start here, where do I go next? ■ Show me one letter. Show me one word. ■ Point to each word as I read this line.	Prekindergarten Kindergarten
	Comprehension	■ Listening comprehension	■ What was the problem in this story? ■ Tell me something you learned about _____.	Prekindergarten Kindergarten

We often gauge our progress across the components of early literacy using more formalized assessments at key points, such as the beginning, middle, and end of the year, as part of program or school's screening assessment. These types of assessments are important for us to consider because a child's acquisition of early literacy skills can predict the trajectory of that child's future reading achievement. Early literacy screening serves three main purposes in that they identify children who may:

- be at risk for reading difficulties,

- need a more thorough assessment, or

- benefit from intervention.

While not an exhaustive list, three easily available literacy assessments that have undergone extensive research and development are *Get Ready to Read!* (Whitehurst, n.d.), *Preschool Early Literacy Indicators* (PELI) (Dynamic Measurement Group, 2019), and *Phonological Awareness Literacy Screening* (PALS) (Invernizzi, Meier, Swank, and Juel, 2001).

ASSESSMENTS	WHERE?	WHO?	WHAT?
Get Ready to Read!	Free online set of downloadable questions http://www.getreadytoread.org/ (an updated print version is available for purchase through Pearson Early Learning)	Children the year before they enter kindergarten (three to five years old)	■ Screening tool ■ Twenty questions focused on print knowledge, phonological awareness, and emergent writing ■ Takes approximately fifteen minutes
PELI	Purchase kit for administration https://acadiencelearning.org/acadience-reading/prek-peli/	Two measures for children: ■ Three to four years old ■ Four to five years old	■ Screening tool and progress monitoring options ■ Measures alphabet knowledge, vocabulary and oral language, phonological awareness, and listening comprehension all within the context of a read-aloud ■ Takes approximately fifteen minutes

ASSESSMENTS	WHERE?	WHO?	WHAT?
PALS	Purchase kit for administration https://pals.virginia.edu/public/tools-prek.html https://pals.virginia.edu/public/tools-k.html	Two measures for children: ■ Prekindergarten (PALS-PreK) ■ Kindergarten (PALS-K)	■ Screening tool ■ PALS-PreK includes name-writing, upper- and lowercase letter recognition, letter sound knowledge and beginning sound production, print and word awareness, rhyme awareness, and nursery rhyme awareness ■ PALS-K includes phonological awareness, lowercase letter recognition, letter sound knowledge, concept of word, and spelling

We also monitor progress day to day with informal assessments. As early childhood educators, we commonly use observation in naturalistic settings. We routinely observe children engage in literacy activities through systematic observation over time. Two common ways we systematically observe are a summary page per child to organize information gained by observations and informal assessments across language and early literacy components, or a sheet focused on one language or early literacy component (for example, alphabet knowledge: letter name, letter sound, letter formation) where you record your observations across all the children. Regardless of how you keep records of your assessments and observations, these can be used to help kick-start and guide your instruction, communicate with colleagues, and share with parents. (See appendix B for examples of checklists.)

After a few weeks of planned observations, you'll have a lot of information on children's knowledge, skills, and interests. Using assessment information to plan lessons and activities makes it much more likely that you will build on children's strengths, meet their needs, and create playful learning experiences. In this way, assessment information allows us to plan successive lessons as well as adapt and individualize curricula and our teaching when children do not make expected progress or are performing at advanced levels. We boost our effectiveness when we use assessment to better understand the children's language and early literacy skills and where these understandings lie with respect to our standards. In other words, we need to understand where children are as well as where they are going.

Standards as Guideposts

Standards help guide us in making decisions about what children should know and when they should know it. I like to think of it this way. When I need directions, I look up Google Maps, and I put in my starting point. Here my starting point is children's language and early literacy skill as informed by initial assessments such as an early literacy screener. Then I put in my destination. My grade-level standards are my destination. Google gives me a route. A comprehensive language and early literacy curriculum that includes activities like the ones in this book provides us with a route to take. Along the way, we have assessments and observations that help us monitor our progress. Continuing with my Google metaphor, sometimes I have to take a

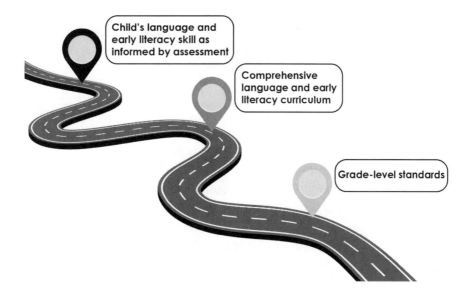

different turn and Google reroutes me, but my destination remains the same. Similarly, our standards are our guideposts in our yearly language and literacy journey.

In this book, I use the National Association for the Education of Young Children (NAEYC) standards for children in the prekindergarten years and the Common Core State Standards (CCSS) to consider achievement in kindergarten. Both NAEYC and CCSS recognize assessment as a core component of early childhood classrooms. As shown throughout chapters 2–7, the standards take the children from emerging in their language and literacy skills to beginning their journey toward skilled, fluent reading and writing.

You can also look to your standards to help you pull together checklists for assessment by literacy components. For example, let's look at a Common Core kindergarten standard for foundational skills, specifically phonics and word recognition (CCSS.ELA-LITERACY.RF.K.3):

Know and apply grade-level phonics and word analysis skills in decoding words:

- Demonstrate basic knowledge of one-to-one letter-sound correspondences by producing the primary sound or many of the most frequent sounds for each consonant.

- Associate the long and short sounds with the common spellings (graphemes) for the five major vowels.

Using these standards, I know children need to work toward quick, accurate recognition of all letter-sound correspondences. I might create a checklist specific to letter names and sounds that I might use with individual children. When I observe the children, I can look for evidence during activities (for example, Alphabet Arc in chapter 4) or during quick, informal assessments.

Let's Take a Look in Some Classrooms!

Let's take a look inside two teachers' classrooms. First, we'll visit Ms. Cheung's prekindergarten classroom with fourteen children and a full-time instructional assistant. Second, we'll explore Mr. Johnson's kindergarten room with twenty-five children and a part-time instructional assistant. Across both classrooms, Ms. Cheung and Mr. Johnson have a handful of guiding principles. They are both committed to providing the children with ample literacy materials and supplies within a well-organized room setup for literacy exploration. Both also use effective procedures and routines to manage the day and implement a strong literacy curriculum that is informed by standards and developmental trends in early literacy. Language and literacy are integrated throughout the day in their classrooms. In addition, they both utilize assessment to help them monitor the children's progress and inform their instructional decisions. Let's head to Ms. Cheung's classroom first.

MS. CHEUNG'S PREKINDERGARTEN CLASSROOM

Ms. Chueng works in a public school as a full-day prekindergarten teacher serving qualifying four-year-olds; qualification is mostly based on household income. Her classroom is lively and literacy rich. This year, she has paid close attention to read-alouds that help teach the children about tolerance and social justice. Some of her favorite additions are *Our Class Is a Family* by Shannon Olsen and *Kindness Is My Superpower* by Alicia Ortego. Language and literacy permeate her classroom all day. For example, upon arrival, children find their names in a pocket chart and immediately practice writing their names to sign in. They look for signs posted indicating where to put trash or recyclables after breakfast, lunch, and snack. Take a minute to review Ms. Chueng's schedule as well as her visual schedule displayed for the children.

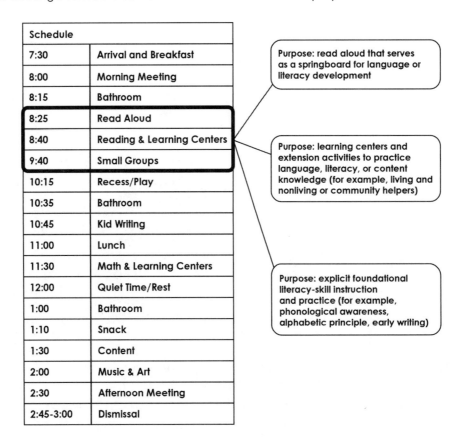

Schedule	
7:30	Arrival and Breakfast
8:00	Morning Meeting
8:15	Bathroom
8:25	Read Aloud
8:40	Reading & Learning Centers
9:40	Small Groups
10:15	Recess/Play
10:35	Bathroom
10:45	Kid Writing
11:00	Lunch
11:30	Math & Learning Centers
12:00	Quiet Time/Rest
1:00	Bathroom
1:10	Snack
1:30	Content
2:00	Music & Art
2:30	Afternoon Meeting
2:45–3:00	Dismissal

Purpose: read aloud that serves as a springboard for language or literacy development

Purpose: learning centers and extension activities to practice language, literacy, or content knowledge (for example, living and nonliving or community helpers)

Purpose: explicit foundational literacy-skill instruction and practice (for example, phonological awareness, alphabetic principle, early writing)

The schedule maps out a block from 8:25 a.m. to 10:15 a.m., which is devoted to language and literacy instruction. To get a feel for Ms. Cheung's language and literacy instruction, let's dive into a day in the life of her classroom. Today, her 8:25 read-aloud is *Fry Bread* by Kevin Noble Maillard. This is their third reading of this book. While she's reading, she's noticing with the children the words that go with our five senses, such as how fry bread looks (round and yellow) and smells (sweet with jam) as well as the sounds you hear when you make it (sizzle and pop). She's taught the children to turn and talk, so she encourages them to talk to each other after she's read about how fry bread is made and how it looks (chapter 2, Talking Partners). She has them stop and think, "What does fry bread make me think about?" She invites the children to turn and talk using the sentence stem "Fry bread makes me think about. . ." When she brings them back to the group to share, she explicitly labels the connection they made between fry bread and foods from their lives and uses a hand gesture to indicate making a connection (chapter 6, Make Connections).

After the read-aloud, the class transitions into reading and learning centers. She begins the time with a whole-group phonological activity in which the children sort pictures of foods by syllable number (for example, eggs—one, pancake—two, banana—three; chapter 3, Syllable Sort). While they sort pictures, she teaches them a new academic term: *category* (chapter 6, Introducing Vocabulary). She tells them a *category* is another word for group of things that go together. To make a connection to previous learning, she reminds them of when they sorted things into circles and squares, explicitly connecting the word *categories* to circles and squares. For example, "We put pennies, pizza, and sun together. They are in the same *category*. They are all circles. So,

their *category* is circles." She uses the word *category* many times during the syllable sort and encourages the children to use it, too.

Ms. Cheung puts the syllable sort with foods in a center. Throughout center time, she engages with children to support their learning and language as she uses oral-language practices such as recasts, expansions, and questions (chapter 2). She uses Paulsen and Moats' Early Literacy Checklist (2018) and makes note of their progress in oral language (for example, the child uses complete sentences with appropriate pronouns), phonological awareness (for example, the child segments words into syllables), and print knowledge (for example, the child identifies uppercase letters).

Then Ms. Cheung brings smaller groups together over two fifteen-minute sessions, bringing roughly half of her class together at a time for more targeted practice. She brings out *fish* from the syllable sort and focuses the children's attention on the beginning sound /f/. She follows the letter introduction from chapter 4, introducing the name, formation, sound, and keyword. Ms. Cheung knows the continuous sound is easier for children, so she "holds on to" the sound /fffff/ as she brings out the letter card for *F* with the keyword *fun*. She says, "*F* says /fff/ like at the beginning of fffffun and fffffish." She follows up with an alphabet review using the Alphabet Arc. While she is working with a small group, the other children have a choice of two activities (Letter or Number or Match It Up) with the support of the instructional assistant, Mr. Hill. See chapter 4 for details on all of these activities.

Ms. Cheung focuses on language and literacy development throughout the day. For example, she teaches uppercase *F* formation using formation language, skywriting, and personal dry-erase boards during Kid Writing at 10:45 (see chapter 6). During morning meeting, she has the children turn and talk with the following sentence starter: "My favorite food is. . . " Then they brainstorm and tally their favorite foods. She adds in hers, figs, shows them a picture as she describes figs, and then models spelling *fig* using Say It, Write It (chapter 7). At 2:30 p.m. as part of her afternoon meeting, she brings the group back together for a Word Train activity (chapter 5). She begins by revisiting the tally of their favorite foods from the morning meeting. Then she chooses their top five to think aloud as she writes the words on a train car. The sentence stem is "My favorite food is. . . " They chorally read the sentence as she moves different favorites in and out (for example, "My favorite food is pizza.").

Throughout the day, Ms. Cheung has included language and literacy activities that work toward her prekindergarten standards, and she maintains her commitment to developmentally appropriate practices. She is thoughtful about keeping the momentum of the group going while also providing time for purposeful play and connecting with children's interests and lives (for example, the Match It Up game or tallying their favorite foods). She also makes sure there is time for them to talk and work with each other during child-directed learning as well as intentional instructional time for teacher-directed learning. As children work with her in small groups, she is observing their performance and making notes about their letter knowledge, including names, sounds, and formation.

MR. JOHNSON'S KINDERGARTEN CLASSROOM

Now let's visit Mr. Johnson's kindergarten classroom. Mr. Johnson works in a large elementary school with grades kindergarten through fifth. He works on a team of seven kindergarten teachers. This year, Mr. Johnson has been working on refining his instructional practice around phonological awareness. He is also growing his read-aloud library to include more books with diverse characters by diverse authors, such as *Thank You, Omu!* by Oge Mora and *The Magical Yet* by Angela DiTerlizzi. Let's take a peek at Mr. Johnson's schedule as he has it posted in his classroom.

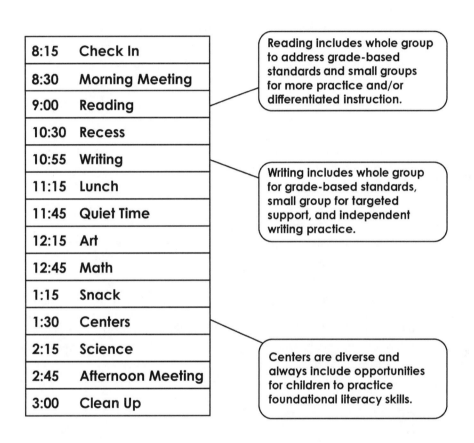

8:15	Check In
8:30	Morning Meeting
9:00	Reading
10:30	Recess
10:55	Writing
11:15	Lunch
11:45	Quiet Time
12:15	Art
12:45	Math
1:15	Snack
1:30	Centers
2:15	Science
2:45	Afternoon Meeting
3:00	Clean Up

Reading includes whole group to address grade-based standards and small groups for more practice and/or differentiated instruction.

Writing includes whole group for grade-based standards, small group for targeted support, and independent writing practice.

Centers are diverse and always include opportunities for children to practice foundational literacy skills.

Mr. Johnson's school has a detailed assessment agenda, including screeners (for example, letter-naming fluency) and measures to monitor progress (for example, letter-sound knowledge and phoneme segmentation). To start the year, he administers a series of tasks as part of his division's adopted literacy screener. This screener provides him with important information about the children's strengths and instructional needs. The screener identifies a number of children in need of additional support.

The class loves animals, and they've recently been learning about how people affect animal lives. At 9:00 a.m., he invites the children to join him on the rug for a read-aloud to start. He is committed to using sophisticated words (chapter 2), so he says, "Let's *gather* at the rug." Today he is reading *Little Turtle and the Changing Sea* by Becky Davies for a second time (chapter 6, read-aloud routine). He begins by having them *contribute* (sophisticated word) to a discussion about what they already learned from the book, using equity sticks (chapter 2) to guide sharing and their KWL chart from the previous reading (chapter 6). Then he teaches the vocabulary word *pollution*. He uses the vocabulary introduction process laid out in chapter 6 as he gives a child-friendly explanation, provides context, asks questions, and encourages the children to make a quick connection. As they read, they *identify* (sophisticated word) examples of pollution.

Then Mr. Johnson engages his class in a quick phoneme-awareness warm-up as he guides the children in Say It! Move It! (chapter 3). For this activity, he has chosen three-phoneme words with particular attention to words with /ch/ as either the beginning or ending sound (for example, *chop, much*). He has taught the children a process of segmenting each sound as they touch thumb to finger and then swipe the thumb across fingers to blend for the whole word. To connect with letters, Mr. Johnson shows the letter card for /ch/ and follows an adapted version of chapter 4's letter introduction, including the sound, the letters that make the sound, and the keyword. "*CH* says /ch/ like at the beginning of *chin*. I need *C* and *H* to make /ch/. Watch me as I underline the letters in *chin* as I say each sound." To end his whole-group time, he uses the activity Where Is It? (chapter 4) as he guides the children in listening for /ch/ in words (for example, *chop* at the beginning and *much* at the end).

Mr. Johnson transitions the children to a three-station rotation for the remaining time of his morning "reading" time. One station is with Mr. Johnson, where he guides the children in a Read Smoothly! activity followed by Blending Lines (see chapter 5 for both). Ms. Ramirez, the class's instructional assistant, leads the second station in Consonant Swap as they build words such as *bat, sat, mat, hat,* and *chat* (chapter 5). For the third station, children work independently on the Picture, Match, and Write activity from chapter 4. The children work together in pairs as they pick a picture (three pictures of previously studied letters and two starting with /ch/), match the letter for the initial sound, and write the letter. Based on developmental readiness, some groups are encouraged to stretch for the whole word.

Mr. Johnson's writing time begins with Say It! Build It! Write It! using words such as *chop, chat,* and *such*. He then invites the children to brainstorm the things Little Turtle sees in the story (for example, fish, plants, bags) and provides them with a sentence frame to fill in as they stretch to write their word: "Little Turtle saw a _____." (See chapter 7 for both of these activities.)

Just like Ms. Cheung, Mr. Johnson knows literacy happens across the entire school day. For example, after his first reading of *Little Turtle and the Changing Sea*, he leads the children in a concept sort about the things Little Turtle sees while swimming when the ocean is his friend and what he sees when it isn't his friend. Mr. Johnson is careful to make an explicit connection to this concept sort (still displayed) when he introduces the vocabulary word *pollution*. During centers time, he encourages the children to do some Nonfiction Writing (chapter 7) using the concept sort from *Little Turtle and the Changing Sea* connecting to the word *pollution*. During afternoon centers time, he regularly brings together a small group of children who were identified by his division's literacy screener to provide additional practice with phonemic awareness and applying alphabet knowledge to decoding and spelling. As you can see, across the day, Mr. Johnson's students have worked to build their phonemic awareness, alphabet knowledge for reading and writing, and foundational fluency as well as world knowledge and vocabulary.

To Sum It Up

Let's think about how Ms. Cheung and Mr. Johnson are addressing the critical components of language and early literacy. Take a look at the following chart that points out the ways they are each incorporating these components in their daily lessons.

COMPONENTS	MS. CHEUNG	MR. JOHNSON
Oral Language	▪ Turn and talk during read-aloud ▪ Turn and talk during morning meeting ▪ Recasts, extensions, explanations during centers	▪ Sophisticated words ▪ Equity sticks
Phonological Awareness	▪ Syllable sort with foods	▪ Say It! Move It! ▪ Where Is It?
Alphabetic Code	▪ Introduction to the letter *F* and its sound /f/ as in *fun* ▪ Alphabet Arc ▪ Letter or Number ▪ Match It Up	Introduction to the digraph *CH* and its sound /ch/ as in *chin*
Word Recognition and Foundational Fluency	▪ Word Train	▪ Read It Smoothly! ▪ Blending Lines ▪ Consonant Swap
Early Writing	▪ Uppercase letter formation *F* with formation language, skywriting, and dry-erase boards ▪ Model writing her favorite food *fig*	▪ Picture, Match, Write ▪ Say It! Build It! ▪ Sentence Frame ▪ Nonfiction Writing
Vocabulary, Comprehension, and World Knowledge	▪ Introduction to *category* ▪ Make connections to their lives with *Fry Bread*	▪ Introduction to *pollution* ▪ Building knowledge about the effects humans can have on animals ▪ KWL Chart

To ensure your daily routines are addressing these critical components, you can use these same categories to reflect on your instructional activities and the opportunities for the children to practice. Keeping track over a few days or even a couple of weeks will help you start to see patterns in your teaching. Ultimately, you are looking for a nice balance across all of these critical language and literacy skills.

The children in our early childhood classrooms are just setting out on their literacy journeys. We are also on a journey as we develop and reflect upon our practice. When we leverage developmentally appropriate practice that is attentive to developmental trends, informed by early literacy assessment, and guided by standards, we can positively affect the early literacy growth of the children in our classrooms. Our goal is to help children reach their full potential. I wish you and the children in your classrooms the very best as you continue along your journeys.

Appendix A: Children's Books

Alber, Diane. 2020. *A Little Spot of Courage: A Story about Being Brave*. Gilbert, AZ: Diane Alber Art.

Aleo, Karen. 2019. *Living Things Need Air*. North Mankato, MN: Little Pebble.

Aleo, Karen. 2019. *Living Things Need Food*. North Mankato, MN: Little Pebble.

Aleo, Karen. 2019. *Living Things Need Light*. North Mankato, MN: Little Pebble.

Aleo, Karen. 2019. *Living Things Need Shelter*. North Mankato, MN: Little Pebble.

Aleo, Karen. 2019. *Living Things Need Water*. North Mankato, MN: Little Pebble.

American Museum of Natural History. 2017. *Wolf Pups Join the Pack*. New York: Sterling Children's Books.

Andros, Camille. 2017. *Charlotte the Scientist Is Squished*. Boston, MA: Clarion Books.

Appleton-Smith, Laura. 2010. *Fran Can Flip*. Manchester, NH: Flyleaf Publishing.

Arbona, Marion. 2020. *Window*. Toronto, ON: Kids Can Press.

Archer, Peggy. 2018. *A Hippy-Hoppy Toad*. New York: Schwartz and Wade Books.

Arena, Jen. 2016. *Marta! Big and Small*. New York: Roaring Brook Press.

Atinuke. 2020. *Catch That Chicken!* Somerville, MA: Candlewick Press.

Baker, Keith. 2010. *LMNO Peas*. New York: Little Simon.

Barnett, Mac. 2014. *Sam and Dave Dig a Hole*. Somerville, MA: Candlewick Press.

Barnett, Mac. 2017. *Triangle*. Somerville, MA: Candlewick Press.

Barnett, Mac. 2018. *Square*. Somerville, MA: Candlewick Press.

Barnett, Mac. 2019. *Circle*. Somerville, MA: Candlewick Press.

Barton, Bethany. 2019. *Give Bees a Chance*. New York: Puffin.

Beaty, Andrea. 2013. *Rosie Revere, Engineer*. New York: Amulet Books.

Beaty, Andrea. 2016. *Ada Twist, Scientist*. New York: Amulet Books.

Beaty, Andrea. 2016. *Iggy Peck, Architect*. New York: Amulet Books.

Beaty, Andrea. 2018. *Rosie Revere and the Raucous Riveters*. New York: Amulet Books.

Beaty, Andrea. 2018. *Sofia Valdez, Future Prez*. New York: Amulet Books.

Beaty, Andrea. 2019. *Ada Twist and the Perilous Pants*. New York: Amulet Books.

Beaty, Andrea. 2020. *Iggy Peck and the Mysterious Mansion*. New York: Amulet Books.

Beaty, Andrea. 2020. *Sofia Valdez and the Vanishing Vote*. New York: Amulet Books.

Beaty, Andrea. 2021. *Aaron Slater, Illustrator*. New York: Amulet Books.

Beedie, Duncan. 2017. *The Lumberjack's Beard*. Somerville, MA: Candlewick Press.

Berger, Samantha. 2020. *ABCs of Kindness*. Honesdale, PA: Highlights Press.

Berry, Cate. 2019. *Chicken Break! A Counting Book*. New York: Feiwel and Friends.

Berube, Kate. 2016. *Hannah and Sugar*. New York: Harry N. Abrams.

Bingham, Kelly. 2012. *Z Is for Moose*. New York: Greenwillow Books.

Bingham, Kelly. 2014. *Circle, Square, Moose*. New York: Greenwillow Books.

Blabey, Aaron. 2016. *Pig the Pug*. New York: Scholastic.

Blabey, Aaron. 2018. *I Need a Hug*. New York: Scholastic.

Boelts, Maribeth. 2016. *A Bike Like Sergio's*. Somerville, MA: Candlewick Press.

Boyd, Lizi. 2015. *Big Bear Little Chair*. San Francisco, CA: Chronicle Books.

Boynton, Sandra. 2020. *How Big Is Zagnodd?* New York: Little Simon.

Brooks, Erik. 2010. *Polar Opposites*. Tarrytown, NY: Marshall Cavendish.

Brown, Monica. 2011. *Marisol McDonald Doesn't Match*. New York: Children's Book Press.

Brown, Peter. 2011. *You Will Be My Friend!* New York: Little Brown Books for Young Readers.

Burgerman, Jon. 2018. *Rhyme Crime*. New York: Dial Books for Young Readers.

Burleigh, Robert. 2018. *Trapped! A Whale's Rescue*. Watertown, MA: Charlesbridge.

Cali, Davide. 2015. *A Funny Thing Happened on the Way to School*. San Francisco, CA: Chronicle Books.

Christelow, Eileen. 1989. *Five Little Monkeys Jumping on the Bed*. Boston, MA: Clarion Books.

Chung, Arree. 2017. *Out!* New York: Henry Holt and Co.

Cleary, Brian. 2006. *I and You and Don't Forget Who: What Is a Pronoun?* Minneapolis, MN: Millbrook Press.

Cleghorne, Vince. 2018. *Bug Soup: What's in Your Lunchbox?* San Diego, CA: Puppy Dogs and Ice Cream Press.

Cole, Henry. 2020. *One Little Bag: An Amazing Journey*. New York: Scholastic.

Colleen, Marcie. 2017. *Love, Triangle*. New York: Balzer + Bray.

Collins, Ross. 2018. *There's a Bear on My Chair*. London, UK: Nosy Crow.

Cornwall, Gaia. 2017. *Jabari Jumps*. Somerville, MA: Candlewick Press.

Danielson, Christopher. 2019. *How Many? A Different Kind of Counting Book*. Watertown, MA: Charlesbridge.

Davies, Becky. 2020. *Little Turtle and the Changing Sea*. Wilton, CT: Tiger Tales.

Davies, Nicola. 2001. *Bat Loves the Night*. Somerville, MA: Candlewick Press.

de la Peña, Matt. 2018. *Carmela Full of Wishes*. New York: G.P. Putman's Sons.

de Regil, Tania. 2019. *A New Home*. Somerville, MA: Candlewick Press.

DiPucchio, Kelly. 2018. *Poe Won't Go*. New York: Little Brown Books for Young Readers.

DiTerlizzi, Angela. 2020. *The Magical Yet*. New York: Little Brown Books for Young Readers.

Dotlich, Rebecca Kai. 2015. *One Day, The End: Short, Very Short, Shorter-Than-Ever Stories*. Honesdale, PA: Boyds Mills Press.

Doyle, Elizabeth. 2015. *AB See*. New York: Little Simon.

Drago, Flavia Z. 2020. *Gustavo, the Shy Ghost*. Somerville, MA: Candlewick Press.

Driscoll, Laura. 2018. *I Want to be a Veterinarian*. New York: HarperCollins.

Dyckman, Ame. 2016. *Horrible Bear!* New York: Little Brown Books for Young Readers.

Ehlert, Lois. 1996. *Eating the Alphabet: Fruits and Vegetables from A to Z*. San Diego, CA: Red Wagon Books.

Engle, Margarita. 2015. *Drum Dream Girl: How One Girl's Courage Changed Music*. Boston, MA: Houghton Mifflin Harcourt.

English, Karen. 2020. *Red Shoes: A Dazzling Journey!* New York: Scholastic.

Entrekin, Allison W. 2011. *For the Love of Dogs: An A-to-Z Primer for Dog Lovers of All Ages*. Chicago, IL: Triumph Books.

Ernst, Lisa C. 1999. *The Letters Are Lost!* New York: Puffin.

Farrell, Alison. 2019. *The Hike*. San Francisco, CA: Chronicle Books.

Felix, Lucie. 2016. *Apples and Robins*. San Francisco, CA: Chronicle Books.

Fenske, Jonathan. 2020. *After Squidnight*. New York: Penguin Workshop.

Ferry, Beth. 2017. *A Small Blue Whale*. New York: Alfred A. Knopf.

Feuti, Norm. 2019. *Do You Like My Bike?* New York: Scholastic.

Fleming, Candace. 2016. *Giant Squid*. New York: Roaring Book Press.

Fleming, Candace. 2017. *Go Sleep in Your Own Bed!* New York: Schwartz and Wade Books.

Fleming, Denise. 2002. *Alphabet Under Construction*. New York: Henry Holt and Co.

Florian, Douglas. 2020. *Ice! Poems About Polar Life*. New York: Holiday House.

Fox, Mem. 2012. *Two Little Monkeys*. San Diego, CA: Beach Lane Books.

Franceschelli, Christopher. 2013. *Alphablock*. New York: Abrams Appleseed.

Fredericks, Arthur D. 2017. *Tall, Tall Tree*. Naperville, IL: Dawn Publications.

Funk, Josh. 2015. *Lady Pancake and Sir French Toast*. New York: Sterling Children's Books.

Gallois, Gina. 2020. *Opossum Opposites*. Atlanta, GA: Moonflower Press.

Gibson, Ginger F. 2013. *Tiptoe Joe*. New York: Greenwillow Books.

Gravett, Emily. 2019. *Cyril and Pat*. New York: Simon and Schuster Books for Young Readers.

Gray, Kes. 2014. *Frog on a Log?* New York: Scholastic.

Green, Agnes. 2019. *Opposites: The Little Book of Big Friends*. April Tale Books.

Guarino, Deborah. 1997. *Is Your Mama a Llama?* New York: Scholastic.

Hall, Kirsten. 2018. *The Honeybee*. New York: Atheneum Books for Young Readers.

Hall, Michael. 2015. *Red: A Crayon's Story*. New York: Greenwillow Books.

Harris, Chris. 2020. *The Alphabet's Alphabet*. New York: Little Brown Books for Young Readers.

Hatanaka, Kellen. 2015. *Drive: A Look at Roadside Opposites*. Toronto, ON: Groundwood Books.

Heavenrich, Sue. 2021. *13 Ways to Eat a Fly*. Watertown, MA: Charlesbridge.

Heling, Kathryn. 2012. *Clothesline Clues to Jobs People Do*. Watertown, MA: Charlesbridge.

Hendra, Sue. 2019. *Cake*. New York: Aladdin.

Henn, Sophy. 2015. *Where Bear?* New York: Philomel Books.

Higgins, Carter. 2018. *Everything You Need for a Treehouse*. San Francisco, CA: Chronicle Books.

Higgins, Ryan T. 2015. *Mother Bruce*. New York: Disney-Hyperion.

Hood, Susan. 2017. *Double Take! A New Look at Opposites*. Somerville, MA: Candlewick Press.

Intriago, Patricia. 2011. *Dot*. New York: Margaret Ferguson Books.

James, Shelly V. 2020. *Fussy Flamingo*. Naperville, IL: Sourcebooks Jabberwocky.

James, Simon. 2019. *Mr. Scruff*. Somerville, MA: Candlewick Press.

Jarvis. 2016. *Alan's Big, Scary Teeth*. Somerville, MA: Candlewick Press.

Jeffers, Oliver. 2016. *The Hueys in What's the Opposite?* New York: Philomel Books.

Jenkins, Martin. 2017. *Bird Builds a Nest*. Somerville, MA: Candlewick Press.

Jenner, Caryn. 2017. *All About Bats*. New York: Dorling Kindersley.

John, Jory. 2019. *The Good Egg*. New York: HarperCollins Children's Books.

Kang, Anna. 2014. *You Are Not Small*. New York: Two Lions.

Kanninen, Barbara. 2018. *Circle Rolls*. New York: Phaidon Press.

Ko, Sangmi. 2015. *A Dog Wearing Shoes*. New York: Schwartz and Wade Books.

Kraegel, Kenneth. 2017. *Green Pants*. Somerville, MA: Candlewick Press.

Kuefler, Joseph. 2017. *Rulers of the Playground*. New York: Balzer + Bray.

Kurtz, Kevin. 2016. *Sharks and Dolphins: A Compare and Contrast Book*. Mt. Pleasant, SC: Arbordale Publishing.

Kurtz, Kevin. 2017. *Living Things and Nonliving Things: A Compare and Contrast Book*. Mt. Pleasant, SC: Arbordale Publishing.

Lake, G.G. 2017. *Gray Squirrels*. North Mankato, MN: Capstone Press.

LaRochelle, David. 2020. *See the Cat: Three Stories About a Dog*. Somerville, MA: Candlewick Press.

Larsen, Andrew. 2016. *A Squiggly Story*. Toronto, ON: Kids Can Press.

Le, Khoa. 2018. *The Lonely Polar Bear*. Mount Joy, PA: Happy Fox Books.

Leopold, Niki C. 2002. *K Is for Kitten*. New York: Putnam.

Lester, Alison. 2019. *My Dog Bigsy*. London, UK: Puffin.

Loewen, Nancy. 2007. *If You Were a Pronoun*. Minneapolis, MN: Picture Window Books.

London, Jonathan. 2015. *Hippos Are Huge!* Somerville, MA: Candlewick Press.

Lozano, Luciano. 2020. *Mayhem at the Museum*. New York: Penguin Workshop.

Ludwig, Trudy. 2013. *The Invisible Boy*. New York: Alfred A. Knopf.

Mack, Jeff. 2012. *Good News, Bad News*. San Francisco, CA: Chronicle Books.

MacPete, Ruth. 2018. *Lisette the Vet*. San Diego, CA: Forest Lane Books.

Maillard, Kevin N. 2019. *Fry Bread: A Native American Family Story*. New York: Roaring Book Press.

Mantchev, Lisa. 2015. *Strictly No Elephants*. New York: Simon and Schuster for Young Readers.

Marsh, Laura. 2016. *Giraffes*. Washington, DC: National Geographic Partners.

Martin, Bill Jr. 1996. *Brown Bear, Brown Bear, What Do You See?* New York: Henry Holt and Co.

Martin, Bill Jr., and John Archambault. 1993. *Chicka Chicka Boom Boom*. San Diego, CA: Beach Lane Books.

Martinez-Neal, Juana. 2018. *Alma and How She Got Her Name*. Somerville, MA: Candlewick Press.

McCloskey, Kevin. 2015. *We Dig Worms!* New York: Toon Books.

McConnell, Patrick. 2017. *The Little Red Cat Who Ran Away and Learned His ABCs (the Hard Way)*. New York: Little Brown Books for Young Readers.

McLeod, Bob. 2006. *Superhero ABC*. New York: HarperCollins Children's Books.

McQuinn, Anna. 2014. *Lola Plants a Garden*. Watertown, MA: Charlesbridge.

Meddour, Wendy. 2019. *Lubna and Pebble*. New York: Dial Books for Young Readers.

Messner, Kate. 2011. *Over and Under the Snow*. San Francisco, CA: Chronicle Books.

Messner, Kate. 2015. *Tree of Wonder: The Many Marvelous Lives of a Rainforest Tree*. San Francisco, CA: Chronicle Books.

Messner, Kate. 2017. *Up in the Garden and Down in the Dirt*. San Francisco, CA: Chronicle Books.

Miranda, Anne. 2019. *Tangled: A Story About Shapes*. New York: Simon and Schuster Books for Young Children.

Mirchandani, Raakhee. 2018. *Super Satya Saves the Day*. Cambridge, MA: Bharat Babies.

Montanari, Susan. 2018. *Hip-Hop Lollipop*. New York: Schwartz and Wade Books.

Mora, Oge. 2018. *Thank You, Omu!* New York: Little Brown Books for Young Readers.

Morris, Suzanne. 2019. *Trapezoid Is Not a Dinosaur!* Watertown, MA: Charlesbridge.

Moyle, Sabrina. 2020. *ABC Dance! An Animal Alphabet*. New York: Workman Publishing.

Muhammad, Ibtihaj. 2019. *The Proudest Blue: A Story of Hijab and Family*. New York: Little Brown Books for Young Readers.

Murray, Alison. 2011. *Apple Pie ABC*. New York: Little Brown Books for Young Readers.

Murray, Diana. 2016. *City Shapes*. New York: Little Brown Books for Young Readers.

Negley, Keith. 2019. *Mary Wears What She Wants*. New York: HarperCollins Children's Books.

Newman-D'Amico, Fran. 2005. *Make Your Own Ice Cream Sundae*. Mineola, NY: Dover Publications.

Olsen, Shannon. 2020. *Our Class Is a Family*. Author.

Ortego, Alicia. 2020. *Kindness Is My Superpower*. Author.

Oswald, Pete. 2020. *Hike*. Somerville, MA: Candlewick Press.

Owens, John. 2020. *One Summer Up North*. Minneapolis, MN: University of Minnesota Press.

Percival, Tom. 2019. *Ruby Finds a Worry*. New York: Bloomsbury Children's Books.

Pernick, Gary. 1996. *Ted's Red Sled*. Carlsbad, CA: Modern Curriculum Press.

Pilutti, Deb. 2020. *Old Rock (Is Not Boring)*. New York: G.P. Putman's Sons.

Rattini, Kristin B. 2013. *Weather.* Washington, DC: National Geographic Society.

Rayner, Jacqueline. 2019. *Hats Are Not for Cats!* Boston, MA: Clarion Books.

Read, Kate. 2019. *One Fox: A Counting Book Thriller.* Atlanta, GA: Peachtree Publishing.

Reidy, Jean. 2019. *Truman.* New York: Atheneum Books for Young Readers.

Reynolds, Aaron. 2017. *Creepy Pair of Underwear!* New York: Simon and Schuster for Young Readers.

Rissi, Anica M. 2019. *Watch Out for Wolf!* New York: Little Brown Books for Young Readers.

Roberts, Justin. 2014. *The Smallest Girl in the Smallest Grade.* New York: G.P. Putman's Sons.

Rosen, Michael, and Helen Oxenbury. 1997. *We're Going on a Bear Hunt.* New York: Little Simon.

Rylant, Cynthia. 2008. *Snow.* Boston, MA: Clarion Books.

Schwartz, Corey R., and Beth Coulton. 2014. *Goldi Rocks and the Three Bears.* New York: G.P. Putman's Sons.

Seuss, Dr. 1963. *Dr. Seuss's ABC: An Amazing Alphabet Book!* New York: Random House.

Shand, Jennifer. 2020. *Rumble, Rumble, Grumble, Grumble: Sounds from the Sky.* Oakville, ON: Flowerpot Press.

Shaskin, Stephen. 2017. *Toad on the Road: A Cautionary Tale.* New York: HarperCollins Children's Books.

Shaw, Nancy. 1986. *Sheep in a Jeep.* New York: Houghton Mifflin.

Shaw, Nancy. 1989. *Sheep on a Ship.* New York: Houghton Mifflin Harcourt.

Snow, Todd, and Peggy Snow. 2007. *Feelings to Share from A to Z.* Oak Park Heights, MN: Maren Green Publishing.

Sobel, June. 2003. *B Is for Bulldozer: A Construction ABC.* New York: Gulliver Books.

Spinelli, Eileen. 2009. *Silly Tilly.* Las Vegas, NV: Two Lions.

Stewart, Melissa. 2017. *Can an Aardvark Bark?* San Diego, CA: Beach Lane Books.

Strathie, Chae. 2016. *Gorilla Loves Vanilla.* Hauppauge, NY: B.E.S. Publishing.

Stutzman, Jonathan. 2020. *Tiny T. Rex and the Very Dark Dark.* San Francisco, CA: Chronicle Books.

Taylor, Sean. 2014. *Hoot Owl: Master of Disguise.* Somerville, MA: Candlewick Press.

Theule, Larissa. 2020. *A Way with Wild Things.* New York: Bloomsbury Children's Books.

Thomas, Jan. 2009. *Rhyming Dust Bunnies.* New York: Atheneum Books for Young Readers.

Thong, Roseanne. 2013. *Round Is a Tortilla: A Book of Shapes*. San Francisco, CA: Chronicle Books.

Twohy, Mike. 2016. *Oops, Pounce, Quick, Run! An Alphabet Caper*. New York: Balzer + Bray.

Underwood, Deborah. 2019. *The Panda Problem*. New York: Dial Books for Young Readers.

Vamos, Samantha R. 2019. *The Piñata That the Farm Maiden Hung*. Watertown, MA: Charlesbridge.

Watkins, Adam. 2014. *R Is for Robot: A Noisy Alphabet*. Los Angeles: Price Stern Sloan.

Wheelan, Susan. 2015. *Don't Think About Purple Elephants*. Auckland, New Zealand: EK Books.

Willems, Mo. 2012. *Goldilocks and the Three Dinosaurs*. New York: Balzer + Bray.

Willems, Mo. 2018. *A Busy Creature's Day Eating!* New York: Hyperion Books for Children.

Williams, Brenda. 2015. *Outdoor Opposites*. Cambridge, MA: Barefoot Books.

Williams, Sue. 1989. *I Went Walking*. San Diego, CA: Red Wagon Books.

Williamson, S. 2020. *Cactus and Flower: A Book About Life Cycles*. New York: Abrams Books for Young Readers.

Wilson, Karma. 2016. *Big Bear, Small Mouse*. New York: Margaret K. McElderry Books.

Wood, Audrey. 1992. *Silly Sally*. San Diego, CA: Red Wagon Books.

Won, Brian. 2016. *Hooray for Today!* Boston, MA: Clarion Books.

Wong, Liz. 2019. *The Goose Egg*. New York: Alfred A. Knopf.

Yim, Natasha. 2014. *Goldy Luck and the Three Pandas*. Watertown, MA: Charlesbridge.

Yolen, Jane. 1987. *Owl Moon*. New York: Philomel Books.

Yolen, Jane. 2018. *A Bear Sat on My Porch Today*. San Francisco, CA: Chronicle Books.

Zolotow, Charlotte. 1994. *The Seashore Book*. New York: HarperCollins.

Zommer, Yuval. 2018. *The Big Book of the Blue*. London, UK: Thames and Hudson.

Zuckerman, Andrew. 2009. *Creature ABC*. San Francisco, CA: Chronicle Books.

Appendix B: Sample Checklists

Name					
Dates					
Consonants					
B					
M					
S					
T					
N					
R					
P					
C					
F					
D					
G					
H					
L					
K					
J					
W					
V					
Y					
X					
Q					
Z					
Vowels					
A					
E					
I					
O					
U					

Names	b	c	d	f	g	h	j	k	l	m	n	p	q	r	s	t	v	w	x	y	z	a	e	i	o	u

Name:

Date:

Name Writing:

Alphabet (letter naming) – upper	Alphabet (letter naming) – lower

Alphabet (letter naming) – upper

M	B	F	X	N	A	
R	T	D	E	Q	C	
Z	G	W	I	K	U	Y
V	O	H	L	P	S	J

Total Correct:

Alphabet (letter naming) – lower

m	b	f	x	n	a	
r	t	d	e	q	c	
z	g	w	i	k	u	y
v	o	h	l	p	s	j

Total Correct:

Alphabet (letter sounds)

m	b	f	x	n	a	
r	t	d	e	y	c	
z	g	w	i	k	u	y
v	o	h	l	p	s	j

Total Correct:

Phonological Awareness

Rhyme Recognition:

Rhyme Production:

Syllable Blending:

Onset-Rime Blending:

Phoneme Blending:

Word Segmenting:

Syllable Segmenting:

Initial Sound Segmenting:

Concepts About Print

Purpose:

Front/Back:

Start Reading:

Left/Right:

Top/Bottom:

Word:

First/Last Letter:

Early Writing

Message:

Linear:

Letter-Like:

Random Letters:

Beginning/Ending Sounds:

Some Vowels:

Spaces Between Words:

Name: Date:

	Letter Name (Upper)	Letter Name (Lower)	Letter Sound	Match Picture (initial sound)	Match Picture (final sound)	Write Letter
b						
m						
s						
t						
n						
r						
p						
c						
f						
d						
g						
h						
l						
k						
j						
w						
v						
y						
x						
q						
z						
a						
e						
i						
o						
u						

References and Recommended Reading

Adams, Marilyn Jager. 1990. *Beginning to Read: Thinking and Learning about Print.* Cambridge, MA: MIT Press.

Adams, Marilyn Jager, Barbara R. Foorman, Ingvar Lundberg, and Terri Beeler. 1998. *Phonemic Awareness in Young Children: A Classroom Curriculum.* Baltimore, MD: Paul H. Brookes.

Administration for Children and Families. 2015. *Head Start Early Learning Outcomes Framework: Ages Birth to Five.* Washington, DC: US Department of Health and Human Services, Administration for Children and Families, Office of Head Start. https://eclkc.ohs.acf.hhs.gov/sites/default/files/pdf/elof-ohs-framework.pdf

Anderson, Richard C., Elfrieda H. Hiebert, Judith A. Scott, and Ian A. G. Wilkinson. 1985. *Becoming a Nation of Readers: The Report of the Commission on Reading.* Washington, DC: The National Institute of Education, US Department of Education. https://files.eric.ed.gov/fulltext/ED253865.pdf

Ball, Eileen W., and Benita A. Blachman. 1991. "Does Phoneme Awareness Training in Kindergarten Make a Difference in Early Word Recognition and Developmental Spelling?" *Reading Research Quarterly* 26(1): 49–66.

Beck, Isabel L., and Mark E. Beck. 2013. *Making Sense of Phonics: The Hows and Whys.* 2nd edition. New York: Guilford Press.

Beck, Isabel L., and Margaret G. McKeown. 2007. "Increasing Young Low-Income Children's Oral Vocabulary Repertoires through Rich and Focused Instruction." *The Elementary School Journal* 107(3): 251–271.

Beck, Isabel L., Margaret G. McKeown, and Linda Kucan. 2013. *Bringing Words to Life: Robust Vocabulary Instruction.* 2nd edition. New York: Guilford Press.

Bereiter, Carl, et al. 2003. *Open Court Reading Pre-K.* New York: SRA/McGraw-Hill.

Biemiller, Andrew. 2006. "Vocabulary Development and Instruction: A Prerequisite for School Learning." In *Handbook of Early Literacy Research, Volume 2.* New York: Guilford Press.

Bishop, Rudine S. 1990. "Mirrors, Windows, and Sliding Glass Doors." *Perspectives: Choosing and Using Books for the Classroom* 6(3): ix–xi.

Blevins, Wiley. 2017. *A Fresh Look at Phonics: Common Causes of Failure and 7 Ingredients for Success.* Thousand Oaks, CA: Corwin.

Bloodgood, Janet W. 1999. "What's in a Name? Children's Name Writing and Literacy Acquisition." *Reading Research Quarterly* 34(3): 342–367.

Both-de Vries, Anna C., and Adriana G. Bus. 2008. "Name Writing: A First Step to Phonetic Writing? Does the Name Have a Special Role in Understanding the Symbolic Function of Writing?" *Literacy Teaching and Learning* 12(2): 37–55.

Cabell, Sonia Q., Laura Tortorelli, and Hope Gerde. 2013. "How Do I Write…? Scaffolding Preschoolers' Early Writing Skills." *The Reading Teacher* 66(8): 650–659.

Carey, Susan. 1978. "The Child as a Word Learner." In *Linguistic Theory and Psychological Reality*. Cambridge, MA: MIT Press.

Catts, Hugh W., Tiffany P. Hogan, and Suzanne M. Adlof. 2005. "Developmental Changes in Reading and Reading Disabilities." In *The Connections Between Language and Reading Disabilities*. Mahwah, NJ: Lawrence Erlbaum Associates.

Copple, Carol, and Sue Bredekamp. 2009. *Developmentally Appropriate Practice in Early Childhood Programs Serving Children from Birth through Age 8.* 3rd edition. Washington, DC: National Association for the Education of Young Children.

Dahlgren, Mary E., and Antonio A. Fierro. 2018. *Kid Lips Instructional guide.* Oklahoma City, OK: Tools 4 Reading.

Dickinson, David K., and Patton O. Tabors. 2001. *Beginning Literacy with Language: Young Children Learning at Home and School.* Baltimore, MD: Paul H. Brookes.

Dolch, Edward W. 1936. "A Basic Sight Vocabulary." *The Elementary School Journal* 36(6): 456–460.

Dynamic Measurement Group. 2019. *Preschool Early Literacy Indicators.* Dallas, TX: Voyager Sopris Learning. https://acadiencelearning.org/acadience-reading/prek-peli/

Elkonin, Daniil. 1971. "Development of Speech." In *The Psychology of Preschool Children.* Cambridge, MA: MIT Press.

Ellefson, Michelle R., Rebecca Treiman, and Brett Kessler. 2009. "Learning to Label Letters by Sounds or Names: A Comparison of England and the United States." *Journal of Experimental Child Psychology* 102(3): 323–341.

Fitzpatrick, Jo. 1997. *Phonemic Awareness: Playing with Sound to Strengthen Beginning Reading Skills.* Cypress, CA: Creative Teaching Press.

Fletcher, Jack M., and G. Reid Lyon. 1998. "Reading: A Research-Based Approach." In *What's Gone Wrong in America's Classrooms.* Stanford, CA: Hoover Institution Press.

Foorman, Barbara, et al. 2016. *Foundational Skills to Support Reading for Understanding in Kindergarten through 3rd Grade.* Washington, DC: National Center for Education Evaluation and Regional Assistance, Institute of Education Sciences, US Department of Education.

Foulin, Jean Noel. 2005. "Why Is Letter-Name Knowledge Such a Good Predictor of Learning To Read?" *Reading and Writing* 18(2): 129–155.

Fountas, Irene, and Gay Su Pinnell. 1998. *Word Matters: Teaching Phonics and Spelling in the Reading/Writing Classroom.* Portsmouth, NH: Heinemann.

Fry, Edward. 1996. *1000 Instant Words: The Most Common Words for Teaching Reading, Writing, and Spelling.* Garden Grove, CA: Teacher Created Resources.

Gillon, Gail T. 2018. *Phonological Awareness: From Research To Practice.* 2nd edition. New York: Guilford Press.

Gough, Philip B., and William E. Tunmer. 1986. "Decoding, Reading, and Reading Disability." *Remedial and Special Education* 7(1): 6–10.

Hall, Anna H., Amber Simpson, Ying Guo, and Shanshan Wang. 2015. "Examining the Effects of Preschool Writing Instruction on Emergent Literacy Skills: A Systematic Review of the Literature." *Literacy Research and Instruction* 54(2): 115–134.

Halliday, Michael A. K. 1993. "Towards a Language-Based Theory of Learning." *Linguistics and Education* 5(2): 93–116.

Hart, Betty, and Todd R. Risley. 1995. *Meaningful Differences in the Everyday Experience of Young American Children.* Baltimore, MD: Paul H. Brookes.

Heckman, James, et al. 2010. "The Rate of Return to the High/Scope Perry Preschool Program." *Journal of Public Economics* 94(1–2): 114–128.

Heroman, Cate, and Candy Jones. 2004. *Literacy: The Creative Curriculum Approach.* Washington, DC: Teaching Strategies.

Honig, Bill, Linda Diamond, and Linda Gutlohn. 2018. *Teaching Reading Sourcebook.* 3rd edition. Novato, CA: Academic Therapy Publications.

Huang, Francis L., Laura S. Tortorelli, and Marcia A. Invernizzi. 2014. "An Investigation of Factors Associated with Letter-Sound Knowledge at Kindergarten Entry." *Early Childhood Research Quarterly* 29(2): 182–192.

Invernizzi, Marcia, Connie Juel, L. Swank, and Joanne Meier. 2003–2017. *Phonological Awareness Literacy Screener–Kindergarten.* Charlottesville, VA: The Rector and the Board of Visitors of the University of Virginia.

Jones, Cindy D., Sarah K. Clark, and D. Ray Reutzel. 2013. "Enhancing Alphabet Knowledge Instruction: Research Implications and Practical Strategies for Early Childhood Educators." *Early Childhood Education Journal* 41(2): 81–89.

Juel, Connie. 1988. "Learning to Read and Write: A Longitudinal Study of 54 Children from First through Fourth Grades." *Journal of Educational Psychology* 80(4): 437–447.

Justice, Laura M., and Helen K. Ezell. 2004. "Print Referencing: An Emergent Literacy Enhancement Strategy and Its Clinical Applications." *Language, Speech, and Hearing Services in Schools* 35(2): 185-193.

Justice, Laura M., et al. 2009. "Accelerating Preschoolers' Early Literacy Development through Classroom-Based Teacher-Child Storybook Reading and Explicit Print Referencing." *Language, Speech, and Hearing Services in Schools* 40(1): 67–85.

Justice, Laura M., Khara Pence, Ryan B. Bowles, and Alice Wiggins. 2006. "An Investigation of Four Hypotheses Concerning the Order by Which 4-Year-Old

Children Learn the Alphabet Letters." *Early Childhood Research Quarterly* 21(3): 374–389.

Justice, Laura M., Paige C. Pullen, and Khara Pence. 2008. "Influence of Verbal and Nonverbal References to Print on Preschoolers' Visual Attention to Print During Storybook Reading." *Developmental Psychology* 44(3): 855–866.

Kagan, Sharon Lynn, Evelyn Moore, and Sue Bredekamp, eds. 1995. *Reconsidering Children's Early Development and Learning: Toward Common Views and Vocabulary.* Washington, DC: National Education Goals Panel.

Kim, Young-Suk, Yaacov Petscher, Barbara R. Foorman, and Chengfu Zhou. 2010. "The Contributions of Phonological Awareness and Letter-Name Knowledge to Letter-Sound Acquisition: A Cross-Classified Multilevel Model Approach." *Journal of Educational Psychology* 102(2): 313–326.

Lane, Holly B., and Stephanie Allen. 2010. "The Vocabulary-Rich Classroom: Modeling Sophisticated Word Use to Promote Word Consciousness and Vocabulary Growth." *The Reading Teacher* 63(5): 362–370.

Learning Without Tears (2018). English print letter charts. https://www.lwtears.com/resources/letter-number-formation-charts

Maclean, Morag, Peter Bryant, and Lynette Bradley. 1987. "Rhymes, Nursery Rhymes, and Reading in Early Childhood." *Merrill-Palmer Quarterly* 33(3): 255–281.

Magnuson, Katherine, and Greg J. Duncan. 2016. "Can Early Childhood Interventions Decrease Inequality of Economic Opportunity?" *RSF: The Russell Sage Foundation Journal of the Social Sciences* 2(2): 123–141.

Marulis, Loren M., and Susan B. Neuman. 2010. "The Effects of Vocabulary Intervention on Young Children's Word Learning: A Meta-Analysis." *Review of Educational Research* 80(3): 300–335.

McBride-Chang, Catherine. 1999. "The ABCs of the ABCs: The Development of Letter-Name and Letter-Sound Knowledge. *Merrill-Palmer Quarterly* 45(2): 285–308.

McGinty, Anita S., and Laura M. Justice. 2010. "Language Facilitation in the Preschool Classroom: Rationale, Goals, and Strategies." In *Promoting Early Reading: Research, Resources, and Best Practices.* New York: Guilford Press.

McKay, Rebecca, and William H. Teale. 2015. *No More Teaching a Letter a Week.* Portsmouth, NH: Heinemann.

Metsala, Jamie L., and Amanda C. Walley. 1998. "Spoken Vocabulary Growth and the Segmental Restructuring of Lexical Representations: Precursors to Phonemic Awareness and Early Reading Ability." In *Word Recognition in Beginning Literacy.* Mahwah, NJ: Lawrence Erlbaum.

Morrow, Lesley M. 2005. "Language and Literacy in Preschools: Current Issues and Concerns." *Literacy Teaching and Learning* 9(1): 7–19.

Morrow, Lesley M. 2019. *Literacy Development in the Early Years.* 9th edition. Boston: Pearson.

Mraz, Kristine, Alison Porcelli, and Cheryl Tyler. 2016. *Purposeful Play: A Teachers' Guide to Igniting Deep and Joyful Learning Across the Day.* Portsmouth, NH: Heinemann.

National Center for Learning Disabilities. n.d. *Get Ready to Read!* http://www. getreadytoread.org/

National Center on Quality Teaching and Learning. 2015. *Language and Literacy Preschool Curriculum Consumer Report.* Washington, DC: Office of Head Start. https://ksdetasn.s3.amazonaws.com/uploads/ckeditor/attachments/12/curriculum-report-II.pdf

National Early Literacy Panel. 2008. *Developing Early Literacy: Report of the National Early Literacy Panel.* Washington, DC: National Institute for Literacy. https://lincs.ed.gov/publications/pdf/NELPReport09.pdf

National Governors Association Center for Best Practices, Council of Chief State School Officers. 2010. *Common Core State Standards English Language Arts.* Washington, DC: National Governors Association Center for Best Practices, Council of Chief State School Officers.

National Institute for Early Education Research. 2021. *The State of Preschool 2020: State Preschool Yearbook.* Rutgers Graduate School of Education. https://nieer.org/wp-content/uploads/2021/04/YB2020_Full_Report.pdf

National Reading Panel and National Institute of Child Health and Human Development. 2000. *Report of the National Reading Panel: Teaching Children to Read: An Evidence-Based Assessment of the Scientific Research Literature on Reading and Its Implications for Reading Instruction.* Washington, DC: US Department of Health and Human Services, Public Health Service, National Institutes of Health, National Institute of Child Health and Human Development.

Neuman, Susan. 2018. *What Effective Pre-K Literacy Instruction Looks Like.* Newark, DE: International Literacy Association.

Neuman, Susan B, and Julie Dwyer. 2009. "Missing in Action: Vocabulary Instruction in Pre-K." *The Reading Teacher* 62(5): 384–392.

Neumann, Michelle M., Michelle Hood, and Ruth M. Ford. 2013. "Using Environmental Print to Enhance Emergent Literacy and Print Motivation." *Reading and Writing* 26(5): 771–793.

Ogle, Donna. 1986. "K-W-L: A Teaching Model That Develops Active Reading of Expository Text." *The Reading Teacher* 39(6): 564–570.

Paulson, Lucy H. 2004. "The Development of Phonological Awareness: From Syllables to Phonemes." Graduate Student Theses, Dissertations, and Professional Papers. https://scholarworks.umt.edu/etd/9522

Paulson, Lucy H., and Louisa Moats. 2018. *Language Essentials for Teachers of Reading and Spelling for Early Childhood Educators*. Dallas, TX: Voyager Sopris Learning.

Pentimonti, Jill M., Tricia Zucker, and Laura M. Justice. 2011. "What Are Preschool Teachers Reading in Their Classrooms?" *Reading Psychology* 32(3): 197–236.

Phillips, Beth M., and Shayne B. Piasta. 2013. "Phonological Awareness and Print Knowledge: Key Precursors and Instructional Targets to Promote Reading Success." In *Early Childhood Literacy: The National Early Literacy Panel and Beyond*. Baltimore, MD: Paul H. Brookes.

Piasta Shayne B., Laura M. Justice, Anita S. McGinty, and Joan N. Kaderavek. 2012. "Increasing Young Children's Contact with Print during Shared Reading: Longitudinal Effects on Literacy Achievement." *Child Development* 83(3): 810–820.

Piasta, Shayne B., David J. Purpura, and Richard K. Wagner. 2010. "Fostering Alphabet Knowledge Development: A Comparison of Two Instructional Approaches." *Reading and Writing* 23(6): 607–626.

Puranik, Cynthia S., Stephanie Al Otaiba, Jessica F. Sidler, and Luana Greulich. 2014. "Exploring the Amount and Type of Writing Instruction during Language Arts Instruction in Kindergarten Classrooms." *Reading and Writing* 27(2): 213–236.

Rasinski, Timothy V., and S. Jay Samuels. 2011. "Reading Fluency: What It Is and What It Is Not". In *What Research Has to Say about Reading Instruction*. 4th edition. Newark, DE: International Reading Association.

Really Great Reading. 2015. Heart Word Magic. https://www.reallygreatreading.com/heart-word-magic

Santangelo, Tanya, and Steve Graham. 2015. "A Comprehensive Meta-Analysis of Handwriting Instruction." *Educational Psychology Review* 28(2): 225–265.

Scanlon, Donna M., Kimberly L. Anderson, and Joan M. Sweeney. 2017. *Early Intervention for Reading Difficulties: The Interactive Strategies Approach*. 2nd edition. New York: Guilford Press.

Shanahan, Timothy, and Christopher J. Lonigan. 2013. *Early Childhood Literacy: The National Early Literacy Panel and Beyond*. Baltimore, MD: Paul H. Brookes.

Shipley, Kenneth G., and Julie G. McAfee. 2015. *Assessment in Speech-Language Pathology: A Resource Manual*. 5th edition. Boston, MA: Cengage Learning.

Solari, Emily, Colby Hall, and Anita McGinty. 2021. "Brick by Brick: A Series of Landmark Studies Pointing to the Importance of Early Reading Intervention." *The Reading League Journal* 2(2): 18–22.

Storch, Stacey A., and Grover J. Whitehurst. 2002. "Oral Language and Code-Related Precursors to Reading: Evidence from a Longitudinal Structural Model." *Developmental Psychology* 38(6): 934–947.

Surles, Jess. 2021. *What's the Best Way to Teach the Alphabetic Principle?* National Center on Improving Literacy. https://improvingliteracy.org/ask-an-expert/whats-best-way-teach-alphabetic-principle

Suskind, Dana. 2015. *Thirty Million Words: Building a Child's Brain.* New York: Dutton.

Tortorelli, Laura. 2016. "What's in a Letter Name? Letter Names and Letter Sounds in Early Literacy." *Reading in Virginia* 38: 7–12.

Treiman, Rebecca, Bruce F. Pennington, Lawrence D. Shriberg, and Richard Boada. 2008. "Which Children Benefit from Letter Names in Learning Letter Sounds?" *Cognition* 106(3): 1322–1338.

Turnbull, K. L. P., et al. 2010. "Theoretical Explanations for Preschoolers' Lowercase Alphabet Knowledge." *Journal of Speech, Language, and Hearing Research*, 53(6): 1757–1768.

University of Oregon. 2020. *Dynamic Indicators of Basic Early Literacy Skills* (DIBELS): *Administration and Scoring Guide.* 8th edition. Eugene, OR: University of Oregon.

US Department of Education, Early Childhood-Head Start Task Force. 2002. *Teaching Our Youngest: A Guide for Preschool Teachers and Child Care and Family Providers.* Washington, DC: Early Childhood-Head Start Task Force, US Department of Education, US Department of Health and Human Services. https://www2.ed.gov/teachers/how/early/teachingouryoungest/teachingouryoungest.pdf

Weizman, Zehava Oz, and Catherine E. Snow. 2001. "Lexical Input as Related to Children's Vocabulary Acquisition: Effects of Sophisticated Exposure and Support for Meaning." *Developmental Psychology* 37(2): 265–279.

Whitehurst, Grover J., and Christopher J. Lonigan. 1998. "Child Development and Emergent Literacy." *Child Development* 69(3): 848–872.

Whitehurst, Grover J., and Christopher J. Lonigan. 2001. "Emergent Literacy: Development from Prereaders to Readers." In *Handbook of Early Literacy Research, Volume 1.* New York: Guilford Press.

Winchester, Simon. 2011. "Has 'Run' Run Amok? It Has 645 Meanings . . . So Far." Neal Conan (interviewer) *Talk of the Nation,* May 30. NPR. https://www.npr.org/2011/05/30/136796448/has-run-run-amok-it-has-645-meanings-so-far

Yokota, Junko, and William H. Teale. 2017. "Striving for International Understanding Through Literature." *The Reading Teacher* 70(5): 629-633.

Zucker, Tricia A., and Susan H. Landry. 2010. "Improving the Quality of Preschool Read-Alouds: Professional Development and Coaching That Targets Book-Reading Practices." In *Promoting Early Reading: Research, Resources, and Best Practices*. New York: Guilford Press.

Index